EXPLORATIONS IN ANTHROPOLOGY OF NORTH EAST INDIA

EXPLORATIONS IN ANTHROPOLOGY OF NORTH EAST INDIA

Edited by
Sarthak Sengupta

GYAN

ISBN : 978-81-212-1242-7

Price : ₹ 900

First Published, 2015

Published by

Gyan Publishing House
5, Ansari Road
Daryaganj, New Delhi-110002
Phones: 9811692060
E-mail: books@gyanbooks.com

Printed at: G. Print Process, Delhi.

Cataloging in Publication Data—DK
Courtesy: D.K. Agencies (P) Ltd. <docinfo@dkagencies.com>

Explorations in anthropology of North East India / edited by Sarthak Sengupta.
pages cm
Contributed articles.
Includes bibliographical references and index.
ISBN 9788121212427

1. Ethnology—India, Northeastern. 2. Tribes—India, Northeastern. I. Sengupta, Sarthak, 1955- editor.
GN635.I4E97 2015 DDC 305.8009541 23

Dedicated to

The Loving Memory of
My Sister-in-law
Preeti Sengupta

Contents

Preface

North East India, the erstwhile greater Assam, presently the land of seven-sister States, covers political units namely, Arunachal Pradesh, Assam, Manipur, Meghalaya, Mizoram, Nagaland and Tripura and is located between latitude 20°N and 22°N North and longitude 89°.E46' and 97°.E05' East. It has an area of 2, 62,179 sq. km., having a hilly and wild topography and comprises about 7.90 per cent landmass of India. The indigenous inhabitants of this region, mostly tribals, are overwhelming in their variety, ethnicity, culture and folklore. The region is perched at the confluence of countries like China and Tibet in the North, Myanmar in the East and North, and Bangladesh in the West and South, and connected by a narrow corridor with the rest of India between Nepal and Bangladesh. The region has about 4,500 sq. km international boundaries across Bangladesh, Myanmar, Bhutan and Tibet. Very recently the State of Sikkim is included in this region. The average population density of North East India is 150 (approx); the literacy rate is 68.50 per cent and the urban population stands at 15.45 per cent of the total population. It is the land of co-existence of the extreme forms of tradition and modernity.

There is a rich assembly of cultures and communities in this rugged expanse of the eastern Himalayas. There are about 200 major tribal groups, which is almost one-third of the total number of listed tribes (635 in number) for the whole of India. The non-tribal plains men of North East India are formed by the caste Hindus, scheduled castes, other backward classes and the Muslims. There is another section formed by the migrant tea garden workers. More than 200 languages or mother tongues are spoken in the region, and some of these have less than 10,000 speakers. The majority of the people living in the regions are Hindus, followed by Muslims, Christian and Buddhist communities respectively. Many tribes of the region still have their own traditional faiths; some have accepted Hinduism while others are Hinduised.

North East India as a meeting place of varied races, people, culture and customs has long been recognised by anthropologists as one of the most dynamic field for research. The history of anthropological research in North East India started more than one hundred years ago.

The British colonial government realised that for effective administration of native North East Indians, understanding of their culture and custom was a must. Thus, when the greater Assam was annexed to the British Empire in 1826, many British scholars in different fields were deputed to carry systematic investigation on human variability in this region. Under the general supervision of an honourary Director of Ethnography of the Government of erstwhile Assam, monographs were prepared on Meiteis; Mikir; Garo; Kacharis; Khasi; Lushai; Angami, Sema, Lotha, Ao, Rengma and Zemi Naga; Lakher and others. However, most of these accounts were prepared by administrators whose primary intention was to generate ethnographic profiles of people they administered and not by professionally trained anthropologists. Several studies suffer from personal bias and other methodologies. The momentum of anthropological research was accelerated with the appointment of von Furer Haimendorf, the first social anthropologist to be commissioned by the Government of Assam to explore and get in touch with the tribes of Subansiri district of the present day Arunachal Pradesh. His monograph on Apatanis of Arunachal Pradesh is extremely valuable. Later, T.C. Das studied the Purum Kuki of Manipur; J.K. Bose reported the Garo social organisation, while K.P. Chattopadhyay published an account on Khasi kinship. Basing on T.C. Das's ethnography, Rodney Needham attempted later detailed analysis of the Purum society and enriched the quality of North East Indian ethnographic studies. Verrier Elwin also wrote several anthropological memoirs on tribes of Arunachal Pradesh, closely followed by P.C. Dutta, Sachin Roy and others that constitute a cross-section of ethnographic studies in North East India. Similarly, Robins Burling studied the kinship and social structure in Garo village in Meghalaya, while Hamlet Bareh reported the ethno-history of the Khasis. D. N. Majumdar studied the socio-cultural change in two Garo villages of Meghalaya. The effect of tea industry on the tribal life has been delineated by R.K. Kar.

The British administrator initiated research into prehistoric part of this part of India. Sir John Lubbock was the pioneer to report the evidence of *Stone Age* tools from upper Assam. Following his footsteps, sporadic finds of polished stone tools were recorded by E.H. Steel, J. Cockburn, J. Anderson, Lt. Barron, H.H. Godwin Austen, Medlicott, H.C. Dasgupta, J. Coggin Brown, R.D. Banerjee, J.H. Hutton, G.D. Walker and others. Based on the antiquities from North East India preserved in the Pitt Rivers Museum of Oxford University, A.H. Dani opines the *Neolithic tools* from North East India shows close affinity with the type found in South East Asia and China. The Neolithic sites from Garo Hills, Meghalaya and Marakdola, North Cachar Hills of Assam were thoroughly explored and excavated. Findings of *Palaeolithic tool* traditions; *Microlithic* industry and *Neolithic* tools from Sarutaru, Kamrup; Dibru valley; Arunachal Pradesh; Manipur were also reported from the region.

Studies on biological anthropology were introduced in the region at the turn of twentieth century when L.A. Waddell carried the first anthropometric works among thirty population groups of Brahmaputra valley. Since then, most of the bio-anthropological studies conducted in North East India are mostly concerned with racial profiling based on either morphological or genetical characters either singly or in combination.

The relevance of anthropological research in the context of massive human diversity in North East India need not be exaggerated. It is true that no other region can boast of such impressive array of monographs, district gazetteers, hand books, research reports. The field of anthropological research in North East India is enormous and unresearched areas are numerous. Whatever, has been done on the life of people has not been adequate enough compared to untrodden and unexplored areas. A cursory glance on the repository of anthropological literature from North East India reveals that information on non-tribal population is scanty, sporadic and sketchy. Research having social relevance, and towards the survival and well-being of population groups living in the region is rarity even today.

The current compilation presents a sixteen research articles offered by eminent social scientists to acquaint with extensive book lovers on ethnic groups living in diverse habitat of North East India. The volume features with abundance of materials and wide-ranging analysis which is extremely stimulative, unique, useful and certainly serves the interest of anthropologists, besides social scientists and many at the teaching and research level with a concern about the indigenous people of North East India. Obviously, the present treatise do not claim or aspire even to cover the whole gamut of anthropological perspective of North East India within limited space. It touches upon some important segments of the vast and varied area of the canvass.

My endeavour will be rewarded if this volume proves to be informative, stimulator, constructive and provoke curiosity among scholars and researchers as well as the administrators and policy makers.

Dibrugarh University
26.01.2014

Sarthak Sengupta

Acknowledgements

I personally owe to those contributors for responding to my request through well-researched articles.

I take this opportunity to put across my deep appreciation to wife Kaveeta, sons Sushruta and Samrat, and daughter-in-law Surovee for their constant enthusiasm, compassion and support throughout the process of editing in this project; Mrs Neelanjana Barua for her pains to arrange the typescript; and to my research student Dr Dali Dutta for going through the typescript. I also wish to appreciate my son Samrat, who helped me in getting photographs for jacket.

It has been possible for my academic quest because of infrastructural facilities extended by the authorities of Dibrugarh University. I avail this opportunity to express my thanks.

Finally, I would like to convey my thanks to Gyan Publishing House, New Delhi for its honest efforts in bringing this volume on time.

Dibrugarh University

26.01.2014 **Sarthak Sengupta**

List of Contributors

Indraneel Banerjee: Royal Manchester Children's Hospital, United Kingdom.

Debashis Basu: Anthropological Survey of India, 27, Jawaharlal Nehru Road, Kolkata, 700 016, West Bengal.

Premananda Bharati: Biological Anthropology Unit, Indian Statistical Institute, 203, Barrackpore Trunk Road, Kolkata, 700 108, West Bengal.

S.B. Chakrabarti: 15/8 Rajkrishna Pal Lane, Kolkata, 700 075, West Bengal.

Nabajit Kr. Das: Department of Anthropology, Gauhati University, Gopinath Bordoloi Nagar, Guwahati, 781 014, Assam.

Rekha Das: Department of Anthropology, Gauhati University, Gopinath Bordoloi Nagar, Guwahati, 781 014, Assam.

Dali Dutta: Department of Anthropology, Dibrugarh University, Dibrugarh, 786 004, Assam.

Michael R. Kolb: Assam Don Bosco University, Guwahati, Assam.

Yashisenla Longkumer: Department of Anthropology, University of Delhi, Delhi-110 007, India.

Mayanglambam ManiBabu: Department of Anthropology, Manipur University, Canchipur, Imphal, Manipur-795 003.

Q. Marak: Department of Anthropology, North Eastern Hill University, Mawkynroh, Umshing, Shillong, 793 022, Meghalaya.

Nitish Mondal: Department of Anthropology, Assam University, Diphu Campus, Diphu, Karbi Anglong.

Barun Mukhopadhyay: Biological Anthropology Unit, Indian Statistical Institute, 203, Barrackpore Trunk Road, Kolkata, 700 108, West Bengal.

Manoranjan Pal: Economics Research Unit, Indian Statistical Institute, 203, Barrackpore Trunk Road, Kolkata, 700 108, West Bengal.

Runjun Patir: Department of Anthropology, Dibrugarh University, Dibrugarh, 786 004, Assam.

Melvil Pereira: North Eastern Social Research Centre, Jagriti, GMCH Road, Christian Basti, Guwahati, 781 005, Assam.

Manis Kumar Raha: Revati F/1, Neelachal Abasan, 98, Rajadanga Gold Park, Kolkata, 700 107, West Bengal.

Geetika Ranjan: Department of Anthropology, North Eastern Hill University, Mawkynroh, Umshing, Shillong, 793 022, Meghalaya.

V.R. Rao: Department of Anthropology, University of Delhi, Delhi, 110 007, India.

Papia Roy: Sociological Research Unit, Indian Statistical Institute, 203, Barrackpore Trunk Road, Kolkata, 700 108, West Bengal.

Sovanjan Sarkar: Department of Anthropology, Vidyasagar University, Medenipore.

Sarthak Sengupta : Department of Anthropology, Dibrugarh University, Dibrugarh, 786 004, Assam

S. Jibonkumar Singh: Department of Anthropology, Manipur University, Canchipur, Imphal, Manipur, 795 003.

Suparna Som: Sociological Research Unit, Indian Statistical Institute, 203, Barrackpore Trunk Road, Kolkata, 700 108, West Bengal.

Chandrajyoti Sonowal: Centre for Study of Social Inclusion and Inclusive Policies, Tata Institute of Social Sciences, Deonar, Mumbai, 400 088.

Deimaphishisha Sun: Anthropological Survey of India, North East Regional Centre, Mawblei, Shillong, Meghalaya, 793 021.

Thokchom Ursa: Department of Anthropology, Manipur University, Canchipur, Imphal, Manipur, 795 003.

About the Editor

Sarthak Sengupta (b.1955) received his M.Sc. (1977) and Ph.D. (1983) degrees in Anthropology from Dibrugarh University and Gauhati University respectively. He worked with the Anthropological Survey of India, Government of India and North Eastern Hill University, Shillong for quite some time and conducted intensive field studies among diverse tribes and castes in Arunachal Pradesh, Assam, Meghalaya, Nagaland, and Uttar Pradesh. He has had to his own credit fourteen well-knit books on North East Indian tribes, over 220 original research papers published in national and international professional journals besides several chapters in edited volumes. He is an active life and executive member of several professional anthropological bodies and members of the editorial boards of *Journal of Human Ecology*, New Delhi (1998-2003); *The Anthropologist*, New Delhi (since 2009) and *The Indian Journal of Anthropology* (since 2013). He is also the Editor of the *Bulletin* of the Department of Anthropology, Dibrugarh University, Dibrugarh.

Dr. Sengupta is at present Professor and Head, Department of Anthropology; and Director (i/c), Centre for North East Studies, Dibrugarh University, Assam. His research interest are genetical demography, globin gene distribution, population genetics, bio-social studies, diet and nutrition, indigenous health practices among tribal population of North East India.

About the Book

The current treatise presents a collection of sixteen articles by eminent social scientists to acquaint booklovers with contemporary anthropological research on ethnic groups living in diverse habitat of North East India.

Under one cover, the present volume features with abundance of materials and wide-ranging analysis extremely useful serving the interest of anthropologists, social scientists teachers and resarchers, as well as planners and policy makers concerred about the indigenous people of North East India.

1
Tribes of North East India : An Overview

– S.B. Chakrabarti

I propose to have a discussion on Tribes and North East India: An overview. If the title is broken down, the three key words would be overview, North East India and tribes. I may be allowed to proceed accordingly. Let me first point out what do I mean by overview. These are :

(i) to see things in broader and larger perspective;

(ii) to involve possible dimensions of space and time in the context of people being discussed;

(iii) time should be great leveler or divider in the interaction of people on space; for the designated space is north-east region of India; and

(iv) one is naturally expected to delimit his 'domain' being thrown open in a time-constrained discussion.

Therefore, in view of limitations, I will briefly draw a rough contour on the diverse factors entailing history, economy, polity and society including the culture of region and its people. These find extremely important for our present discourse.

When we consider historical context, we may bear in mind the following citation. The great historian E.H. Carr observes, "Great history is written when the historian's vision of the past is illuminated by an insight into the problems of the present". B.S. Cohn, a noted anthropologist-cum-historian while discussing ethno-history points out, "In recent years, regions and regionalism has become one of the prime concerns of all social scientists in the study of India and Indian culture". Joseph Schwartzberg, a geographer, on Regions and Regionalism in South Asian Studies remarks, "The word 'region' have has significantly different meanings in various contexts. It is most important that scholars understood these meanings when dealing with regions in an area like South Asia, where such a remarkable degree of regional diversity exists, where so many old instituted boundaries have been swept away in the wake of Independence, where peoples, 'perceptions' of what should constitute the new regional order are so often at variance and still in a state of flux, and where regional sentiment often runs dangerously, if not suicidal".

Robert I. Crane, a historian looks at the region in the following words, "the use and misuse of demographic, ethnic, linguistic and other 'evidence' to support conflicting claims to greater or lesser territorial enclaves highlights the importance of scholarly sober enquiry regarding the bases for and appropriate definitions of regions".

Prof. Nirmal Kumar Bose, a noted anthropologist and social historian through an *All India Survey on Cultural Traits* found the spread of material cultures of the people of rural India cut across the linguistic divide of the existing geographical regions and "there is more unity in India's variety than one is likely to admit in moment of forgetfulness". He sincerely feels a deep acquaintance with social facts gives birth to meaningful social science research.

When we think of economy we need to keep the region known as North East as really not isolated in space. The existence of Silk Road or Silk Route during various historical periods would bear testimony to this pointer. This road or route happened to be a channel of trade and commodity transfer from one area to another from East to West Asia starting from China to Mediterranean Sea involving areas like Tibet, Bhutan, Burma (now Myanmar) and Indo-China and their people. Gurdon, who studied the Khasis in early twentieth century, mentioned about the export of iron from Khasi Hills to other places. The colonial rulers rightly assessed the commercial interest of many other tradable commodities such as timber, coal, tea and oil.

While considering polity, we may bring in the existence of a number of trans-border communities since long before independence. These communities were made familiar as the 'forest tribes' by colonial rulers and later by the administrators-cum-anthropologists like, Risley. It was evident in 1901 Census report that forest tribes were by and large considered as the 'animists'. In 1921 Census report, the term animist was changed in favour of 'tribal region'. To the colonisers in general Assam and its hilly terrain in the east were known as the land of jungles in blanket term and its people as the savage, primitive, and uncivilised. The entire area was considered as the 'backward' till 1930. One would simply fail to understand how a section of such people met the Simon Commission in Assam, in 1929, and placed their grievances therein. The levels of their consciousness and intellectual preparation would be revealed from the number of Memorandum submitted by them. This very point was emphatically highlighted by P.R. Kyndiah, the former Speaker of Meghalaya Assembly as well as the former Governor of Mizoram, in his publication, which brought the debates held in the Constituent Assembly just prior to independence and immediately after during early 1947 till late 1949. The scathing attack perpetrated against the tribal autonomy in the Hill Areas by using the fitting phrases only matched the initial assessment of tribes by the colonial rulers as mentioned earlier.

Indian leaders who engaged themselves in the struggle for freedom were trying to understand the real problem of nation building in these less visited areas. Pt. Jawaharlal Nehru, for example, was initially caught in a dilemma between 'protectionism' of the tribes unleashed through the policy reflected in the Government of India Act, 1935 and promoted the people like Verrier Elwin and 'integration' with main-stream socio-economic forces, envisioned in the constitution and promoted by scholars like G.S. Ghurya and others. This very debate is agog in the deliberations of social scientists at large, even today. Meanwhile, lot of changes took place with regard to the question of 'identity', even within inter and intra-group relations–Assam, Manipur, Nagaland, Mizoram and Tripura figure out in everyday national dailies on the matter. Among other things, migration and partition have occupied central place in this discussion. A lot of publications are available which have been authored by historians, political scientists, anthropologists, economists and others of academic disciplines. Alexander Mackenzie's report of 1884 down to B.K. Roy Burman's Census publication of 1961 and some other publications of scholars like H.K. Barpuzari, Amalendu Guha, S.K. Chaube, B. Pakem, Mahadev Chakravarti, Sanjay Hazarika, Sanjib Baruah, Udayan Mishra bear testimony to changing political contexts and compulsions of various governments vis-à-vis the growing political consciousness among the local people.

The next component that comes in the present chapter is what is North East India geographically, historically, politically and socio-economically speaking? Let me briefly recapitulate the otherwise known facts:

It is already known that North East India comprises seven sister States, such as Assam, Nagaland, Meghalaya, Manipur, Tripura, Mizoram and Arunachal Pradesh and one brother State, i.e., Sikkim.

People by and large know how the present administrative units evolved by stages since the rule of the Ahom Kings for about 600 years beginning in the early thirteenth century via annexation of Assam by the British in 1826 till the attainment of India's independence. Even after 1947, lots of changes have taken place. Assam province with its outlying hilly terrains with two principalities i.e., Manipur and Tripura passed through reshufflings in political governance including the granting of new statehood to old union territories. Thus came Nagaland (1963), Meghalaya, Manipur, Tripura (1972), and Mizoram and Arunachal Pradesh (1986). and Sikkim as a new State in 1975.

There is some confusion as reflected through historical documents with regard to the term North East and its inclusive regions prior to independence of India. After the independence, it was officially formalised with the establishment of North Eastern Council (NEC) in 1971. The colonial rulers experimented through a policy of 'Non-interference' and proceeding through 'Forward Policy' till the attainment of full economic and political control over the region (1865 – 1914). By and large, there were three spatial enclaves, namely Brahmaputra – Surma valley", Excluded and Partially Excluded areas, and two princely States – Manipur and Tripura.

Let me move on to another component i.e., 'Tribes' of this region:

Going round the world there has been a debate on the criteria ever since the issue of 'primitivity' was attached long back in the history of human sciences. Now, an additional qualifier is offered aloout is the indigenous population. India was no exception. It attracted administrators, planners as well as scholars alike especially during the colonial era.

Initially, the decadal census in the later part of nineteenth century attempted to classify certain people – both of the hills and of the plains, who were virtually isolated from the so called 'mainstream' in terms of their exclusive living as basically tribes people having low level of technology and literacy and certain 'worldview' approximating to animistic beliefs. In fact, any attempt of defining tribe from that perspective has been ineffective. Even now this could not be so without a controversy. The only standard format has been the constitutional category which includes a list of 'scheduled' tribe(s) prepared on the basis of the recommendation of the President of India.

These tribes (scheduled or otherwise) form a formidable eight per cent of the tribal population. If one looks at the scenario in North East India it would be a microcosm or mini India. About 200 of India's 635 tribal communities have been reported (one can consult the *People of India, National and State Volumes*, published by *Anthropological Survey of India*). There are 175 spoken languages in the north east region out of 325 Indian languages. We get earlier designated 'racial' strains such as Mongoloid and the language families such as Austric, Tibeto-Burman etc. We get many trans-border communities who have migrated many generations back. The north east region have three fourth hilly and rugged terrains out of 2,55,000 sq. km and about 4,500 sq. km international boundaries across Bangladesh, Myanmars, Bhutan, and Tibet.

In north east region, one gets greater diversities in ecology, economy, society and polity. Patri-matri structural pattern in social relations, and clan-community type of ownership in basic resources i.e., land and forest are some of the unique features available even now. Traditional political governance is combined with the autonomous institutions granted under the Sixth Schedule aside with the democratic national framework of federal States.

Inspite of rich socio-cultural heritage and natural abundance, the familiarity of north east region to an outsider is primarily is as the land of political turmoil, terrorism, insurgency, drug trafficking and so on and so forth.

The dissidence on identity and political autonomy that started before the independence during the colonial rule is somewhat continuing in diverse ways and means, inspite of having the scheduled self–governance through the Sixth Schedule in number of places. The purpose of colonial rulers of dividing people from one another in pre-independence period in getting them participated to a considerable extent in certain areas on certain time and among certain population groups. Those tendencies of internalisation of olden day issues during lesser exposure to the outside world are being externalised during much expressed and interactive globalised world. This process has been advanced fast through the improved technology of communication.

Tribal studies are no more the exclusive preserve of the anthropologists. Now, scholars of many collateral academic disciplines show vigourous interest including some NGOs and individuals on tribal issues in general and North East India in particular. Even some World Conventions are being held since the International Labour Organisation (ILO) initiated major discussion from 1957 by introducing the term 'Indigenous and Tribal Communities'.

In the twenty-first century, we have experienced the impact of two major global factors on the economy, society and polity throughout the country. These factors, namely bio-demographic and technological revolutions, which first emerged since the later part of twentieth century have been instrumental in lessening spatial distance among the people, ensuring wider and closer economic participation and cultural blending. The demands of more democratic rights and greater political autonomy enlarge and go through various tests of time. Apprehensions of loss of community identity are increasing in different magnitude at the local, regional, national and international level.

In these transformation scenarios, if one taks up meaningful research on North East India, the traditional research approaches could be inadequate. The intellectual preparation of the present generation of anthropologists should be far more precise, time saving and inter-disciplinary in nature. Only the clan and kinship on the one hand and reservation issues of all kinds on the other would not suffice to understand comprehensively the basic changes among diverse population groups, specially the tribes of North East India. To understand the entire processes holistically, one has no option but to take up the question of political economy of the region and its linkages, within and without the regional spheres. This approach would situate the tribes in the context of North East India in the right perspective. Prof Nirmal Kumar Bose, a renowned scholar on anthropology in this country emphasise's, the lessons of great bio-physicist, Sir Jagadish Chandra Bose, on the intimate observation of the phenomena around and on asking the right kind of questions before coming to any conclusion. Probably then, Abraham Lincon would re-appear to say, "This nation, under God, shall have a new birth of freedom, that government of the people by the people and for the people shall not perish from the earth".

References

Barua, Sanjib Kumar. 1994. *'Éthnic Conflict as State-society Struggle'.* In Modern Asian Studies.

Borpujari, H.K. 1981. *Presidential Address*. First Session of North East India Historical Association.

Bose, Nirmal Kumar. 1961. *Peasant Life in India*. Calcutta: Anthropological Survey of India.

Carr, E.H. (quoted in Mahadev Chakravarti's *Social Change in North East India*, NEIHA, Shillong, 2008).

Chakravarti, Mahadev. 2008. *Social Change in North East India*. Shillong: NEIHA.

Chaube, S.K.1993. *Hill Politics in North East India*. New Delhi: Mittal Publications.

Chaudhury, Abhijit. 2002. 'The contextual dimension of the sixth schedule'. In *Contemporary India*, Vol. 1, Number IV, New Delhi: Nehru Memorial Museum and Library.

Choudhury, D.P. 1978. *The North East Frontier of India (1865-1914),* Calcutta: The Asiatic Society.

Cohn, Bernard. 1967. 'Regions subjective and objective', In R. I. Crane (Ed): *Regions and Regionalism in South Asian Studies*. Duke University.

Crane, R.I. 1967. 'Íntroduction', *ibid.*

Elwin, Verrier. 1957. *A Philosophy for NEFA*, Shillong: Directorate of Research, Government of Arunachal Pradesh.

Ghurey, G. S. 1950. *Caste and Class in India*, Bombay.

Government of India Act – 1919 and 1935.

Guha, Amalendu. 1977. *Planter Raj to Swaraj: Freedom Struggle and Electoral Politics in Assam 1826-1947,* New Delhi: Indian Council of Historical Research.

Gurdon, P.R.T. 1914. *The Khasis*, London : David Nutt.

Hazarika, Sanjay. 1994. *Strangers of the Mist*. New Delhi: Penguin India.

International Labour Organisation – Resolution of 1957.

Kyndiah, P. R. 1993. *Rev. J. J. M. Nichols Roy : Architect of District Council Autonomy,* New Delhi: Sanchar Publishing House.

Mackenzie, Alexandar. 1884. *History of the Relations of the Government with the Hill Tribes of North East Frontier of Bengal.* Calcutta.

Mishra, Udayan. 2001. *The Transformation of Assamese Identity: A Historical Survey,* Shillong : NEIHA.

Pakem, B. 1997. *Insurgency in North East India.* New Delhi : Omsons Publications.

Risley, Herbart. 1901. *Census of India,* (reprint).

Roy Burman, B. K. 1971. *Demographic and Socio-Economic Profiles of the Hill Areas of North East India.* Delhi : Census of India.

Schwastzberg, Joseph. 1967. 'Prolegomens to the study of South Asian Regions and Regionalism'. In Robert I. Crane (*ibid*).

Singh, K. S. 1998. *India's Communities.* Delhi : Oxford University Press.

2
Megaliths and Living Cultural Traditions

– *Q. Marak*

Introduction

The word "*megalith*", from ancient Greek *megas* meaning large and *lithos* meaning stone, stands for large stones either standing alone or assembled to form a structure or monument. These structures are found in different parts of the world and have multiple meanings–funerary, commemorative, religious and ceremonial. They generally belonged to prehistoric times, while some continue to have modern-day relevance to living communities. The meanings in them are varied, and studies have given diverse insight into socio-political, economic and ideological life of prehistoric societies. Much of these studies are concerned with how they played major role in the emergence of early agricultural communities, and complex polities (Renfrew, 1976). Chapman (1981) noted megalithic monuments in Neolithic Europe acted as territorial markers controlled by kinship-based corporate groups. Some authors (Flemming, 1973; Sherrat, 1990; Nelson, 1999) see them as representation of an elite class of individuals and groups. Few studies focused on the symbolism inherent (Hodder, 1990; Bradley, 1998), while a few others contended they were used for astronomical observations (Thom, 1966; MacKie, 1997).

The problem of megaliths is complex in India, where a living tradition is additionally found. In an article in 1945, Christoph von Furer-Haimendorf (1945) discussed this problem, synthesising the archaeological and ethnographical data of his time. He distinguished two types of independent megalithic cultures–one, which was still living tradition in eastern and central India, and two, which was documented with the help of archaeological remains in south India. The two groups clearly had no connection. Ramachandran (1971) supported and stated that the south Indian megaliths form a class of its own. Here, iron and black-and-red pottery occur in direct association with megaliths and hence the term Iron Age is used. Radiocarbon dates place megalithic cultures in south India between 1000 BC-1000 AD.

In North Eastern India, megaliths are found widely distributed in the Khasi-Jaintia Hills of Meghalaya (Godwin-Austen, 1872; Gurdon, 1914), in Naga dominated areas of the districts of Chandel, Ukhrul, Tamenglong, Senapati and Churachandpur in Manipur (Singh, 1985; Devi, 2011), in North Cachar Hills and Karbi Anglong districts of Assam (Mills and Hutton, 1929; Bezbaruah, 2004), and in Kohima and Phek districts of Nagaland populated by Angamis and others (Dewar, 1966; Jamir, 1998). In these areas there exists a living tradition among the tribal communities in the erection of megalithic monuments and linked beliefs—this cultural practice associated with the megaliths among living communities is referred to as *living megalithism* (Marak, 2012). Thus this living tradition existent among megalithic users of the region makes an interesting study.

Despite large number of communities having such traditions, it is impossible to correlate with the use of stones in the diffusion of a particular linguistic family, for the Khasis and Jaintias speak Mon-Khmer, while Nagas speak Tibeto-Burman, Gonds and Gadabas are speakers of Dravidian while Saoras and Mundas speak Mundari; or a supposed universal religious stage either a "fertility cult" or a "stone worship". The only shared feature between the socio-political organisations is the lineage-based tribal division of the society articulated with a respect, if not a cult, for ancestors. Within these societies, the ancestors occupy a respected position, and thus it is not by chance that stones are erected to commemorate, not those who died recently, but precisely the ancestors who were united with the lineage during the secondary funerary ceremonies. In these societies, the stones literally stand for the ancestors' presence, and at the same time for the status of the living members of their family (Rousseleau, 2012).

Notwithstanding its importance among communities in North Eastern India, these structures have more or less been relegated to the background after the coming of Christianity and modernity, and generally referred to as "backward" by them[1]. The sorry state of affairs seen in Khasi Hills in Meghalaya is however not seen in the Jaintia context[2], a sub-tribe of the greater Khasi group. This chapter takes up the Jaintia situation and discusses the megaliths found among them and their living traditions. In doing so, it uses the post-processual approach. The discussions follow the anthropological empirical traditions of village ethnography;

therefore in this context, Nangbah, one of the oldest Jaintia villages situated in Jaintia Hills District, Meghalaya is discussed. This is an exploratory study with one-month fieldwork in January 2010, when ethnographic and ethno-archaeological data was collected and analysed. This village is located to the north east of Jowai town, which is the capital of the district, on the JNKK (Jowai-Nartiang-Khiap-Khanduli) road about 13 kms from Jowai towards Khanduli.

The village of Nangbah has a population of 4,279 individuals, half of whom are followers of *Niamtre*, and the rest converts to Christianity. *Niamtre* is the traditional Jaintia religion which believes in ancestor and spirit worship, with accompanying beliefs and practices. There is a preponderance of female principle in their religion, thus the supreme god; *U Blei Nongtaw* is represented by a goddess *Ka Blei Synshar*. Female deities are agents of familial, social well-being and collective economic endeavour, whereas male deities are connected to state activities, administration and territorial defence (Sen, 2004). Jaintia matriliny has been much studied and debated for "unique" system of marriage, popularly referred by anthropologists as "visiting husband marriage". This is termed so since post-marital residence is partial; even though the husband moves into the house of the wife, for all practical purposes including economic ventures, he continues to be an important member of his mother's house. As in other systems of matriliny, inheritance of property, lineage, and residence after marriage is in the female line. In such matrilineal system, the inheriting daughter is the youngest (*khadduh*), who assumes the role of custodian of family property and the responsibilities towards aged parents, maternal uncles, brothers, sisters and their children.

Besides the family (*iing*), which is the smallest and most important social unit, the clan (*kur*) is of great importance; some families are grouped into lineages (*kpoh*) or sub-clans, which are further grouped into the larger clan. All clans trace their origin from common ancestress and their descent is from mother to daughter; sons trace their descent from mother as well. In the village, there are twenty clans out of which it is likely that originally there were only twelve clans since these are represented in the form of "clan stones" in the sacred grove of Iawmusiang.

Morphological and Functional Classification

The megaliths in Nangbah total over five hundred in number, mostly found in Iawmusiang, though a few are found in other localities and groves of the village. The megaliths of Iawmusiang represent the twelve clans of the village—these were erected by village ancestors during different periods of time. In the centre of these twelve "clan stones" lie a large dolmen called *sangap*, where the god/goddess of Iawmusiang resides. This grove is not only geographically located at the centre of the village, but is also at the centre of all socio-religious activity.

Just like the *sangap* stone, the megaliths in Nangbah are all locally named–either singularly or as an assemblage–thus reiterating the cultural importance of these stones. These are usually prefixed with the word "*moo*" (stone). Morphologically, these stones can be classified into various types, which include menhirs, *moopynieng* (upright standing stones), commonly found in the village. Some menhirs are also known as *mooshyarang* (male stones) found in association with dolmens. Some of the notable menhirs found in the village include: *u-moo-thulelane* (stone of Thule lane), the tallest menhir in Nangbah, standing at a height of 563 cms. *Moopyllaitsyier* (stone where the cock is set free) is another noteworthy menhir measuring 192 cms from the ground located at Khlopano locality. This stone is named so since at this menhir, a ritual is held after which the proffered cock is set free.

Dolmens, known as *mooknor* (flat stones), are found in association with menhirs either singly or in a group, while a few of them are known as *mookynthai* (female stones). One of the notable dolmens found in the village is *bleiiawmusiang*, or the stone where the god/goddess of Iawmusiang resides, popularly called the *sangap* stone. This is the first megalith placed in the village in the grove of Iawmusiang, measuring 351 × 232 × 27cms at a height of 20 cms from the ground. One other notable dolmen is *moolyngdoh* or the lyngdoh stone located in Iawmusiang grove opposite the big dolmen of *sangap*, measuring approximately 137 × 161 × 20 cms at a height of 20 cms.

Alignments are found in various shapes and sizes in the village with a combination of menhirs and dolmens, or menhirs and dolmens alone. One of the alignments is a group of fifteen stones in a straight line which represent the clan stones of the Susngi clan comprising menhirs, dolmens and stone slabs or capstones. Other menhirs measuring 60-152 cms in height are seen as alignments, but are put up to mark the boundary of an area, or as path stones leading to clan cists. The stone circle found in Iawmusiang comprises a circular arrangement of nine menhirs in association with eleven dolmens and two stone slabs.

Another category of stones commonly found include cists, essentially stone chambers, varying in size from 182-213 cms to 304-365 cms, which are opened periodically by removing one of the vertical stones placed in front for depositing bones of the deceased ancestors. The variation in size depends on the functional capacity of the cists – whether it is a family or a clan repository.

Capstones (large slabs of stones) of various shapes and sizes are found in clusters varying from 91-152 cms in length and 60-152 cms in breadth. One miscellaneous structure is *ramshyllong*, an oblong stone found in Iongbiam locality of the village. The size of the stone is ten times that of a football, and essentially has various religious associations. *Mookhrah* (stone balls) found in Iawmusiang are round in structure and twice the size of a football, the circumference being approximately 52 and 58 inches respectively. These two *mookrah* are never taken out of the grove, but used on ceremonial occasions.

On the other hand, on the basis of functions, megaliths in Nangbah can be classified into various types. The *moobuhshieng* are burial or funerary cists directly associated with the post-cremation rituals, where the remains of the deceased are kept. These are normally of three types – the one belonging to a family, the sub-clan or lineage, and the clan.

Megaliths such as *moolyngdoh*, *ramshyllong* and *moopyllaitsyier* are religious stones, the touching of which is a taboo. *Moolyngdoh* is a sacred stone, where the *lyngdoh* (priest) performs all religious ceremonies and rituals connected to village welfare during festivals of *Pam Iawmusiang* and *Knia Lyngdoh*. *Ramshyllong*, on the other hand, is a menhir at whose feet animals are sacrificed and offered in the early hours of the day on the occasion of above mentioned festivals. *Moopyllaitsyier* is located at Khlopano and associated with rituals when women die during pregnancy. In such cases, a cock is made to scratch the stone and let off to roam, which will appease the dead souls of the mother and the child.

In addition to the complex of ritualistic and funerary megalithic practices, they also build a series of stones commemorating certain important social and political events. Such memorial stones are put up by the clansmen to commemorate an event of public interest — social, political, ideological and others. For instance, *bleiiawmusiang* is in memory of *Sangap* and *u-moo-thulelane* is in memory of a Jaintia hero.

A large number of resting stones meant for sitting or resting purposes are also present. This type of stone signified other socio-religious functions such as the "clan stones" of Iawmusiang. Resting stones found were either dolmen or capstone types, which can be classified as clan sitting stones, where in clan members sit during ceremonies; or sitting stones, when a weary traveller can rest during his/her journey from one village to another. On the other hand, some menhirs in association with dolmens acted as path stones to guide someone to the different clan cists.

Judiciary stones are found in several places in Jaintia Hills. In the village, *khimdan*[3] is one such stone which is a combination of three menhirs in association with a huge flat and narrow stone placed in front. Nangbah, prior to British rule, was one of the biggest market in the Jaintia kingdom. During that period of time, duty was imposed on merchants who entered and exit the village as import and export tax. The tax collector who was in charge of this procedure collected all duties at this particular location. This stone, which is no longer in use, is still known as the "tax collector stone".

Besides, some stones found in Nangbah have recreational values. *Mookhrah* refers to stone balls found in Iawmusiang which are used for a traditional sport held annually during *Knia Lyngdoh* festival, just before the harvest season. These stone balls are lifted and carried, and the person who carries it farthest is declared the strongest man of the village.

A Post-processual Cultural Interpretation

Post-processual archaeology developed as a critique to processual archaeology in the 1970s. This critique aimed at redefinition of social practice, social units and groupings, and of the nature of culture, all seen to be the heart of social archaeology aiming at the reconstruction of societies on the basis of material remains. Society was not seen as an extra-somatic means of adaptation, but a communicative medium (Shanks, 2008). The first studies in post-processual archaeology were of symbolism interpretations of the meaning of things, of prehistoric burial practices, of house design, of pottery decoration. This was a cognitive archaeology of the mind (Gabora, 2008), and symbolism demanded not a fixed specification of singular meaning but a more subtle range of exploration of possible meaning.

Post-processualist Miller (1984) believed the positivist approach of the processualists in holding that which could be sensed, tested and predicted as valid, only sought to produce technical knowledge that facilitated the oppression of ordinary people by elite. Similarly, Miller and Tilley (1984) believed that by putting forward the concept that human societies were irresistibly shaped by external influences and pressures, archaeologists were tacitly accepting social injustice. Many processualists took this further and criticised the fact that archaeologists from wealthy, western countries study and write the histories of poorer nations in the second and third world. Hodder (1984) stated that archaeologists had no right to interpret the prehistory of other ethnic or cultural groups, and that they should instead simply provide individuals from these groups with the ability to construct their own views of the past.

The crux of Jaintia megaliths is its ancestor worship and post-funerary functions. Among them, the dead are cremated and their bones interred into the stone cists. Generally, three ceremonies are held in connection with the deposition of the calcinated bones of the deceased, each time into a cyst of superior size compared to the previous and corresponding to larger kinship group — that of the household or family, matrilineal sub-clan/lineage, and matrilineal clan. Therefore, three different type of bone repositories exists : (i) *mookynroh*, a simple individual cist near the house, receiving only the deceased's bones, (ii) a second *mookynroh*, a larger repository collecting the bones of the dead members of the matrilineal lineage sometime after the first ceremony; and (iii) *moobah* (great stone) or *mooniam* (ceremony's stone), the most important cist receiving finally the bones of matri-clan members.

When a man dies, his body is washed by his male relatives, dressed in ordinary clothes, and taken to the cremation ground. Once the body is cremated, and the fire stamped out, the bones are collected with the help of an iron pincher by a man and received by a woman who holds out a white cloth which must not touch the ground. If the cremation is performed by the clansmen of the deceased, the bones are collected by his mother's brother, brother, or sister's son, and received by his mother's sister, sister, or sister's daughter. When a man is cremated by his children, the bones are collected by his son and received by his widow provided she has no plans of remarriage. If she decides to remarry, then her daughter receives the bones. If she decides to remarry after having already received the bones, then she has to hand over the bones to her husband's clan before she remarries. These bones are carefully kept in the individual family *mookynroh*, until they are handed over to the deceased's maternal relatives after the performance of certain rites. When a woman dies, her husband does not conduct the cremation, which is done by her children and clansmen. A woman who dies without children may be cremated by the husband but he cannot collect nor receive the bones which will be done by the deceased's clansmen and women. From these individual cists, the bones are collected in a year or even later and placed in a larger cist of the sub-clan/lineage. After some years when the clan members are able to gather sufficient money for the ceremony, these bones from family and sub-clan cists are gathered and laid to rest in the *moobah* (clan cist). Thus, an individual born into a clan will likely travel thrice if not at least twice to reach its final resting place at the clan cist, even if it takes some years to do so. The above ceremonies reiterate the importance of the clan system, and therefore a person born into a clan will likely remain there in even after death.

The belief in life after death is re-enforced in their funeral ceremonies, where the dead are given food and drinks for their journey to the after-world. As the deceased is cremated, a raw egg meant for the deceased, followed by other food items (such as maize, bananas and areca nut) are thrown into the fire. After the body is consumed and the bones collected in a white cloth, it is properly wrapped and then interred into the family cist, which are later re-deposited in the clan cist. Inside the repository, a flat stone called *moosiangsangia* (flat stone for the soul) is seen. This is a stone table, where food and drinks are offered to the souls of the deceased on their onward journey. Food items are also offered for dead ancestors, which the recently deceased will carry and deliver.

Besides the funerary practices connected to the cists, another form of ancestor worship is the erection and maintenance of the "clan stones". These are monuments built in honour of the matrikin consisting of a set of three menhirs and a dolmen; five menhirs and a dolmen. Sometimes, the number of menhirs and dolmens go up to fifteen and ten respectively. In all cases, the central menhir, *mookni* (uncle stone), is always taller than those flanking on either sides, and represents the maternal uncle of the clan. The maternal uncle has a high status in Jaintia society, since he wields powers in matters of the family, and the decision-maker in matters of the clan. The menhirs flanking the maternal "uncle stone" represent the younger male members of a clan such as brothers or nephews. These stones called *moobud* (accompanying stones) represent the lower status of male members, by their shortness in height, in comparison to the maternal "uncle stone". The dolmen, placed in front called *mookynthei* (female stones), stand in contrast to the menhirs. These dolmens are referred to as "ancestress stones", and the matrilineal clan ancestress, though at times they could be found alone without the standing stones. If two dolmens are placed side by side, the one to the left represent the root ancestress and the one to the right, the younger ancestress, i.e., ancestress of the sub-clan or family. These are two groups of such structures. *Moolynti* is a path stone constituted by three standing stones: one "uncle stone" and two "accompanying stones", and one flat stone representing the root ancestress. Invariably this type of alignment is set up in order to guide clan members towards the cists – members both living and dead – and while travelling to rest. Due to such function, this type of alignments is concentrated along roads leading to clan cists. *Moobynna*, on the other hand, refers to an alignment comprising at least five standing stones and two flat stones. The standing menhirs represent the maternal uncle and other male kin while the flat stones represent the matrilineal root ancestress (on the left) and the younger ancestress of the lineage or family (on the right). In Iawmusiang, the twelve clusters of "clan stones" follow the principle of the *moobynna*.

This unique system of matri-clan unity is witnessed at various levels during festivals such as *Pam Iawmusiang*, when different clan members gather at their own "clan stones" to pray for their respective clans by calling upon the ancestors. This takes place in the months of February and March, during which each of the twelve clans, represented by its male members, occupies its own stone. The *lyngdoh* (priest) performs rituals on the *moolyngdoh* dolmen to appease the goddess of Iawmusiang, calls upon the ancestral spirits to protect the respective living clan members from all evils, diseases and calamities, and to bring prosperity to them.

Other Socio-cultural Connotations

Jaintia megaliths are associated with other socio-cultural meanings. One such association witnessed in the village under study is with social merit. The powerful are seen to build monuments such as *u-moo-thulelane*, erected by Kat Treiaw's uncle, to commemorate his victory over a cruel giant, but at the expense of his slave Thule Lane[4]. The story of the *sangap* stone[5], equally interesting, tells how a husband had to leave his wife's house in the dead of the night in accordance to custom. It was as a mark of respect for the strength and valour of this strong man that the goddess of Iawmusiang is said to reside herein.

These local stories reveal cultural meanings besides merit. At one level, it reveals the existence of social hierarchy among individuals (or clans), such that the warrior's uncle sacrificed his slave by deceit, while at another level, the society acted as a great leveler. Thus, the elite not only showed their power over the rest through the erection of megaliths but also used deceit to exploit slaves. Slavery was said to be very common in Jaintia Hills during the pre-Colonial times, when human sacrifices were commonly made. Many hapless non-Jaintia travellers would be captured, failing which the slaves of the elite were sacrificed. These sacrifices were made to appease several gods and goddesses such as the river goddess of Kupli towards the north of the studied village. However, the leveling mechanism existent in society equalised such that the stone (*u-moo-thulelane*) came to be known after the slave and not the hero in whose name it was erected. Regardless of differences in wealth and power among the rulers and the ruled, death played a great leveller. Thus a ruler would be finally interned in the same repository as the ruled, if they belonged to the same clan.

Similarly, the story of a husband being asked to leave the wife's house portrayed the dilemma of husbands in Jaintia families. Husbands were seen as visitors outside the purview of the needs, requirements, and functions of the family of procreation, except for biological reasons[6]. This position of the husband is reiterated even in death when he dies in his wife's home and village. In such cases, his bones rest only temporarily in the family cist, and travels to his mother's clan cist for final resting place. Additionally a widow, who intends to remarry, does not receive the husband's bones after cremation, reiterating that the relationship being transitory, served only when he was alive.

Among the different Naga groups living in neighbouring States of Manipur and Nagaland, erection of megaliths takes place after a series of feasts of merit by the merit seeker for whom this becomes a status symbol (Dewar, 1966; Singh, 1985; Jamir, 1998; Devi, 2011). However, megaliths among Jaintias are not set up by an individual for personal merit, rather they are set up communally to commemorate an event, an occasion, or in honour of a dead ancestor/ancestress. These structures, therefore, indicate some form of leadership and affluence which guided the people in the past. The commonness and the widespread presence of these stone structures indicate certain authoritative power or an ideology that forced them build these structures uniformly. Possibly the emergence and establishment of *syiemships*, Jaintia kingdoms set up by dominant clans, were linked with megalithic activity on a larger scale. This was likely possible through the surplus generated by trade particularly in iron, lime, and other products from southern areas in the Khasi Hills, while in the Jaintia Hills through surplus generated from the control over plough agriculture of the Sylhet plains. Megalithic-building of this phase, according to Mawlong (2004), is associated with the establishment of markets at important centers such as Nongskseh, Laitlyngkot, Nongkrem, Mylliem, Cherrapunji, Sutnga, Raliang, Nangbah, Shangpung, Nartiang, Jowai, etc.,; at intra–tribal boundaries such as Shillong and Jowai; and at ecological boundaries such as Mawsmai, Cherrapunji, Jaintiapur etc. One of the well-known sites in Jaintia Hills is Nartiang (Rousseeau, 2012), where hundreds of standing stones and equally large stone tables are seen. The original aim of this architecture seems to have served as large selling platforms or stalls during festivals. Every site of the market, marked with numerous stone structures was the former seat of a local political power, presided over by a particular clan or *syiem* (king). Each week on the market day, tax was collected over the goods. The *syiem* and the council of elders (each having a status title) shared the tax before eating together on the large stone table in front of the highest slab. The founding stone of the place received some offerings before the opening of the market. This stone was considered as the seat of the presiding market goddess. This has similarity with the Nangbah *khimdan* stone which till today is referred to as the "tax collector stone".

Sacralisation of the Past

Christianity entered the Khasi-Jaintia Hills in the early nineteenth century. It brought about a change in the socio-cultural life of the people. As a result of the spread of Christianity and the missionary zeal to dispel ignorance, superstition and the worship of evil spirits, the megalithic tradition was seriously eroded and gradually disappeared (Mawlong, 2009). However in the village under study, the cultural practices are still alive. Understandably, Christian families no longer follow ancestral practices of periodical bone collection of the dead, and the dead instead are buried in accordance to Christian rituals. The diminishing interest in the traditional beliefs and practices among Christians is mirrored in the lessened sanctity of these stones. A Christian does not take part in any prayer or ritual to appease gods and goddesses residing in various sacred spaces including stones. However half of the studied population was *Niamtre* believers, and therefore the importance of these lithic structures were still alive. Ritualistic behaviours towards these stones were still in practice and the deposition of the deceased's family and clan repositories were still followed by the traditionalists. A fortnight before the present fieldwork, a woman passed away, and not only were her burnt remnants still visible in the cremation ground, but her bones placed in the repository were still afresh in the minds of witnesses.

During the festivals of *Pam Iawmusiang* and *Knia Lyngdoh* when several gods and goddesses are worshipped to bring prosperity and good health to the people, the Christians abstain from ritualistic regalia, but take part in the celebratory feasts and sports which take place in Iawmusiang. Many Christian men are also known to take part in traditional sports to test their strength against other men of the village. However, irrespective of their religious affiliations, men and women take care not to break a taboo – whether it is connected to behaviour inside a sacred grove, or the touching of the sacred stones. The clan stones whether it is *moolynti* or *moobynna* are still used for resting/sitting and as guidance and even younger members, notwithstanding religious affiliations, recognised their own "clan stones".

An interesting development in recent time is the revivalism in past cultural practices within the fold of Christianity which earlier was the strongest opponent. The Catholic church in recent times made efforts to preserve and conserve some of the surviving megalithic monuments, which stand within the church premises like the monument at the Lailyngkot church compound in Jaintia Hills. Additionally, the Catholic church at Laitumkhrah in the city of Shillong erected a set of menhirs and a dolmen within its premises to mark the centenary celebrations of the Catholic church in the Khasi-Jaintia hills in 1990 (Mawlong, 2009). This indicates the secularisation of megaliths, once solely connected to socio-religious life of the *Niamtre* Jaintias. Thus, the stones which traditionally had religious connotations were made "secular" by taking away its meaning and putting it up within church premises as mere tokens. Similar efforts by the State government was seen when a few monoliths were set up in 1975 in the centre of the city under its patronage to commemorate the centenary of the State capital of Shillong (Rao, 1991).

In this continuance of past tradition, the politics of culture is inherent. No doubt, the colourful nature of these structures has comparatively gone down since a sizeable number of the population are now Christians, who do not adhere to the customs of post-crematory rituals, and other religious practices. However, on certain occasions, the Christian churches and the State government itself are reviving these traditions. This revivalism, does not in any way reflect a re-sacralisation of traditional symbols —but rather a token to counter the challenges of the traditionalists, especially, the Seng Khasi proponents[7]. This was a counteractive step so that the church could be viewed as pro-tradition. This social reality is supported by the fact that except the structure (megalith), no other socio-religious activity of the past survives within the Christian complex. The ceremonies connected to the erection of megaliths within the church premises are marked by Christian prayers and hymns. Thus, this is a re-invention of tradition, where responses to novel situations take the form of reference to old situations or that establish their own past by quasi-obligatory repetition. This reality finds parallel in the revivalism of "folk culture" traditions among the Jaintia, such as songs and dances, dress and ornaments, celebrations and rituals, leading to a quasi-sacralisation of the past.

Among the *Niamtres*, on the other hand, a sacralisation of the past is evident when the "living" nature of the megalithic culture is analysed. No new megaliths have been erected, but the existing ones have not only been maintained, but associated practices were still observed. When "clan stones" fall, some members take care to re-erect it; when religious stones are displaced, then accompanied with rituals conducted by the priest, the villagers set it up again. An interesting change that is witnessed is the renovation of the cists (both family and clan), with the use of newer materials. For instance, when a clan cist breaks down, more often cement and mortar are being used to re-build it. In fact, years of renovation has led to a total facelift to cists of some clans. Thus, the prehistoric structures found in Nangbah are still seen to carry many socio-religious interpretations. This brings the *living* nature of these structures to the fore.

Conclusion

Post-processual approaches in archaeology are many and varied, however, they can go a long way in giving archaeology culture-specific interpretations instead of sweeping the whole process under one blanket. This chapter is an attempt to see how much of a culture is revealed through the study of a group of megaliths. Many traditional archaeologists acknowledge that artifacts (including megaliths) are ultimately expressions of ideas to each cultural and historical context. This was found to be true in the present study, where the use of these structures is very much alive and a part of their religious and cultural life. The story of how the *sangap* stone came into place is interesting and reveals their unique marriage system. The clan stones indicate how much of their social life is structured around the clan system, and how a group of clans alone can be a force of solidarity and cohesiveness for the welfare of the village. The male-female dichotomy, seen in the ancestress and maternal uncle stones, though passively stressed is also interesting, since it symbolises not only the inherent natural forces, but how they come together as one. Women did have real power, at least as founder-mothers, as expressed by the innumerable presence of female representation (in the form of the ancestress stone). The specific position and reverence given to ancestors who are called upon and worshipped through the stones that have been set up for them is an interesting phenomenon. The size and position of the structures indicate their importance and prestige, not only in the clan, but also in the village as a whole.

Megaliths in Jaintia Hills seem to reify territoriality for cists, whether belonging to a family or clan, are found in a coursed manner in certain well-laid areas. While no evidence of hierarchy within a clan is visible—such that all members of a clan are laid to rest in a single cist—stratification in terms of prestige and ranking (during rituals) among and between clans in terms of its history and numerical strength do exist. Prominent families of the *syiem* and other functionaries had their elaborate family cists, and dominant clans had clan repositories and elaborate funerals to not only worship, but also commemorate the ancestors and their deaths. Besides the funerary connotations, symbols of territoriality, i.e., marking an area out, are repeatedly seen in the clan stones (meant for a particular clan), path stones (the pathway to the clan repository), places for ceremonies (such as Iawmusiang for annual rituals), and even market places (such as the *khimdan* stone). In Nartiang, a few kilometers away from the village, the market place is strewn with menhirs and dolmens of different shapes and sizes. The identification of markets through stones assumes prominence since the Jaintias achieved prosperity through trade and commerce in the pre-Colonial days.

It is the funerary stones that differentiate the Khasi-Jaintia megaliths from their northeastern counterparts, and the striking absence of structures raised though feasts of merit, which are common among the various Naga tribes of the region. It is likely that the earliest Jaintia megaliths were probably the *moobuhshieng* (cists), of the *moókynroh* and *moobah* variety where bones of ancestors were stored, built by prominent families and dominant clans, since ancestor worship forms a very important part of their religion. The construction of these structures was probably followed by other lithics, such as the clan stones, the commemorative stones and stones for miscellaneous purposes.

Despite the different types of megaliths, it is the system of matriliny which is highly underlined in the Jaintia megaliths. The underlying feature being twofold: the veneration of the dead ancestors, and the unification of the matrilineal members of a clan. This social fact is rather strong such that a person once born into a particular clan will die and remain in that clan forever. Consequently, the dead are interred in their clan repositories, and it is seen that the unity of the matrilineal kin even after death is of utmost importance. Non-funerary megaliths, such as clan stones, has also a strong connection to the matrilineal system – such that there are stones in memory of the ancestress and maternal uncles "reiterating the social position of the matrilineal kin.

In conclusion, the present study reveals that the crux of this prehistoric culture is still maintained by the present day megalith users in Jaintia Hills due to its connectedness with the social system that of matriliny and worship of matrilineal ancestors. Despite various factors of change, such as Christianity and modernisation, this culture is still alive through the processes of revivalism and sacralisation of the past.

Note

1. Most Khasi Christians felt they were superior in every way to the orthodox Khasis. In fact, the latter were called "pagans" and "heathens" by their own Christian brethren (Natarajan, 1977: 90). Mawlong (2009 : 199) states, "The process of deculturation that slowly began with the spread of Christianity in the Khasi Hills in particular, is now complete... Here, *mawbahs* or the most sacred of the Khasi megalithic structures embodying concepts of clan solidarity and their matrilineal ancestry now function as pig sties and as public conveniences. Some local people when questioned about these structures were totally unaware of the significance in traditional society."
2. In Jaintia Hills, there is greater significance of the megaliths, and sites are better preserved and looked after possibly because the traditional religion is strong, and Christianity never had the same impact as it had in the Khasi Hills (Mawlong, 2009: 200).
3. "*Khimdan*" comes from two words, "khim" meaning "handful or fistful"; "dan" meaning "tax". However, this stone is not only the tax collector stone, but also one where some decisions, regarding the market were made / taken.

4. There was once a cruel giant named Shai Rangmut, who lived in Madan Saphlang Nongjngi, a place bordering Nangbah village. The last of his atrocities included the kidnapping of *bei lyngdoh*, the female priestess, whose absence brought drought and famine in the village. Not being able to bear such sufferings, the villagers of Nangbah under the leadership of Kat Treiaw of Thubru clan declared battle against the giant, who was defeated, killed and beheaded. His head was hung in the village for days together till scavengers finished it off. As remembrance of this event and in honour of the warrior, it was decided to erect a menhir at the spot, where the head of the giant was hung. This stone was carried from Wahiajer village some 40 kms away by pulling it with pumpkin stalks, as the priest–chanted prayers. On reaching Nangbah, a pit was dug to place the stone. However, despite numerous efforts to place it, the stone refused to stand. A ritual was conducted in which it was revealed that the stone wanted a human sacrifice and that it would stand only on a human body.On this revelation, Kat Treiaw's uncle hatched a plan to sacrifice his slave, Thule Lane, in order that the menhir could be erected. He sat near the pit and pretended that his *dabi shun*, a small container where he stored lime, had slipped from his hand and asked his slave to jump into the pit and bring it back. As Thule Lane jumped inside the pit at his master's bidding, the huge stone was pushed inside the pit and placed atop the slave.
5. Sangap, who hailed from the village had a wife at Shangpung and according to their visiting husband marriage system, he would visit his wife at night and leave early in the morning. Once when there was torrential rains, he asked his wife for a rain shield (*knup*) made of bamboo and cane, which his wife refused. She is said to have told him, out of anger, to use stone as cover. Sangap searched long and hard for a large, flat stone in the pelting rain and on finding one used it as a rain shield and carried it all the way to Nangbah. Notwithstanding the incredulous feat of Sangap who is credited with carrying the stone alone in the dead of the night in torrential rains,

it reveals the unique custom of marital residence that the Jaintias follow.

6. A Khasi-Jaintia family was primarily a family of mother, children and uncles. A father who should be the leading member of the family became less significant because of his role as an uncle on the one hand and the incompatibility of his clan code with that of his wife on the other hand. Whereas his status in the house of his sisters, among his nephews and nieces is supreme, authoritative and decisive, he is nevertheless a mere dummy in the house of his own wife (Snaitang, 1998: 56).
7. Established in Shillong in 1899, the founders of the *Seng Khasi* were men who were the products of the time — men who had a liberal education, business opportunities and had found government employment. The *Seng Khasis* were witness to the zealous efforts of missionaries propagating the faith and were concerned that large numbers of Khasis were being converted to Christianity. The *Seng Khasi* which remains an active religious group has over the years been able to retain the "primal" Khasi religion, something that most other tribes were not able to do (Syiemlieh, 2005: 147). Having initiated the process of revivalism and reformation of the Khasi religion, the *Seng Khasi* encouraged the people to abide by the matrilineal system of descent, to respect the kith and kin on the maternal and paternal side, to believe in God, and to serve God through service of humankind. The *Seng Khasi* flag came to depict a crowing cock in white and red setting. The red signifies courage and white represents the world. The *Seng Khasi* started organising archery competitions and traditional dance performances such as "Ka Shad Suk Mynsiem" and the "Nongkrem Dance" (Das, 2009:4).

References

Bezbaruah, D. 2004. *Megalithic Remains in Karbi Anglong District, Assam: A Study in the Context of Karbi Culture.* Unpublished Ph.D Thesis, Gauhati University.

Bradley, R. 1998. *The Significance of Monuments: On the Shaping of Human Experience in Neolithic and Bronze Age Europe.* London; Routledge.

Chapman, R. 1981. 'The emergence of formal disposal areas and the 'problem' of megalithic tombs in prehistoric Europe'. pp. 71-82, in R. Chapman, I. Kinnes and K. Randsborg (Eds.): *The Archaeology of Death.* Cambridge; Cambridge University Press.

Das, N. K. 2009. 'Identity politics and social exclusion in India's North-East: The case of re-distributive justice', *Bangladesh e-Journal of Sociology,* 6, 1.

Devi, P. B. 2011. *Megalithic Culture of Manipur.* Delhi; Agam Kala Prakashan.

Dewar, S. 1966. 'The ceremony of erecting a megalith among the Angami Nagas', *Folklore,* 77, 4: 264-69.

Flemming, A. 1973. 'Tombs for the living', *Man,* 8, 2:178-93.

Furer-Haimendorf, C. 1945. 'The problem of megalithic cultures in middle India', *Man in India,* 25, 2: 73-86.

Gabora, L. 2008. 'Mind'. pp. 283- 296, in R.A. Bentley, H.D.G. Maschner and C. Chippindale (Eds): *Handbook of Archaeological Theories.* Plymouth, UK; Altamira Press.

Godwin-Austen, H.H. 1872. 'On the stone monuments of Khasi hills tribes', *Journal of the Royal Anthropological Institute,* 1:122-36.

Gurdon, P.R.T. 1914. *The Khasis.* London; Macmillan.

Hodder, I. 1984. 'Burials, houses, men and women in the European Neolithic'. pp. 51 – 68, in D. Miller and C. Tilley (Eds): *Ideology, Power and Prehistory.* Cambridge; Cambridge University Press.

Hodder, I. 1990. *The Domestication of Europe: Structure and Contingency in Neolithic Societies.* Oxford; Basil Blackwood.

Jamir, W. 1998. 'Megaliths in Nagaland', *Purattatva,* 28:104-10.

MacKie, E. 1997. 'Maeshowe and the winter solastice: Ceremonial aspects of the Orkney Grooved Ware culture', *Antiquity,* 71:338-59.

Marak, Q. 2012.' Megaliths of North East India'. pp. 34 – 53, in T.B. Subba (Ed.): *North-East India: A Handbook of Anthropology.* New Delhi; Orient Blackswan.

Mawlong, C.A. 2004. 'Megaliths and social formation in Khasi-Jaintia hills'. pp. 35 – 56, In M. Momin and C. A. Mawlong (Eds.): *Society and Economy in North-East India* Vol. I. New Delhi; Regency Publication.

Mawlong, C. A. 2009. 'Christianity and megalithic tradition in the Khasi-Jaintia hills: A preliminary study of the processes of deculturation and enculturation'. pp 194 – 202, in T. B. Subba, J. Puthenpurakal and S. J. Puykunnel (Eds.): *Christianity and Change in Northeast India*. New Delhi; Concept Publishing Company.

Miller, D and C. Tilley. 1984. *Ideology, Power and Prehistory*. Cambridge; Cambridge University Press.

Miller, D. 1984. 'Modernism and suburbia as material ideology'. pp. 37 – 50, in D. Miller and C. Tilley (Eds): *Ideology, Power and Prehistory*. Cambridge; Cambridge University Press.

Mills, J. P and J. H. Hutton. 1929. 'Ancient monoliths of North Cachar', Journal of Asiatic Society of Bengal, 25, 1: 185-300.

Natarajan, N. 1977. *The Missionary among the Khasis*. New Delhi; Sterling Publishers.

Nelson, S. M. 1999. 'Megalithic monuments and the introduction of rice into Korea'. pp. 147 – 165, in C. Gosden and J. Hather (Eds.): *The Prehistory of Food: Appetites for Change*. New York; Routledge.

Ramachandran, K. S. 1971. *Bibliography of Indian Megaliths*. Madras; State Department of Archaeology.

Rao, S.N.1991. 'Megalithic practices among Khasis and Nagas of North-Eastern India'. pp. 106 – 123, in J. P. Singh and G. Sengupta (Eds.): *Archaeology of North-Eastern India*. New Delhi; Vikas Publishing House.

Renfrew, A. C. 1976. 'Megaliths, territories and populations'. pp. 198- 220, in S. J. De Laet (Ed.): *Acculturation and Continuity in Atlantic Europe*. Bruges; de Tempel.

Rousseleau, R. 2012. 'Megalithic landscapes, cultures and identity in North East India'. pp. 17 – 35, in N. Laine and T. B. Subba (Eds.): *Nature, Environment and Society: Conservation, Governance and Transformation in India*. New Delhi; Orient Blackswan Private Limited.

Sen, S. 2004. *Khasi-Jaintia Folklore: Context, Discourse and History*. Chennai; National Support Folklore Centre.

Shanks, M. 2008. 'Post-processual archaeology and after'. pp. 133 – 46, in R. A. Bentley, H. D. G. Maschner and C. Chippindale (Eds): *Handbook of Archaeological Theories*. Plymouth, UK; Altamira Press.

Sherratt, A. 1990. 'The genesis of megaliths: Monumentality, ethnicity and social complexity in Neolithic North-West Europe', *World Archaeology*, 22, 2: 147-67.

Singh, O. K. 1985. 'A live megalithic culture in Manipur'. pp. 491-496, in V. N. Misra and P. Bellwood (Eds.): *Recent Advances in Indo-Pacific Prehistory: Proceedings of the International Symposium held at Poona, December 19-21,* 1978. New Delhi; Oxford and IBH Publishing Company.

Snaitang, O. L. 1998. 'The impact of Christianity on the Khasi-Jaintia matrilineal family'. pp. 54-73, in P. M. Chacko (Ed.): *Matriliny in Meghalaya: Tradition and Change*. New Delhi; Regency Publications.

Syiemlieh, D. R. 2005. 'Christian missions and tribes in the hills of North-East India'. pp. 147-156, in T. B. Subba and S. Som (Eds.): *Between Ethnography and Fiction: Verrier Elwin and the Tribal Question in India*. Hyderabad; Orient Longman.

Thom, A. 1966. 'Megaliths and mathematics'. *Antiquity*, 40: 121-28.

3
Cultural Transmission and Social Contexts of Pottery Making among Andros of Manipur, India

– Mayanglambam ManiBabu

Introduction

Studies on craft skill learning (Shennan and Steele, 1999) and situated learning (Lave and Wenger, 1991; Wenger *et al.*, 2002), etc., are the two important aspects amongst the myriad fields of anthropological studies on learning and cultural transmission. At its simplest, situated learning is the learning takes place in the same context in which it is applied. Lave and Wenger (1991) argue that learning should not be viewed as simply the transmission of abstract and decontextualised knowledge from one individual to another, but a social process whereby knowledge is co-constructed. In addition, they *(op. cit.)* suggest that such learning is situated in a specific context and embeded within particular social and physical environment. In the situated learning approach, knowledge and skills are learned in the contexts that reflect how knowledge is obtained and applied in everyday situations. In addition, in the domain of cultural transmission the impact of the gene-culture co- evolutionary (Cavalli-Sforza and Feldman, 1981; Stone and Lurquin, 2005; MacEachern, 2000) and dual inheritance approaches to cultural evolution (Richerson and Boyd, 2005; Boyd and Richerson, 1985) are the two significant developments. By way of interaction, cultural elements are learned, shared and transmitted spatially by individual members in a society. Through a cultural system that is, certainly developed to an unprecedented degree among the humans, they acquire tendencies to a particular mode of behaviour. This behaviour is perceived as one of the dual inheritance frameworks of humans (Boyd and Richerson, 1985; Richerson and Boyd, 2005) where cultural transmission acts like an inheritance system, bringing out significant similarities between those passing on the information and those learning, which could not be accounted for by genetic transmission on continuity of environment (Boyd and Richerson, 1985; Rindos, 1984, 1989). It is held that cultural transmission, like particular gene distribution, can persist in the face of changing environmental conditions to which different practices would be better adapted (Boyd and Richerson, 1985; Edgerton, 1971; Guglielmino *et al.*, 1995; Henrich and Gil-White, 2001 Henrich *et al.*, 2001). Though the routes of cultural transmission towards evolution can be modelled mathematically in similar ways to that of genetic transmission, using (variations on existing population) genetic and epidemiological models (Boyd and Richerson, 1985; Cavalli-Sforza and Feldman, 1981) – there are limits to strictly biology-based models of cultural evolution, because the analogue of the processes that affect gene frequencies in population (such as, mutation, selection, and drift) do not exhaust the set of processes that affect cultural attribute frequencies (Bentley and Shenan, 2003). Here, even if culture is treated as system of information transmission following Darwinian rules parallel to and independent from genetic transmission, this should not be taken to be synonymous with the cultural evolutionism theory of Morgan, Taylor and Spencer (Leonard, 2001). Eerkens and Lipo's (2007) argument regarding the cultural transmission processes is that these are greatly affected by the content, context, and mode of transmission and fundamental structure variation in material culture.

Since pot-making technology is a process replicated and transformed through learning, the propensity of Darwinian concept of cultural transmission is appropriately extended to the spatio-temporal continuity of the ceramic technological tradition, since within a pot-making population people possess inherited information related to the art through the mechanism of social learning. Significantly, the study of cultural transmission of ceramic technology lies with type-variety system of ceramic taxonomy, where the combined value forces of the total configuration (the inherent cultural bias) are striven for, as desired norms in ceramic manufacture (Gifford, 1960:346). The cultural transmission enables to move naturally from specific pottery-making preferences by one or a few potters to a widely and culturally accepted ceramic category reflecting widely shared value orientations.

The significances of examining the social parameters relating the training period have been felt by many workers (such as, Bril and Roux, 1993; Carr, 1995; David *et al.*, 1991; Dietler and Herbich, 1989; Gosselain, 1998; Herbich and Dietler, 1991; Hosler, 1996; Lave, 1988; Lave and Wenger, 1991; MacEachern, 1996; Mahias, 1993; Sackett, 1990; Wallaert-Petre, 1999a, 1999b; etc.). Wallaert-Petre (2001) proposes an etic-emic approach involved in handmade pottery making which may give 'a useful tool to evaluate the influence of teaching period on the making and reproduction of material culture' (pp. 472). Here, the etic approach corresponds with all the processes shred by human beings, who are learning technical behaviours (which psychologists refer to as cross-cultural patterning of apprenticeship) and the emic approach refers to the intra-cultural parameters of apprenticeship that are shaped by cultural contexts. Many workers (Coy, 1989; Lave and Wenger, 1991; Moll, 1990; Rogoff, 1990; Rogoff and Lave, 1984; Vygotsky, 1978; Wenger, 1998; etc.) have put forward myriad frameworks to explain how individuals become skilled practitioners and how learning occurs through participation in activity within social context.

It is suggested (Van der Leeuw, 1994) that the major concepts involved in the manufacture of a ceramic vessel are typology (shape), patronomy (how the vessel is divided into sections) and sequence (order of manufacture). Four types of learning frameworks have been proposed by Schiffer and Skibo (1987:597) such as, self-teaching by trial and error, observation/imitation, verbal instruction/explanation, and hands-on demonstration. Others (Kramer, 1997; Rogoff and Lave, 1984; Vygotsky, 1978, etc.) have discussed the role-played by the use of visual observation and verbal communication during apprenticeship and their impact on teaching and learning strategies and behaviours. In non-state societies, observational learning and imitation of adept potters is probably the most common form of transmitting knowledge (Bunzel, 1972; Crown, 1999; DeBoer, 1990; Fortes, 1938; Goody, 1989; Lave and Wenger, 1991). Three vectors of cultural transmission characterise transfer of knowledge,–two that focus on intergenerational transmission (*vertical, oblique*), and one that involves the transfer of knowledge within a generation or peer group (*horizontal*). These terminologies have their genesis to the Darwinian approaches in characterising and comparing cultural transmission, particularly for studying apprenticeship and other learning frameworks (Stark *et al.*, 2008). In *vertical transmission* cultural knowledge moves from parents to children within the family; primarily occurring throughout infancy and early childhood, this process reflects parent-child proximity and attachment, is powerful, and is thought to be relatively conservative (Cavalli-Sforza *et al.*,1982; Guglielmino *et al.*,1995; Hewlett *et al.*,2002). In *oblique transmission,* cultural knowledge moves from 'a member of given generation to a member of the next (or later) generation, who is not his or her child or direct descendant', such as formal teacher-student interactions (Cavalli-Sforza and Feldman, 1981:54). *Horizontal transmission* involves the transfer of knowledge between members of the same generation or age group, whether these individuals are related biologically or not, such as in peer group learning (Cavalli-Sforza *et al.*, 1982; Guglielmino *et al.*, 1995).

The present chapter endeavours to give a brief ethnographic account of pottery production, and to explain the vectors that involve the transfer of knowledge of pottery making in terms of the patrilocal set up among pot-making population of Manipur, the Andro, among whom pottery is a part-time, women-oriented occupation.

The People

The Andros are one of the important constituent ethnic groups of the larger *Loi* (or, Chakpa) population of Manipur and inhabit the village of the same name – perched on the eastern down slopes of the Nongmaiching hill range of the Imphal East district (Manipur), at an altitude of about 2,700 meters above sea level. The patri-oriented agrarian Andros are mainly agriculturists whose craft forms the major occupation of livelihood. Rice is the only main cereal that dominates the agricultural landscape of Andro that surrounds the village. Other important economic pursuits of the Ando include pot making and distillation of country-liquor (*yu*). The two activities pursued by the females form the substantial economy of the Andro family coffer. Women excel in the art of pot making on part-time basis in the dry seasons when they are free from the agricultural work. The people (population: 8,313 souls – Census of India, 2001) live in a compact and well-ordered village with a well-marked boundary in as many as 23 hamlets (*leikais*). An Andro *leikai* is principally a small territorial unit, which is demarcated by some territorial lines of division, based usually on the geo-physical features of natural settings, such as lanes, marshes, lakes, streams/rivulets, etc. In every *leikai*, one comes across a number of lineages (*yumnaks*). Thus, lineage ties cut across the territorial ties, and members of the same lineage have a great deal of 'horizontal solidarity' that exists in common. The Andro have seven exogamous corporate groups, clans (*salai*), namely - Mangang (or, Ningthouja), Luwang, Khuman, Moirang, Kha-nganba, Chenglei and Angom. As many as eighteen lineages[1] are known to exist, each affiliating to either or the other of the seven exogamous groups. Each clan has a head, called *Piba*, who are the ultimogenitural male issue of an Andro lineage/clan. Another remarkable feature of the Andro society, that traces its genesis to primordial days, is the existence of the local organisation of *pana* institution, firmly based on the *yumnaks*. In reality, *pana* is a *yumnak*-level organisation and every Andro male is automatically enrolled as a member of a *pana* by birth. The Andro *pana* can also be taken as lineage segmentation, a principle of micro-political structure. Another significant feature apparent in the Andro social system is the existence of a permanent network of alliance between the 'wife-giving' and 'wife-receiving' *yumnaks* / families in respect of the disposal of the dead.

System of Ceramic Production

Pottery manufacturing among the Andros is one economic strategy to meet household economic needs. The people use a wide range of earthen vessels in their daily chores. In addition, some of these are the indispensable items in the religious affairs. They classify their pottery based on the design of the pots, which is, largely, the morphological projection of their usage. This functionally based classificatory system focuses on such features of the ceramic vessel as size, shape, presence or absence of decoration and other factors. Based on the function, the Andro pots, made by hand and beater technique may be classified into utilitarian and non-utilitarian group. The vessels of the first group include that of the cooking, drinking, storing, carrying pots, water-transport vessel, serving and eating vessels, etc.; and ritual wares are the main items of the non-utilitarian group.

(*a*) (*b*)

Figure 3.1: Andro potters exploiting resources from the specific resource sites – (*a*) Leitan (clay), (*b*) Leichreng (tempering material)

The Andro system of ceramic production, organised at the level of the nuclear or extended family, is a complex process and sets of principles govern the organisational networks of production. The sets include cultural, environmental and economical factors that make the production a part-time, seasonal and specialised craft. Andro ceramics are modeled by using the potters' finger and thumb. The process is simple rather, but labourious and time-consuming. The raw material of the Andro pottery consist of *leitan* (clay class) co-mingled with *leichreng* (the tempering material) at a given proportion of 1 : 1.25 for the sole effect of achieving workability, counteracting ill-effects of shrinkage and facilitating drying process of the finished product. The craft is solely in the realm of female household activities, forming main economic pursuit and province of married females. Married women, who have completed six months of their married life can only make the earthen vessels. They engage in this craft on part-time basis in consonance with the systematically patterned network of cultural, economical and climatical stipulation. The manufacturing processes of Andro ceramics consist of the processing of the primary resources—such as cleaning and dipping, mixing and pounding, and kneading. Fashioning of the vessel is done with potter's naked hand and the stuffs are processed in a series of stages using a combination of strip, and traditional technique of paddle and anvil (hand-beater technique). Adept potters are well acquainted with this technique of ceramic production. The thoroughly kneaded paste of *leitan* and *leichreng* is first made into a number of flattened and elongated clay slabs (called *charei*) on a wooden plank. Each strip is of about 45 cm to 50 cm in length. The local way of keeping the normal length of each *charei* is about one *khudup* (that is, the length measured from the tip of the middle finger up to the elbow in stretch position). The number of the *chareis* prepared is made in consonance with the desired size of the product. A special strip (which they called *phei*), which is a little larger than the other clay strips (*chareis*), is made by adding more paste. This special strip *(phei)* is the one with which a pot is initially made. The two ends of the elongated *phei* (having about 3" to 5" in height) are joined forming a ring (Fig. 3.2 b). The ring of strip *(phei)* is then placed on an inverted pot (Fig. 3.2 d). Any medium sized earthen pot may be used for the purpose, and this particular pot is locally called a *phuhou chaphu* (literal meaning: a pot upon which pot making is to start). The two ends of the clay strip (*phei*) are so well amalgamated by the potter's thumb and fingers that any suture left on the outer wall is expunged (Fig. 3.2 c). On this *phei* (the first clay strip in pot making), a *charei* is placed, keeping one end overlapping laterally on the other end. The overlapping portion is then removed and joining part is made even by moving the index finger with slight pressure. Already prepared strips are then placed one upon another with a little pressure to fuse. Rolls of strips are appended till the required height of the vessel is attained (Fig. 3.2 e). Now, it takes the shape of a large cylinder, with hollow ends.

(a)

(b)

(c)

(d)

(e)

(f)

(g)

Fig. 3.2: (a-g) : An adept Andro potter at work.

Before shaping the body portion of the pot, the rim part is first shaped right from the uppermost part of the strip. The neck and rim portions are shaped with the hand- beater technique. Initially, the uneven portion of the uppermost border is outlined with a knife or a bamboo split to make the edge consistent and uniform. A water-damped beater (*tetap*) around all border is flapping the uppermost borderline of about 11/2" or 2", which shall be made into the rim portion. The beater on one side does fluttering on the edge skillfully and categorically and the potter's fingers (pressed oppositely) on the other side of the wall that an outcurve constricted neck, flaring rim and a rounded lip are ultimately yielded. A final retouch of the rim and neck part is duly given with a wet rag (called *petep*) held in between the potter's thumb and the other fingers. While rubbing and shaping the rim and neck portion, the potter walks around the molding pot. The process of making the rim and lip part is known as *mapan peba*.

The globular body part of a pot naturally gets its form through the paddle-and-anvil technique. The convex surface is achieved by the outward pressures of an oval pebble given from the inner surface by the potter's left hand against the mild blow given with the beater by the other hand on the outer surface of the pot.

The shoulder part of the green pot is also made with the same technique. While shaping the green pot - the beater, the oval pebble and the surface of the pot are wetted frequently in order to avoid stickiness and cracking on the pot. In general, the shaping is done with plain beaters.

The base part is shaped by keeping the pot in an inverted position. The base is gradually mould by tapering the thickened area of the paste deposited at the lower base of the body. Mild pressure given by the beater and the rounded pebble from the opposite sides of the wall makes the base tapered . In addition, the act continues till only a little portion of gap/hole is left, which is filled finally with a piece of flat paste. The potter's thumb and fingers mend so skillfully the portion that no trace of sutures is seen at the outer and inner walls. Besides, roughness of inner surface is reduced with *unio* shell to bring forth a good profile.

The process and techniques described above are for making large and medium-sized pots. The process for fashioning smaller vessels is different, and simpler than that of larger ones. In this case, the base is molded first, and gradually makes the body, shoulder and neck portions. The whole process of pot making takes place on the potter's lap, with the same technique of hand- beater. Here ends the general shaping of the green pots, which is followed by decoration and drying vis-à-vis beating stages.

After the general shaping, the pot is dried in the shade for about 1-2 hours, after which the second and final shaping starts. According to the sizes, shaping and beating are done with the plain beater (*tetap*), on the outer surface of the pots in such manner that the force of beater is counteracted from the inner wall with an oval-shaped stone anvil held by other hand. The surface of the pot, the beater and the oval stone are frequently wetted while undergoing beating process in order to avoid stickiness and cracking of the pot. The purpose of beating is obviously to enlarge the size of the green ceramics further cohesion to its clay wall. Beating, however, is not done at a stretch but in three or four stages, whose number of stages may be reduced or increased to potter's convenience and perception as well as to the size of the vessel. Moreover, the interval of beating depends upon the weather condition and the amount of work the potter has for the day. Initially, plain beaters are used in every beating stage. The decorative patterns are stamped on the soft wall of the green pot with beater having engraved mark of designs. The designs include the motifs of comb, cord, button, fish bone, etc. Stamping with engraved beater is done after the completion of final shaping and beating. Linear marks on the serrated mouth of pots are incised with bamboo splits. In some pots, impressions with bamboo branches are seen. In rare cases, decoration of ceramics with perforation, pinching of relief and appliqué bosses are seen. Various designs of perforation comprise round, triangular and floral motifs, accomplished by the bamboo split. Ritual vessels are embellished with appliqué designs and engravings and in designing the appliqué bosses - lugs, formed separately for the purpose are luted at the shoulder part of the undried green pot, keeping intact till these are affixed into oneness with the pot.

Drying of green pottery is not done quickly under the direct sunshine just to avoid the chance of cracking of finished stuff. Such undesirable damages are easily avoided by drying these objects in the shade. Drying is normally carried out in the shade for a couple of days or so, or even longer in case of large pots. Duration of shade drying may vary according to the size of the pot as well as the weather condition. Normally, a medium-sized vessel is required to go through the air-drying for five to seven days during dry weather. Fully dried and polished vessels are ready for firing. As a rule, Andro pot is not fired singly. Potters baked their pots collectively at a time, that is, a number of dried pots (ranging usually from 15 to 60) that belonged to different potters are accumulated and arranged for firing. Firing is performed in the open space according to the potters' convenience - either at the surrounding paddy field, near the foothill or at the large open space within some habitation site *(ingkhol).* The Andro fuel resources consist of readily available unwanted by- products of subsistence activities. The fuel for firing comprises straw from harvest, dry cow dung cakes and husk. The female potters and their children collect dry cow dung cakes from the nearby pasture well before the day of firing. Normally, Andro women fire their earthenware in the afternoon. Before the act of firing, it is mandatory on the part of potters to pray the Mother Earth to get good outcome of baked pot and save them from being cracked. It is strongly observed in the society that *phuhings* (*phu* - earthen vessels, *hing* or *ahingba* - live: literally means the unfired green pots) should not be dispensed – either by giving away or by selling to someone. A *phuhing,* among the *Loi* (and among the larger Meitei community), is believed to have magical value used by local shaman (*maiba*) occasionally in accusation of witchcraft and sorcery (ManiBabu, 1994). During dry, clear days making of medium-sized earthenware takes about 12 to 16 days - right from its initial stage of mixing/pounding till the end of firing.

The fabrication-time needed to produce different types of Andro pots is shown in Table 3.1, revealing the mean value of both the actual time spent in fabrication and the elapsed time.

Table 3.1: Time needed (Mean value) to produce handmade earthen vessels among the Andros

TYPES OF POTS		Mean Values of the				NO	Mean Values of the				
		Vessel height	Maxm Diam	Neck Diam.	Body circum ference		Actual time spent (including firing time)		Elapsed time		
							Hrs	Min	Days	Hrs	Mns
Cooking pots:	Large	26.8	27.8	27.1	87.5	7	21	13	13	18	34
	Small	20.6	23.4	14.2	73.7	7	19	26	9	20	16
Water carrying jar		23.2	31.6	11.4	99.7	7	22	49	12	13	12
Storage vessel		53.2	47.8	23.4	153.1	7	28	52	16	20	15
Liquor carrying jar		31.3	30.9	10.7	99.6	7	24	18	12	23	52
Globular jar	Medium	26.2	25.9	16.9	92.3	7	20	49	12	20	25
	Small	13.5	15.8	11.6	52.9	7	9	54	7	10	18
Serving vessel		8.1	26.2	31.3	85.6	7	7	39	7	22	35

Source : Field Data.

Here, the elapsed time, the actual time spent to fabricate vessel includes the firing time. A larger globular cooking pot, - with a vessel height of 26.8 cm, maximum diameter of 27.8 cm, neck diameter of 27.1 cm and body circumference of 87.5 cm, - formed by the strip, and paddle and anvil technique requires a fabrication-time of 21 hrs 13 minutes stretched over 13 days 18 hours and 34 minutes (Table 3.1). The serving vessels (such as Kamuk, Koklou, Kambi, etc.,) – the smallest of the Andro ceramics, require 7 days, 22 hours and 35 minutes with actual spent mean time of 7 hours 39 minutes. It is also seen that the mean time needed to produce large storage vessels is 28 hours and 52 minutes (*ibid.*). Painting or colouring of Andro ceramics is done after firing while the baked pots are still hot. No sooner the pots are taken out of fire, the *kuhi* solution is sprinkled with a broom of straws, made for the purpose. The solution of *kuhi (Pasania pachyphyla*, kurz.) is prepared well before the firing. In making this maroon coloured solution, the barks of *kuhi* are pounded and soaked in water for five to eight days. Sometimes, it may also be boiled. The *kuhi* tree is readily available to potters, as these are grown abundantly in the nearby hill. Colouring / painting is done by sprinkling and pouring the *kuhi* solution over the shoulder of the red-hot pots, usually on plain pots.

In terms of context, one of the four general parameters for the characterisation of the mode of ceramic production proposed by Costin (1991), the craft specialisation of Andro ceramic production may be conceived as an attached one in contrast with the independent one. The implication of concepts has been generally focused on extending the economic and socio-political contexts of craft production. Attached specialists refer to those whose production system, including raw materials and technology, the location of production activities, are partly or wholly under the direct control of the elite (Arnold and Munns, 1994; Brumfiel and Earle, 1987; Costin, 2000; Earle, 1987), whereas in the system of independent production, artisans are constrained by such direct institutional or elite control (*ibid.*). In fact, resource-procurement strategy among the Andros is a complex system. Clay and temper are not just picked up according to the potters' convenience of time and space, but are to be exploited duly with cultural categorisations from two particular exploitation sites. Resource-procurement activities are under the direct control of the Andro lineage heads the *Pibas*,

Fig. 3.3: Andro Pibas performing exploitative ritual at the clay collection site.

who are the ultimogenitural male issues of an Andro lineage/clan. And collection of these (clay and temper) is regulated by the culturally prescribed rituals (Fig. 3.3) performed by the three *Pibas* of Ningthoujam, Phanjoubam and Khunungmayum lineages, who have the prerogative of patronising the exploitative rituals by virtue of being members of *Mangang* clan to which King of the State belonged. Thus, the performance of two rituals marks the general approval of the exploitation of resources for the year's potting season. The first collection of potting clay (*leitan*) of a potting year begins only after the performance of a ritual locally known as *leitan-leipak hangba*. The performance of this ritual complex comprising two consecutive ritual acts namely *lei-yengba* and *leiphu phatpa* on the morning of the fifth day of Andro lunar month, *phairel* (January-February) under the ritual supervision of the *Pibas* of the three Andro lineages, viz., Phanjoubam, Ningthoujam and Khunungmayum—marks the general approval of the collection of clay for the coming potting season. This ritual, performed under the ritual headship of the *Piba* of Phanjoubam, is also customarily joined by the *Khullakpa* (the village chief) and other officials of the village council. The first ritual act of *le-yengba* is followed by the performance of second and concluding ritual, named, *leiphu-phatpa* or, *leibak-thong-hangba*. A nominal spade-deep digging at the site only once by the three *Pibas* with spade marks. It heralds symbolically the beginning of the collection of clay for the current potting season. Thus, the ceramic production system of Andro is characterised by an attached mode of production.

Social Context of Learning

Cultural transmission process of pot making in the population may be explained within two socio-cultural perspectives, such as, one, the social rule of debarring Andro unmarried females in excelling the craft, and two, the patrilocal rule of post-marital residence. Under the first rule, girls are debarred from practical learning from elders though they are not restricted to have visual and informal learning of the craft while their female elders are still working with the clay. The restriction of the craft to the unmarried Andro females has cultural significance, which may be perceived as a boundary–maintaining mechanism of the tradition within the community. If the girls are taught to, and excelled in the craft, and if married outside the community after acquiring the knowledge of pottery-making techniques—there are chances of spreading the craft to their husbands' family and community. However, enthusiastic girls in the craft have the opportunity to see the processes and techniques, while their grandmothers, mothers, sisters-in-law are engaging in the work. Though they are forbidden from practical learning, many of them possessed informal and theoretical basic knowledge of the craft through visual learning–which they utilise fruitfully when they come after marriages in their families of orientation. Andro craftswomen are allowed to join the works of pottery making after six months of marriages when respective husbands attained the ascribed status of *pana thou-chanba-mee*. Only through a confirmatory rite called *hirukaba,* an Andro male can become socially recognised working member *(thou-chanba-mee)* in his respective *pana*, a local organisation of lineage segmentation. Remarkably, the existence of *pana* institution is based on the *yumnak*, and every Andro male is automatically enrolled as member of one of the two *panas* of the society by birth. All the eighteen Andro *yumnak* are equally affiliated to two Andro *Panas*, the Ahallup (*ahal*-old men, *lup*-group/club) and Naharup (*Naha* - young men, *rup* or *lup*-group/club). In each *pana* (that is, Ahallup and Naharup), there exists two groups, called Laipham and Khabam, which have their own council of dignitaries. Each council has nine official positions, which are in the order of hierarchy and the manner of filling up any vacant position, whenever available because of either the death or resignation of an incumbent is in such a way that the seniormost dignitary from the next lower position is entitled to occupy the position. Those newly married males, who have gone through the *hirukaba* rite after six months of marriage, are newly enrolled as *thoumi*, the lowest official position in the council.

Andro women practically learn the craft from their in-laws (mother and sisters) and from neighbours/non-clan members. The network of ceramic learning models (Table 3.2) encompasses the system of communication of mental templates of Andro ceramic tradition. Pottery making among the Andro, being a hand-modelled one, is not as easy to carry out, as it first seems simple looking. And one needs mental preparation, skill, and aptitude of the craft to become an adept potter. Hence, a formal learning of the

Table 3.2 :
Learning model of andro pottery making.

Model	Persons from Whom Learning is Transmitted	Number of Cases Recorded: Visual Learning (pre-marital)	Number of Cases Recorded: Practical Learning (post-marital)	TOTAL
(i) Consanguineal Kin Model	*Mo*	-		34
	Fa Mo	2	-	
(ii) Affinal 5 Kin Model 1	*Br Wi*	-		
	Fa Br Wi	-		
	Fa Br So Wi	-		
2	*Hu Mo*	-	42	
	Hu Fa Mo	-	9	
	Hu Fa Br Wi	-	7	
	Hu Br Wi	-	15	
	Hu Fa Br So Wi	-	4	85
(iii) Non-kin Model	Neighbours/ Non-clan members	4	9	13
	Total	**6**	**86**	**132**

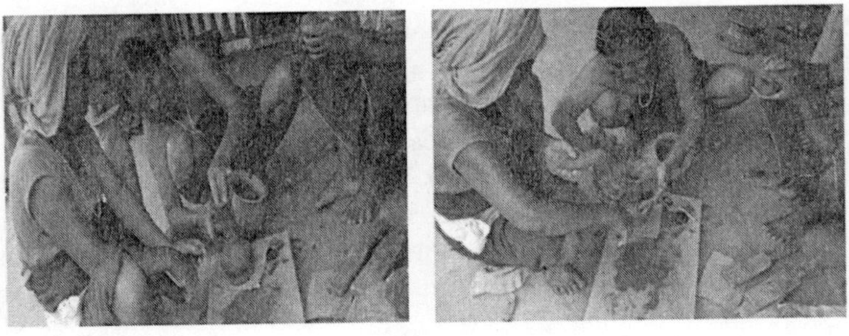

(*a*) (*b*)

Fig. 3.4: (a-b) : Formal, practical learning of pot making among the Andros: Mo-in-law to Da-in-law. An enthusiastic neighbour potter (right) also joined during the act.

mechanical skill on the art is a prerequisite of every amateur potter. Two forms of learning of Andro pottery making are recognised visual and practical learning. The pre-marital visual learning system is an informal one, which is of non-cognisance in the society. The process is a simple pursuance of the pot making by enthusiastic unmarried females while married women in their households are executing the craft. The pottery-making processes executed by their consanguinal kins (Mo, FaMo) and affinal kins (BrWi, FaBrWi, FaBrSoWi, etc.,) are learnt through observation while they are in their families of orientation. In the second system of post-marital practical learning - a beginner, generally a daughter-in-law learns formally the art of pot making from her affinal kins that comprise mothers-in-law (HuMo, HuFaBrWi), grandmothers-in-law (HuFaMo), sisters-in-law (HuBrWi, HuFaBrSoWi), etc. Neighbours (non-kins), who are taken to be the good potters are also involved in some cases. It is quite natural that many mothers-in-law do teach their daughters-in-law. It is also quite significant that none of the potters have formal, practical learning from their mother - they never go to natal home for the purpose. The two systems of learning networks reveal patrilocal background of formal pottery-making among the Andros. Here, the most common ways of transmission are —

1. Mother → daughter (informal / visual learning),
2. Mother-in-law → daughter-in-law (formal/practical learning),
3. Sister-in-law → sister-in-law (in both formal and informal learning).

The first one, however, is not socially sanctioned way of learning, but individual enthusiastic learners do at their own discretion while elders engage in the work.

Discussion

The Andro ceramic production is a result of the interaction between the ceramic tradition percepts and the potters' idiosynchratic perception. Ceramic production is entirely a feminine activity, and the learning process occurs primarily within domestic family groups through the transmission of knowledge of the art in both the vertical and horizontal ways. Each Andro household is a ceramic production unit wherein married females, either individually or work jointly. A production team usually comprises the wife of the head of household, her daughter(s)-in -law and sometimes, neighbouring married women. The learning models (Table 3.2) signify the production unit.

Males are out of the scene in the production of the craft. The craft monopoly of the Andro females can be explained in the light of role expectation and division of labour by age and sex in the society. The craft of clay, being tied to the household task, is found to be a women-oriented job, and an ideal Andro man is never expected in any female-oriented role and activities, such as the household related works of childrearing, cooking, washing, water fetching and so on. Andro women are the custodians of household tasks and responsibilities, including distillation and piggery. As seen in many populations (Arnold, 1985; Skibo and Schiffer, 1995), this part-time feminine craft of pottery production is more compatible with other household activities than with subsistence activities, which take place away from home and undertaken predominantly by men. The way in which pottery production was organised and the extent of craft specialisation also influence the method of forming.

The social identity of the artisans has direct bearing on the social organisation, that is, the patriarchal set-up of the society. A woman attains the status of a full-fledged and socially accepted craftsperson only when her husband earns a social status (*thou-chanbamee*) in the society after six months of his marriage. In other words, the status of being potter is achieved socially by woman consequent upon the attainment of social position by her husband, and the identity of the artisans has, largely, rooted in the patri-oriented social systems of the society. This social rule of craft monopoly of married women and not the girls exhibit significant ethno–genetic signal with sharply defined cultural boundaries. In addition, this gave rise obviously to the ethnic boundary to the spatial transmission of craft beyond the village.

The Andro ceramic craft tradition is an outcome of the processes of teaching and learning, which is long and complex. The craft production strategically corresponds with the extent of cultural norms and need. The pot making schema provides the trellis for storing, retrieving and transmitting the art of craft within patterned cultural perceptions. The Andro way of visual learning of pot making comes within the arena of pre-marital informal and post-marital formal-practical learning as well. In the first case, the learning pattern is both vertical and horizontal in nature, however practical learning of the art commences only when she marries to an Andro man. The required steps in pottery production – such as knowledge and motor skills have attained with imitation, instruction, demonstration by the adept instructors, etc. The acquisition of skills may proceed through series of stages. Observation of different stages of pot making while the skilled potter is working is a basic component of the teaching-learning system of production knowledge. As observed in other ethnographic contexts (Pryor and Carr, 1995; Roe, 1995), it is also seen among the Andro that the more control the instructor has over the learner during the process of learning and making an item' the more similar the objects they produce will look.

The technique of Andro ceramic production shows standardised procedure. The technique includes the preparation of potting raw materials, the proportionate mixing of ceramic resources, steps involved in manufacturing technology, firing technique and duration, etc. These expositions reflect specialised mass production of Andro earthen vessels. Categorical steps towards the production of vessels mainly include —

(i) Initial formation of the paste into mundane framework of emical mental template of a vessel,
(ii) Addition of subsequent lump of flattened paste/clay accordingly to make a pre-conceived vessel morphology,
(iii) Manifestation of emical perception of vessel forms that are structured in consonance with the normative value system of the people,
(iv) Beating and streaking of semi-dried green pots within given intervals of drying period,
(v) Categorisation of the shade-drying period according to the vessel size,
(vi) Emical and potters' sense of perception to the firing time-period through the senses of sound and smell that emits from the firing vessels.

The multiple stages of vessel fabrication have provided the potters with several opportunities for adjustment, whenever necessary, with vessel shapes and dimensions. Once a paste of clay and temper had been modeled into a vessel-framework and semi-dried, the potters could make proper correction in respect of variation in wall thickness, distortion due to handling, shrinkage during drying, and rim deformation during the trimming process. These final modifications have assured maximal standardisation for the entire run of production. The thickness and standardisation of shape and dimensions indicate high level of skill of hand movements and pinching activities of potters. A craft specialist could check uniformity in vessel wall thickness, shrinkages or deformities of pot during beating stage. These show maximal standardisation in the entire run of ceramic production. Moreover, the dense and impermeable Andro wares are achieved by firing them to a point of partial vitrification. Therefore, it is very much the potter's knowledge of perception that works the situation accordingly. Participation in such auxiliary activities makes learners aware of the basics of the craft. Moreover, each step in the process requires knowledge and practical experiences.

At the early stages of learning, the novice has to start making miniature vessels imitating the general features of the actual vessel through stages of production. In the process of production, novices are taught about the control of hand movement, pressure required to exert by hand in making the body part specially and in the moistening of clay to make it workable. Some pottery forms find more difficult to materialise by the novices than others, and in such situation a higher level of skill including intricate designs. In many a case, Andro earthen vessels, made by inexperienced craftsperson, usually exhibit uneven thickness, irregular body surfaces (specially the inner ones), imperfect rotundity, etc.

Amateur Andro potters have discerned patterned behaviour of craft technology through formal learning processes. The craft-knowledge, an esteemed cachet of Andro craftsperson, is transmitted culturally by way of prescribed post-marital-learning models (Table 3.2). Potters share new and old items of information through mechanisms of social learning within some spatial and temporal range. This cultural transmission of information, in general, constitutes an inheritance system (Boyd and Richerson, 1985; Rindos, 1984, 1989). As pottery-making information is transmitted through an inheritance system, ceramic traditions must be subject to mechanisms of change peculiar to inheritance systems (Neff, 1993). Andro vessels show more or less phenotypic uniformity within a type as their shapes are made after emical understanding of potters, which to a large extent, a cognitive ability derived from tradition kept alive to meet the demands of natural as well as social environment. However, variation among potters in respect of strict observance of rules for making pots within the Andro ceramic traditions and resultant variations, if any, in shape and form of pots within a type may arise from the variation in enculturation process at the individual level. In fact, pottery-making practice among the Andro is perpetuated through time by way of following social model based on inheritance pattern and this result in similarities in the vessel shape and morphology within a type.

During the teaching process, a great 'concern with the technique excellence' (Bunzel's term, 1972:60) in terms of controlled teaching, constant verbalisation and demonstration from the instructors relating to techniques, as well as on the results to be reached in each of the productive stages are a must. Unskilled learners however, demand greater skill in achieving outwardly convex vessel body and in tapering the hollow base towards its filling with flat piece of clay paste. The so-called proper learning stage lies with the general process of making a pot. However, general ideas about the mode of procurement and selection of ceramic resources, processing of the clay and tempering materials and their proportionate mixing and moistening to make it workable are necessary. Learning to make pottery requires mastering complex series of tasks, which potters naturally perceived through repeated actions and experiences. For instance, drying of green pot is such crucial/ important stage in pot making, which is not done very quickly under direct sunshine just to avoid the chance of cracking of finished stuff. Drying is normally carried in the shade for a couple of days or so or even longer in case of larger pots. Again, the drying period may vary according to the weather condition, while the pot is under the process of making. Naturally, the period of drying during the foggy/rainy period will differ from that of the bright sunny period. Thus, not only the size of pot under making but the weather condition during the same will have different drying period of the green pot. Since Andro potters are not full-time specialists, the acquiring of theoretical as well as practical knowledge by novices takes months or years long time, where they are to learn and work within an influential context of specific mundane parameters outlined by socio-cultural system. Not only is the transmission of wholesome knowledge of production but also of the symbolic meaning of the pottery in the society is the basic component of the teaching-learning system. Certainly, symbolism in the act of pottery making and in its products and uses often seems to be a factor in female domestic pottery.

The present ethnographic study has ceramic ethno-archaeological significances, since it may highlight some of the aspects of the archaeologically non-observable record. Obviously, recognising cultural transmission in archaeological record is not an easy task, yet archaeological research provides an excellent data for exploring processes of cultural transmission (Eerkens and Lippo, 2007). Obviously, attempt may be made indirectly through the units of the type-variety system or alternative taxonomic approach to ceramics (Neff, 1993). The archaeological significance of analysing learning framework of pottery making lies on the identification of potential source of variability in their ceramic assemblages, and obviously 'different instruction methods and goals result in different material outcome' (Minar, 2001:376), which is an important archaeological issue advocated by many workers (DeBoer, 1990; Greenfield, 1984; Roe,1995; Wallaert-Petre, 2001; etc.). Here, ceramic ethno–archaeology has immense contribution towards explaining cultural transmission. The question of identity of artisans is of central importance in ceramic ethno archaeological studies that focus on power, economic organisation and the role of material culture in social relations (Costin, 2000: 395). Artisans play central role in materialising ideology and social meaning through the creation and transformation of material objects, and archaeological studies do address the identities of the workers (Costin, 1996; Costin and Wright, 1998). However, unlike in archaeological research, in ethnographic studies the artisans themselves are directly visible. Ethnographic analogy has traditionally been a primary means of many methodological and substantive tools with which ethno archaeology may provide insight into the identification of artisans. (Costin, *loc. cit.*).

Note

1. The eighteen Andro lineages (*yumnaks*) are – Chingakham, Thokchom, Puthem, Maibam, Leisungbam, Samjetsabam, Laishram, Salam, Heigrujam, Asheibam, Hijam, Ningthoujam, Phanjoubam, Khunungmayam, Sagolsem, Sarubam, Sarungbam, and Yumkhaibam. The first nine are the lineages affiliated to the Ahallup *pana* and the remaining nine to the Naharup *pana*.

References

Arnold, D. E. 1985. *Ceramic Theory and Cultural Process*, Cambridge; Cambridge University Press.

Arnold, J.E, J.E. and A. Munns. 1994. 'Independent or attached specialisation: The organisation of shell–bead production in California'. *Journal of Field Archaeology*, 21, 4: 473-489.

Beck . E. and M.A. Neupert. 2009. 'Identifying pottery clay from rice fields: An example from southern Luzon, the Philippines'. *Journal of Archaeological Science*, 36, 3: 843-849.

Bentley, R. and S. Shennan. 2003. 'Cultural transmission and stochastic network growth'. *American Antiquity*, 68:459-486.

Boyd, R. and P. J. Richerson 1985. *Culture and the Evolutionary Process*. Chicago; University of Chicago Press.

Bril, B. and V. Roux, 1993. 'Competences impliquees dans l'action: Les cas de la taille des perles en Pierre Dure (Khambat, Inde)'. *Raisons Pretiques: Les Objets dans 1'Action*, 4: 267-286.

Brumfiel, Elizabeth, M. and T.K.Earle. 1987. 'Specialisation, exchange, and complex societies: An introduction'. In Elizabeth, M. Brumfiel, and T. K. Earle (Eds.): *Specialisation, Exchange, and Complex Societies*. pp. 1-9. Cambridge; Cambridge University Press.

Bunzel, R. 1972. *The Pueblo Potter: A Study of Creative Imagination in Primitive Art*. New York; Columbia.

Carr, C. 1995. 'Building a unified middle-range theory of artifact design: Historical perspectives and tactics'. In C. Carr and J. Neitzel (Eds.): *Archaeological and Ethnological Perspectives*. pp.151-170. New York; Plenum Press.

Cavalli-Sforza, L.L. and M.W. Feldman. 1981. *Cultural Transmission and Evolution: A Quantitative Approach*. Princeton, NJ; Princeton University Press.

Costin, Cathy Lynne and R.P. Wright, 1998. *Craft and Social Identity*. Archaeological Papers of the American Anthropological Association, No. 8. Washington DC.

Costin, Cathy Lynne. 1991. 'Craft specialisation: Issues in defining, documenting, and explaining the organisation of production'. In M. B. Schiffer (Ed.): *Archaeological Method and Theory*, Vol. 3, pp. 1-56., New York; Academic Press.

Costin, Cathy Lynne. 1996. 'Exploring the relationship between gender and craft in the complex societies: Methodological and theoretical issues of gender attribution'. In R.P. Wright (Ed.): *Gender and Archaeology: Essays in Research and Practice*. pp.111-142. Philadelphia; University of Pennsylvania Press.

Costin, Cathy Lynne. 2000. 'The use of ethno archaeology for the archaeological study of ceramic production'. *Journal of Archaeological Method and Theory*. 74 , 377-403.

Coy, M.W., 1989. *Apprenticeship: From Theory to Method and Back Again*. Albany; State University of New York Press.

Crown, P.L. 1999. 'Socialisation in American Southwest pottery decoration'. In J.M. Skibo, and G.M. Feinman (Eds.): *Pottery and People: A Dynamic Interaction*. pp. 25-43. Salt Lake City; University of Utah Press.

David, N' K. Gavua, S. MacEachern, and J. Sterner. 1991, 'Ethnicity and material culture in North Cameroon', *Canadian Journal of Archaeology*, 15: 171-177.

DeBoer, W. 1990. 'Interaction, imitation, and communication as expressed in style: The Ucayali experience'. In M. Conkey and C. Hastorf (Eds.): *The Uses of Style in Archaeology*. pp. 82-104. Cambridge; Oxford University Press.

Dietler, M. and I. Herbich. 1989. 'Tich Matek: The technology of Luo pottery production and the definition of ceramic style'. *World Archaeology*, 21: 148-164.

Earl, Timothy K. 1987. 'Specialisation and the production of wealth: Hawaiin chiefdoms and the Inka Empire'. In Elizabeth, M. Brumfiel and T.K. Earle. (Eds.) : *Specialisation, Exchange, and Complex Societies*. pp. 64-75. Cambridge; Cambridge University Press.

Eerkens, J.W. and C.P. Lipo. 2007. 'Cultural transmission theory and the archaeological record: Providing context to understanding variation and temporal change in material culture'. *Journal of Anthropological Research*, 15, 3: 239-274.

Fortes, M. 1938. 'Social and psychological aspects of education in Taleland'. In M. Fortes (Ed.): *Time and Social Structure and Other Essays*. pp. 201-259. London; Athlone.

Gelbert, A. 1999. 'Technological and stylistic borrowings between ceramic traditions: A case study from north eastern Senegal'. In, L.R. Owen and M. Porr (Eds.) : *Ethno-Analogy and the Reconstruction of Prehistoric Artifact Use and Production.* Urgeschichtliche Materiale Hefte, 14, pp.207-224. Germany, Tubingen; Mo Vince Verlag.

Gibson, J. J. 1977. 'The theory of affordances'. In R. Shaw and J. Bransford (Eds.): *Perceiving, Acting and Knowing*. Hillsdale, NJ; Erlbaum.

Gifford, J.C. 1960. 'The type-variety method of ceramic classification as an indicator of cultural phenomena'. *American Antiquity*, 25:341-347.

Goody, E.N. 1989. "Learning, apprenticeship, and the division of labour". In M. Coy (Ed.): *Apprenticeship: From Theory to Method and Back Again*. pp. 233-255. Albany; State University of New York Press.

Gosselain, O.P. 1998. 'Social and technical identity in a clay crystal ball'. In M. T. Stark (Ed.): *The Archaeology of Social Boundaries*. pp. 78-106. Washington, DC; Smithsonian Institution Press.

Greenfield, P.M. 1984. 'A theory of the teacher in the learning activities of everyday life'. In B. Rogoff and J. Lave (Eds.): *Everyday Cognition*. pp, 117-138. Cambridge; Harvard University Press.

Guglielmino, C.R.; C. Viganotti; B.Hewlett; and L.L. Cavalli-Sforza. 1995. 'Cultural variation in Africa: Role of mechanisms of transmission and adaptation'. *Proceedings of the National Academy of Sciences., USA*, 92:7585-7589.

Henrich, J. 2001. 'Cultural transmission and the diffusion of innovations: Adoption dynamics indicate that biased cultural transmission is the predominant force in behavioural change'. *American Anthropologist*, 103: 992-1013.

Henrich, J.and F.J. Gil-White. 2001. 'The evolution of prestige: Freely conferred difference as a mechanism for enhancing the benefits of cultural transmission'. *Evolution and Human Behaviour*, 22: 165-196.

Herbich, I. and M. Dietler, 1991. 'Aspects of the ceramic system of the Luo of Kenya'. In H. Ludkte and R.Vossen (Eds.):

Topferei-und Keramikforschung, Vol. 2. pp. 103-135. Bonn; Habelt.

Hosler, D. 1996. 'Technical choices, social categories and meaning among the Andean potters of Las Animas'. *Journal of Material Culture*. 1: 63-93

Lave, J. 1988. *Cognition in Practice*. Cambridge, England; Cambridge University Press.

Lave, J. and E. Wenger. 1991. *Situated Learning: Legitimate Peripheral Participation*. Cambridge, England; Cambridge University Press.

Leonard, R.D. 2001. 'Evolutionary Archaeology". In I. Hodder (Ed.) *Archaeological Theory Today*. pp. 65-97.Cambridge; Polity.

MacEachern, S. 1996. 'Foreign countries: The development of ethno-archaeology in sub-Saharan Africa'. *Journal of World Prehistory*, 10,3, : 243-304.

Mahias, M.C. 1993. 'Pottery techniques in India: Technical variants and social choice'. In P. Lemonnier (Ed.) *Technical Choices: Transformation in Material Cultures since the Neolithic*. pp. 158-180. New York; Routledge.

ManiBabu, M. 1994. 'Post-cremation-urn - burial of the Phayengs (Manipur) – A study on mortuary behaviour'. *Eastern Anthropologist*, 47, 2 : 157-171.

Minar, C.J. 2001. 'Learning and craft production: An introduction". *Journal of Anthropological Research*, 57, 4: 369-380.

Moll, L.1990. *Vygotsky and Education: Instructional Implications and Applications of Socio-historical Psychology*. Cambridge, England; Cambridge University Press.

Neff, H. 1993. 'Theory, sampling, and analytical techniques in the archaeological study of prehistoric ceramics'. *American Antiquity*, 58,1: 23-44.

Pryor, J., and Carr, C. 1995. 'Basketry of Northern California Indians'. In, C. Carr and J. E. Neitzel (Eds.): *Style, Society and Person*. (Archaeological and Ethnological Perspectives). pp. 259–296. New York, London; Plenum Press.

Richerson, P. J. and R. Boyd. 2005. *Not by Genes Alone: How Culture Transformed Human Evolution*. Chicago, IL; University of Chicago Press.

Rindos, D. 1984. *The Origins of Agriculture: An Evolutionary Perspective*. New York; Academic Press.

Rindos, D. 1989. 'Undirected variation and the Darwinian explanation of cultural change'. In M. B. Schiffer (Ed.): *Archaeological Method and Theory*. Vol. I., pp.1-45. Tucson; University of Arizona Press.

Roe, P. 1995. 'Style, society, myth, and structure'. In C. Carr and J. Neitzel (Eds.): *Archaeological and Ethnological Perspectives*. pp. 27-76. New York; Plenum Press.

Rogoff, B. 1990. *Apprenticeship in Thinking: Cognitive Development in Social Context*, New York; Oxford University Press.

Rogoff, B. and J. Lave 1984. *Everyday Cognition: It's Development in Social Context*. Cambridge, Mass.; Harvard University Press.

Sackett, J.R. 1990. 'Style and ethnicity in archaeology: The case for isochrestism'. In M. Conkey and C. Harstorf (Eds.): *The Uses of Style in Archaeology*. pp. 32-44. Cambridge, England; Cambridge University Press.

Schiffer, M.B. and J. Skibo. 1987. 'Theory and experiment in the study of technological change'. *Current Anthropology*, 28:595-622.

Shennan, S.J. and J. Steele. 1999. 'Cultural learning in Hominids: A behavioural ecological approach'. In H. O. Box and K.R. Gibson (Eds.): *Mammalian Social Learning: Comparative and Ecological Perspectives*. pp. 367-388. Cambridge; Cambridge University Press.

Skibo, J. M., and M. B. Schiffer, 1995. 'The clay cooking pot: An exploration of women's technology'. In J. M. Skibo; W. H. Walker and A. E. Nielsen, (Eds.): *Expanding Archaeology*, pp. 80-91. Salt Lake City; University of Utah Press.

Stark, Miriam T., B. J. Bowser, and L. Horne. 2008. 'Why breaking down boundaries matters for archaeological research on learning and cultural transmission: An introduction'. In M. T. Stark, L. Horne and B. Bowser (Eds.): *Cultural Transmission and Material Culture: Breaking Down Boundaries*. pp. 1-16. Tucson; University of Arizona Press.

Van Der Leeuw, S.E. 1994. 'Cognitive aspects of the development of higher psychological processes technique'. In C. Renfrew and E.B.W. Zubrow (Eds.): *The Ancient Mind: Elements of Cognitive Archaeology*. pp. 135-142. Cambridge; Cambridge University Press.

Vygotsky, L.S. 1962. *Thought and Language*. Cambridge, MA; MIT Press.

Vygotsky, L.S. 1978. *Mind in Society*. Cambridge, Mass.; Harvard University Press.

Wallaert-Petrie, H. 1999a. 'Ethnoarcheologie et apprentissage de la Paterie', December 1998- March 1999. *Nyame Akuma*, 50:2-9.

Wallaert-Petrie, H. 1999b. 'Manual laterality as a first learning rule prescribed to potters: A case study in handmade pottery from northern Cameroon'. In L. R. Owen and M. Porr (Eds.): *Ethno-Analogy and the Reconstruction of Prehistoric Artifact Use and Production*. Urgeschichtliche Materiale Hefte, 14, pp.63-84. Germany, Tubingen; Mo Vince Verlag.

Wallaert-Petrie, H. 2001. 'Learning how to make the right pots: Apprenticeship strategies and material culture: A case study in handmade pottery from Cameroon'. *Journal of Anthropological Research*, 57, 4:471-493.

Wenger, E. 1998. *Communities in Practice: Learning, Meaning, and Identity*. Cambridge; Cambridge University Press.

4
Tribal Law, Property Rights and Gender Issues of North East India

– R.P. Athparia

The customary law plays an integral role in tribal identity and has given some basic concepts and issues which resolves around them. These concepts and issues are important to understand the dynamics of interface with modernity and its impact on women's status.

However, the encounter with the "modern" formal law is not uniform throughout the North East India. Most tribes of the region live according to their customary law but only a few have been constitutionally recognised. In 1963, the thirteenth Amendment to the Constitution recognised the customary laws of Nagaland through Article 371-A. The fiftythird amendment of 1986 recognised those of Mizoram through Article 371-G. This recognition includes laws governing marriage, divorce, inheritance and other social and cultural practices and rights like community ownership. No Act of the Union Parliament concerning the religious or social practices, procedures, administration of justice involving customary law ownership and transfer of land and resources applies to them unless their legislative assemblies agree (Fernandes and Bharali, 2008).

In order to understand the gender dimensions, we shall define customary laws, take a look at the role, tradition and the constitution assigned and study the reality in each State among the fourteen tribes. We shall include a diverse enough number to make it representative of the region. It will lay the foundation of good understanding of women's right in the customary laws (Fernandes *et al.*, 2005: 23).

Role of Customary Laws

Customary laws have a gender dimension that define the roles of men and women. In this chapter, we shall not include all the aspect of gender issues, but limit ourselves to a few issues that will define the role and status of women in tribal society and their interface with modernity. These issues are related to their ownership and inheritance, role in religion and politics.

Meaning of Customary Law

Customary law, by one definition, is 'customs that are accepted as legal requirements or obligatory rules of conduct, practices and beliefs that are so vital and intrinsic a part of a social and economic system that they are treated as if they are laws.'

By another account, "customary law consists of established patterns of behaviour that can be objectively verified within particular social setting. The modern codification of civil law developed out of customs, or *coutumes* of middle ages, expressions of law developed in particular communities and slowly collected and written down by local jurists. Such customs acquired the force of law, when they became the undisputed rule by which certain entitlements (rights) or obligations were regulated between members of a community."

Another term used is 'consuetudinary law' (from the Latin, consuetudo: custom), referring to law, the validity of which is established by custom (in contrast to specific legislation or statutory law). A recent workshop defined customary law as "locally recognised principles, and more specific norms or rules, which are orally held and transmitted, and applied by community institutions to internally governor, guide all aspects of life."

Custom is the oldest form of law making. Briefly speaking, customs is a continuing course of conduct observed by the community. The word 'custom' is used to apply to the totality of behaviour patterns, which are continued by tradition and lodged in the group, as constructed with the more random personal activities of the individual. It is to be said that customs relates to society and law is concerned with the State. In its origin, customary laws appear to be only a differentiated form of general custom (Bhowmick, 2002: 15).

Social customs grew up by a gradual process. When customs are already in operation, judicial authority adds to the sanction of general recognition. The historical school of Savigny has held customary law as a spontaneous expression of the genius of the people. It arises from the people's juristic consciousness and posits that rules shall be regarded as legal. This school of jurisprudence claims that customs was the main vehicle of legal development. As per historical views, we endorse that law is not made but evolved from the bottom of the society and not imposed from the top. Savigny reiterated that a legal system is a part of culture of a people. Customary law is followed because it is convenient, conducive and helpful to the society as it reflects societal norms and values (*ibid:* 19).

Tribal Customary Law in India

Regardless, of its formal status, most tribes regulate their community and social affairs according to the 'customary law' and treat it as integral to their culture and basic to their identity. This law reinforces the tribe's age-old traditions and binds together through normative rules by regulating the social and personal relations of its members. Through the institutions such as the village council based on it, the leaders manage the internal affairs of the village. Culture is a community's expression of worldview i.e. its interpretation of the reality around or what can be called its philosophy, expressed through customs, social relations and organisation, language, rituals, festivals, dress, ornaments and arts. It culminates in its identity. Both the customary law and culture have changed over time (Fernandes *et al.*, 2005: 23).

Customs and customary laws are not synonyms. There may be various customs without any legal authority whereas the customary laws have the sanctions of the bulk of the society and if not obeyed, such violator is to be punished. The early history of mankind prove that the human being was individualistic and nomadic. There was nothing known as group living in society. In individualistic style of living, no human being was dependent on other and there was no norm to regulate any style of living other than laws of nature. By experience, human beings gradually learn particular mode of behaviour and conduct as conducive and beneficial to collective living. On the march of time, some particular patterns of behaviours emerged and by consistent adherence, such behaviour achieved the status of some obligatory norms spontaneously and consciously followed by the members of the group. This is the stage where the customs acquired its existence. Customs are of family, of caste, of community or of guild. Customs are also source of law. Sometimes, custom prevails even over law as we see Mohammedan Law or tribal custom of possessing more than one living wife (polygamy) having recognised against Hindu Law allowing only one living wife. Hence, customs have also force of law in certain communities including tribes (Narwani, 2004:31-32).

Customary laws were laid down by ancestor with the sole objectives of maintaining internal unity and peaceful living and preserving their social as well as religious ceremonies, rites and practices based on their concept of ethics and interpretation of the supernatural belief. They are conscious that these traditions have passed down from generation to generation without any alteration or amendment. Breach of traditions is neither contemplated nor tolerated by any as it is regarded as a crime against the society (Narwani, 2004:33).

According to S.L. Doshi, in his book 'Tribal Ethnicity, Class and Integration', has described the traditional unifying bonds of tribal society as well as social customs as under :

1. Scattered pattern of living.
2. Religion
3. Language
4. Isolation and lifestyle oriented to hills and forests
5. Marriage and its related aspects
6. The ethnicity of drinking liquor
7. Ethnic core of economic life.

Impact of Modernisation

In Fernandes and Bharali's article, they have quoted Roy's words describing, "The interface of the customary law with the formal systems has to be situated in the context of an egalitarian society that had also seeds of inequality. Some inequalities such as women's subordinate status have been modernised. Among the forces influencing changes are the individual-based formal laws, administrative systems, education and religion. Most changes began in the colonial age. For example, the office of the village leader or *gaonburah* created two centres of power, since he is rarely the same as the traditional chief. Its other examples are colonisation and appropriation of common lands and forests through military campaigns or legal fictions, and their eviction from territories. These changes at times are accelerated by the rapid integration of economies with the national and global markets especially in the age of globalisation. This rapid integration continues to expose them to economic exploitation, because they are either excluded from the processes of trade and governance or are marginal actors in them" (Fernandes and Bharali, 2008).

In an individual's life, right from birth till death, based on some customs, observed faithfully without conscious effort. Some customary rules are being followed without being enforced by an outsider authority. These are self-imposed. Sometimes, it undergoes modifications of change in response to emergent needs of changed socio- economic and ritual cultural scenario (Goswami, 1986: 5). For example, in Garo matrilineal society, men do not own or inherit the ancestral property though they are the head in the family as according to customary laws usually women inherit but with the change of time, they (men) inherit especially the one who looked after his parents (Marak, 2000:165).

The interface between indigenous peoples' customary laws and mainstream legal systems, at the national and international levels, is complex. There are instances of acute conflict between the systems, while there are many arrangements in which customary law systems operate within the relatively benign oversight of the State legal and judicial systems. In addition, there are occasions, where the relationship is one of mutual suspicion and disdain (Roy, 2005:21).

Constitutional Safeguards

With the dawn of independence and adoption of the Constitution of free India, the British policy of isolation and non-interference was replaced by the policies of integration and development. The Constitution of India provided several types of safeguards to the tribal communities. There are the Protective Provisions shielding them from all forms of social injustice and exploitation, the Developmental Provisions promote education and developmental activities, the Reservation Provisions ensure their representation in legislative bodies and government jobs, and the Administrative Provisions under the Fifth and Sixth Schedules provide for special administrative set up to provide autonomy of self-governance according to customary traditions.

The tribal people live in contiguous areas unlike other communities. So, an area approach was adopted for administrative and developmental purposes. Under the Constitution "Scheduled Areas" are declared by the President after consultation with the State Governors. These Areas have been designated to protect the interests of Scheduled Tribes regarding their land and other social issues and are governed through provisions of either Fifth or Sixth Schedule. The Scheduled Areas of the North East India are covered under the Sixth Schedule provisions; other Scheduled Areas are covered by the Fifth Schedule laws. The administrative structure is different in the two Schedules.

State Governors have a special constitutional protective role in all Scheduled Areas. They are empowered to make regulations prohibiting or restricting transfer of land from tribals to non-tribals and prevent exploitation of the tribal communities. Since these Scheduled Areas are supposed to enjoy autonomy protected by the Constitution, the laws passed by parliament and the State legislatures do not automatically apply to them. Hence, the Fifth Schedule defines Governors' powers to adapt laws to these areas.

Administrative Structure : Sixth Schedule Areas

The Sixth Schedule areas are governed through Autonomous District Councils, which have wide ranging legislative and executive powers. As a result, they work almost like a "mini Parliament". They have complete freedom to allow village level bodies to run according to customary laws. The verdicts of district and lower level courts can only be challenged in the high court. At present, Sixth Schedule Areas exist only in four North-Eastern States: 1) Assam, 2) Meghalaya, 3) Mizoram, and 4) Tripura. These Areas are administered through Autonomous Districts/Regional Councils. Except Meghalaya, other three States have only certain selected areas covered under Sixth Schedule.

Fifth Schedule Areas

Unlike the Sixth Schedule areas, there are no institutional autonomous bodies in the Fifth Schedule areas. However, an Act of 1996 has empowered the local village level Panchayats, particularly the Gram Sabhas in the Fifth Schedule tribal areas to act as local bodies of self-governance. But, they lack the protective umbrella of a district level body (like the District Council of the Sixth Scheduled areas); as a result, their decisions are routinely ignored or overruled by the State officials.

Constitutional Protection

Tribal people are simple, honest and naive by any yardstick of modern society. Besides, they have traditionally lived in close contact with nature, in the hills and forests. In this sense, they are different from the rest of mainstream people; they have historically tried to avoid contact with "outsiders" to preserve their traditional community based living in which they feel more secure. The Sixth Schedule of the Indian Constitution offers them local autonomy through the system of autonomous district and regional councils, which have extensive legislative as well as executive powers to protect land and tribal traditions. It was a path-breaking effort when launched in the 1950s and offers better protection than the Fifth Schedule provisions.

Women's Land and Customary Law

In 2007, Indo-Global Social Service Society initiated a process to know the status of the land and housing rights of women in India and explore the possibility of building platform to raise issues for networking, advocacy and ground level interventions.

Land is a State subject in India. There are lots of small civil society organisations and State or regional networks working on land rights of marginalised and backward people. Landlessness is invariably connected with inequality and poverty, more so in the case of women. The rights of women over land, housing, and other resources are essential not only to reduce their poverty but also to increase their financial efficiency. This shall, in turn, bring about gender equality and equity in the society. Land and housing rights are generally explained within a patriarchal framework – without giving due recognition to gender equity. It was observed during the study that women's rights over land, particularly agricultural land, are important in rural settings, since it is a source of livelihood.

Agarwal (1995) argue that, "The issue of women's rights in housing and land has been largely neglected in both research and policy. In almost all developing countries, large-scale surveys and agricultural census collect property-related information only by households, without disaggregating by gender. In most of South Asia, including India, dependency upon small-scale surveys and village studies to assess women's access to land cannot be undermined. These sources reveal typically few women owning arable land and even fewer have any effective control over them. In the Indian context, female workforce participation rates, rather than property rights are widely used as the main indicator of women's economic status".

In the Indian context housing right is now recognised as fundamental human right. As a primary user, a woman's requirements rank the highest in a house. Beyond being a shelter, a house has multiple dimensions for her. It is a place of livelihood. It is the point for social interaction. It serves as a refuge from social instability, sexual exploitation and legal authority. There are seven elements as regards the rights of women towards housing. They are–establish the house, use the area, manage, dispose, regulate, sanction and perform rituals therein. If a woman is able to exercise these rights, only then her right to house is vouched.

Women's right to housing has to be understood in terms of their access to and control over housing and property. 'Legal rights in housing and property' broadly refers to security of tenure, i.e., right to own, lease, rent, mortgage or dwell in house and property, and the right not to be forcibly evicted. In general, the condition of Indian women, (both rural and urban) has been pathetic as far as their land and housing rights are concerned.

According to the approach paper to the Eleventh Five-Year Plan, women constitute 40 per cent of the agricultural workforce. This percentage is rising due to large scale migration by men, preoccupation of men in non-farm activities and rapid industrialisation. An estimated 20 per cent of rural households are *de facto* female-headed due to widowhood, desertion, or migration of males. The increasing number of women in agricultural work needs to be seen in the context of concentration of unskilled women in this sector. This leads to decline in agricultural produce, which leads to further poverty.

In defining the customary laws of the North East India, our objective is to understand women's rights, particularly over property. Amid their diversity, they have some commonalities, the most important being patriarchy (Fernandes *et al.*, 2005: 29). Apart from legal status and the presence or absence of protective mechanism, the general state of tribal customary laws varies according to the nature and extent of application and the manner in which they are invoked and adhered to. Among the first to change are the land relations because except in the Sixth Schedule areas, the formal law recognises only individual ownership, while central to the culture of most tribes is community control over the common property resources (CPR). Since, the culture of equity and the relatively high status of women depend on the CPRs, changes in the management have implications for these values (Fernandes and Bharali, 2008).

Customary Laws, the Gender Issue and Property Rights

The customs and its laws vary from region to region and so is the case for North Eastern region. The Seven Sister States is diverse in the form of practicing different customs and traditions in order to retain their identity from one another, and these variations make the region unique in its own way. Ethnic and cultural diversity ensure differentiation in tribal socio-cultural and economic identity. Focusing on the status of women in tribal society undergoes great diversity. In most of the tribes of this region, women share in property rights are very minimal. They enjoy very limited or at times no control over landed properties, as we are bounded by patrilineal practices and ideologies, where man enjoys the overall power in the family. But, the situation and this practice of patriarchy contradicts totally when it comes to matrilineal societies like the Garos, the Khasis, the Jaintias or the Lyngngams from the State of Meghalaya.

Women are often associated or considered as a homemaker. Nath (2003) in his book, 'Rural Women Workforce in India' talks about the dual role of women both in home as well as outside home. He says, "In the social context, due to the low status attached to manual labour in our society and the cultural value associated with women's confinement to home, the work of rural and urban as wage labourers, unskilled factory workers and menials are not conducive to a better status. The average woman in rural can give little attention to the upbringing of her children. With dual roles and without any mechanical aids for house-work, she is really overworked. So also are the women engaged in unskilled or semi-skilled work in organised and unorganised sectors attitude of unconcern about the public affairs, is responsible for the limited participation of women in activities like those of Trade Unions or political parties" (Nath, 2003:13).

However, recently we have witnessed significant changes in the government, the Church and the society. Although, the Mizoram Presbyterian church, the largest Christian denomination in the State, is yet to okay woman ordination, a significant number of women have been included in its high committees and as Sunday school teachers. "A number of churches have now allowed women to preach in the church", Sangkhumi said.

The Mizoram Legislative Assembly has also made some landmark decisions such as legislating the Mizoram Women Commission, adopting the parliamentary act known as the Protection of Women against Domestic Violence Act, 2005.

The Mizo women have also given a hats-off to the Mizo Divorce Ordinance 2008, which would put an end to certain divorce laws under the "male-friendly" Mizo Customary Law which are highly unfavourable to women. "The Ordinance was a major milestone in the history of Mizoram, and was the result of concerted efforts of the women wings of different political parties and a number of highly learnt Mizo women", Sangkhumi said. "Under the existing customary laws, when a man divorces his wife the latter leaves the house without virtually anything even if she had contributed a lot to the family's assets. All this will be abolished with the new Mizo Divorce Law". Thanks to the women's campaign, the Mizoram Baptist church has agreed to ordain women as Kohhran Upa or church elders even though woman ordination for pastors or priests seems a far cry.

Conclusion

This bird's view of tribal inheritance shows that the status of most North East Indian tribal women is higher than that of their counterparts elsewhere in India. Most customary laws confer significant economic rights and impose burden on them. Some say that the burden outweighs the rights while others hold that the rights make them equal to men. In reality, the tribes of the region are egalitarian in the sense that they are less stratified than 'advance' communities. So, tribal women enjoy more rights than what those in other societies do but are not equal to men. Besides, their situation has changed with 'mainstream' intervention. It causes a contradiction between their law and social reality and also raises some issues.

The first issue is tribal women have greater voice that most others do. A sign of their relatively high status is the division of labour which is controlled by women. They decide what to grow and how to use the produce. The close link between their hold over the family livelihood and their role in agriculture makes land basic to their status. However, today agriculture and forests do not cater to many of their needs. Land is today bought and sold as commodity but not treated as livelihood. That affects women's control over it since their relatively high status and the identity of the tribe are inter linked. Their alienation and change through deforestation and commercialisation affect the tribe negatively, but women lose more since by and large men control the new technology and marketing systems. These processes can result in women losing traditional rights and control over livelihood and strengthening patriarchy and weakening equality (Barbora and Fernandes, 2002: 123-125).

The second issue is the impact of modernity on women. Haimendorf (2004) is of the opinion that their relatively high status emanated from the important role they play in family economy but it does not equte them to men. So many tribal women oppose going back to the customary law. They feel that though women have played an important role in shaping history they have remained invisible in public life. They do not participate in the village council and cannot often take decisions in the family without consulting husband (Gupta, 2002). They do not have inheritance rights and practice the customs that men legislate.

The issues are of great importance in the North East India because many tribal communities want to go back to customary law in search of new identity. Some want to codify customary law because of its close link with their identity.

Thus, each approach has its own merits and demerits. Experience shows that documentation without recognition is useless. Many conflicts in the North East India originate from this contradiction. Recognition is an integral part of the peace process, because it is also a sign of acceptance of their identity. Moreover, documentation of customary laws is a flexible process that keeps their law open to ongoing interpretation according to the changing situation. This ongoing process can protect their identity without stagnation.

References

Barbora, Sanjay and Walter Fernandes. 2002. 'Modernisation and tribal women's status in North East India'. In *Modernisation and Women's Status in North East India: A Comparative Study of Six Tribes*. Guwahati: North Eastern Social Research Centre.

Bhoumick, P.K. 2002. *Customary Laws of the Austric Speaking People*. Delhi: Kalpaz Publications.

Fernandes, Walter and Gita Bharali. 2008. 'Customary law - formal law interface: Impact in tribal culture'. In T.B. Subba, Joseph Puttenpurackal and Joseph Puykunnel (Eds): *Christianity and Change in North East India*. New Delhi: Concept Publications.

Fernandes, Walter; Melvil Pereira and Vizalenu Khatso 2005. *Customary Laws in North East India: Impact of Women*. New Delhi: National Commission for Women.

Haimendorf, Christoph von Furer. 2004. *The Naked Nagas*. Guwahati: Spectrum Publications.

Narwani, G.S. 2004. *Tribal Law in India*. New Delhi: Rawat Publications.

Nath, Madhuri. 2003. *Rural Women Workforce in India*. Delhi: B.R. Publishing Corporation.

5
Tribal Land Laws with State Laws: Implications for Tribal Forest Conservation

– *Melvil Pereira*

Introduction

It is well-known that despite harsh living conditions on steep hills and difficult environment, the tribal communities have managed to sustain an existence in ecologically fragile areas (Deruyttere, 1997:7; Kerkhoff and Sharma, 2006). One of the factors in the successful adaptation of tribal communities to hilly and difficult terrains is the easy access to Indigenous Knowledge (IK) that has come down from past generations. It is the IK that has helped the tribal people survive difficult terrains wherein they inhabit. Studies have revealed that behind the IK lies a well-oiled customary law system that has evolved gradually over the centuries (Dzüvichu, 2003: 6; Pereira, 2009: 130 - 154).

However, with the introduction of modern legal system the tribal customary laws are gradually but significantly losing hold over practitioners. This chapter argues the forays made by modern legal and administrative systems have had an adverse impact on the tribal customary laws leading to changes in land ownership system and has resulted in the weakening of forest conservation tradition of tribal communities of North East India.

This chapter is divided into four sections. The first section gives a brief background to the communal land holding system and the guiding norms. It discusses the significance of tribal customary law to adherents all over the world. The second section deals with the customary law and land ownership system in some communities of North East India. The third section deals with the interface of customary land laws with the formal laws of State and its impact on tribal forest conservation with special reference to the Garo of Meghalaya. The final section deals with search for solutions in the context of the adverse impact of formal laws on the tribal customary law.

Tribal Land Laws and their Significance

The land ownership system in tribal societies is mostly communal. Although, there was variation in how the system of communal ownership system got translated in practice, the general ethos guiding the system was community oriented and not individual based. While some communities like the *Angami* gave proprietary rights over terrace fields to individual families, the *Aka* of Arunachal Pradesh gave usufruct right over land to its members (Fernandes and Pereira, 2005: 112). In other communities like the *Kuki*, the land belonged to the village chieftain and he would allot the land to families for *jhum* cultivation (Haokip, 2009: 304-308).

As noted, in most of these land ownership systems, the community owned the land and distributed it to the families and clans in the village according to needs. The community had the right to claim the land back from individuals. This system denied absolute ownership rights of land to individuals. The communal ethos guided their land use pattern and led to egalitarian values being practiced in societies. It contributed to the conservation of flora and fauna and resulted in maintaining rich biodiversity. This went on for centuries together and kept the communities well-knit and united.

The edifice of communal land ownership system was built on tribal customary laws from which the indigenous knowledge system evolved. Scholars have maintained that these customary laws evolved gradually over a period of time in response to the needs and requirement of specific land and forests (Krishnan, 2004: 48). They are place-specific and time-specific. Their origin lies in catering to the needs of community while not undermining the needs of individual families. It paid attention to intra–generational as well as inter-generational requirements. Hence, its approach to land use was sustainable.

In the past, indigenous people all over the world had made use of customary laws to regulate the society, to conserve natural resources and to resolve conflicts within the community. They treated customary law as a useful tool to protect the common resources and promote harmony in the community. Specific to it is its role as a social organisation mechanism. The role of customary law in social organisation and maintaining harmony in the community has been well documented (Human Development Report, 2004: 59). It plays a significant role in determining the ownership of land and regulating the use of forests. It articulates the rules of access, extraction and the use of natural resources ensuring sustainable management (D'Souza, 2001). The customary law is thus the repository of values and ideals of a tribe and is central to its identity. The role it plays in managing and conserving forests is the main reason why the customary law is increasingly being studied by social scientists (Ostrom, 1990; D'Souza, 2001; Orebech, 2005).

Most tribal societies have their own customary laws. As mentioned, these laws are anchored in a specific place. Because of it, the tribes develop appropriate rules and regulations to suit that particular environment. Their social and political organisation is shaped around the management of natural resources. Thus most customary laws originated in response to the needs of particular group of people settled in specific place at given point of time. That makes them location-specific, people-specific and time-specific (Krishnan, 2004: 48). Most of these laws came into existence through the interaction of people among themselves and with the natural resources that they were bestowed with. So, they contain guidelines for ownership, use and protection of natural resources.

Management and regulation of forest and other natural resource based sustenance was the primary concern of indigenous communities. They could not afford to harvest these resources as the industrial agents do. To industrial agents, these resources are only a raw material and a source of profit. The industry-based approach to natural resources is extractive and does not lay stress on the renewal of natural resources (Guha and Gadgil, 1996 : 34–35).

Some criticise customary laws as being rigid and static or as getting caught up in age–old beliefs and traditions and not allowing the community to develop. This criticism can be levelled against all the formal or statutory laws. While critiquing the customary laws, it is important to note these laws originated in response to specific need in particular context. So, they are subject to change according to requirements of practitioners (Sheleff, 1999: 84–88). Referring to the Canadian Amerindians, Borrows (2002: 27) argues that 'First Nations legal traditions are strong and dynamic and can be interpreted flexibly to deal with real issues in contemporary

Canadian law concerning Aboriginal communities'. He adds that the customary law, their living document, changes and evolves according to needs and on terms.

Customary Law and Common Property Resources in North East India

It is well-known that *jhum* cultivation is widely practiced in North East India. It has traditionally been successful in North East India and South East Asia because people adhered to the practice of setting fixed number of years aside for cropping and fallowing. They strictly held on to *jhum* cycles which helped in keeping the soil fertile (Gangwar and Ramakrishnan, 1992:101-102). Such practices were found on the basis of time-tested customary laws. Studies have noted the role played by customary law in the protection and conservation of natural resources (Jodha, 1986; D'Souza, 2001). Some studies have highlighted their instrumentality in the sustainable development of the natural resources (Orebech, 2005).

In the context of the North East Indian tribal communities, customary laws of various tribal communities employed intricate mix of land and forest management systems like ownership of land and forest by individuals, clans, *khels* and villages (Fernandes *et al.,* 2005: 27-47). It is true that due to the influence of market and commercial forces, these different systems of land ownerships are at different transitional stages from communal ownership to individual land holding system (Buragohain, 1990: 10). However, it is important to note that in some tribal communities of North East India communal ownership of land is intricately intertwined with private ownership of land. Thus, one has to be careful not to straightjacket land ownership system in North East India as communal in nature.

Among the Aka of West Kameng district of Arunachal Pradesh, land is owned by the village. The individual families have usufruct rights over the land (Fernandes and Pereira, 2005: 112). This is not the case among the Angami of Nagaland. Among the Angami, the individual families have absolute right over terraced land which is used for rice cultivation but forest land is owned by clans and village. Among the Garo of Meghalaya, the *nokma*[1] is the owner of the village land. It is the *nokma* who allots land to individual families for cultivation.

Like the Akas of Arunachal Pradesh, among the Tangkhul Nagas in Manipur, community land is an important component of the village. A village dweller is free to use such land for cultivation but after the cultivation, the plot of land automatically reverts as community land (Shimray, 2009: 248). In case an individual has made some permanent improvement on a plot of land for agricultural purposes, like converting into terrace fields, then such land is eventually considered as individual land holding (*ibid*: 249). All operations relating to land and forest come under the jurisdiction of village chief and council, who are bound by customary laws of the community.

Among the Garo of Meghalaya, there are broadly two types of land, the hilly land and the plain land. While the hilly land, also known as *a.king*[2] land, comprises 95 per cent of the total land, the rest is plain land. The plain land is governed by the provisions of the Assam Land and Revenue Regulation Act of 1886, which was later adopted by the Garo Hills Autonomous District Council[3] in 1952 (Nongkynrih, 2008: 29). The ownership of *a.king* land is vested in the founding clan of that *a.king*. The *a.king nokma*, the husband of inheritress of the founding household, is recognised as the custodian of the *a.king* land. The members of the clan only have usufructury rights over the *a.king* land. The *nokma,* with the help of clan members, identifies the land for swidden or shifting cultivation and apportions to members of the *a.king*. After cultivation, the land reverts to the *a.king nokma*. Thus the property is communally owned and not individually transferable (Agarwal, 1995:102; Sangma, 1981:149). Within the *a.king*, everyone has equal access to land and equal right to use it.

Among the Kuki in Manipur, land is owned by the chief of the village and his legal heirs inherit the land after his death. The village chieftain is the owner of the village land, the guardian of law and the ultimate arbitrator in case of conflicts (Haokip, 2009: 304-308). His ownership of land was not absolute but custodial in nature. He played the role of distributing the land for shifting cultivation. His leadership in the village is linked to identity and territoriality among the Kukis since chieftainship is considered the source of Kuki customary laws (*ibid*).

Experience has shown that such mix of ownership patterns of land and forest has positive impact on the protection of natural resources and on forest conservation. There are various norms, techniques and mechanisms applied in the sustainable use of land and forest. For instance among the Angami of Nagaland, access to forests and its resources is determined by customary laws. As noted above, the Angami customary laws have an interesting mix of individual and communal ownership of land and forests.

At present, terrace fields and the greater part of *jhum* lands are owned by individuals. Similarly, a certain area of forest is owned also by individuals. But, there is also a considerable amount of *jhum* land and forest owned by clans, and certain amount by the village as a whole. While individual ownership of terrace fields is treated as absolute, ownership of *jhum* fields and forests is usually not absolute because others have access to such fields and land under certain circumstances (D'Souza, 2001: 44).

As the above quote illustrates, customary law regulation of land and forests among Angami maintains balance between individual and communal ownership of land. While making sure that no individual is given a free hand to accumulate land, it ensures the requirements of each and every individual family in the village are met. This arrangement of ownership of land between the individual units and community maintains balance between fields and forests. Such balance between land allotted to fields and forests is considered essential for successful cultivation of fields (D'Souza, 2001: 56). The forests are singularly protected and conserved in order that the terrace fields are able to obtain sufficient water for rice cultivation. Such land and forest regulation mechanism is not unique to the Angami community of Nagaland. Mention has already been made about the Akas of Arunachal and Tangkhuls of Manipur who also follow similar land ownership pattern.

The section above briefly summarised various land ownership systems among tribal communities of North East India. It highlighted the norms and rules that guided these land holding systems. It stressed the significant role played by tribal land laws and IK in the sustainable use of land and forests which catered to the need of every family in the village. The next section deals with the interface of tribal customary laws with the formal land laws that were introduced by the British and later by the Government of India.

Interface of Customary Land Laws with Formal Laws

One of the contentions of this chapter is that an entirely alien system which is based on the concept of private property, the individual, the written word and with profit as its prime motive was imported by the colonial regime and imposed on the tribal communities. The Indian Government continued this process after independence in the name of national development. Changing land laws was basic to the colonial system that was meant to turn India into a supplier of raw material and a captive market for finished products of the Industrial Revolution. Laws had to be changed to ensure easy land transfer to British plantation and mine owners for producing raw materials. They succeeded in doing so in the plains through several measures, the first one being the *Permanent Settlement* 1793.

Similar processes were set in motion after the formal entry of the British into this region with the Anglo-Burmese Yandabu Treaty, 1826. They took control of the North East India gradually beginning with Assam where they saw its potential for tea and later petroleum and mines. The tea plantations and extraction of oil meant acquisition of large tracts of land that belonged to indigenous people of the region. The colonial regime acquired land for tea in the latter half of the Nineteenth century from the Ahom, Koch, Bodo and others on highly exploitative terms (Jha, 1996). The major efforts at extraction of oil and coal came after 1947 (*ibid.*). The legal tool they used to acquire land was the *Assam Wasteland Rules* 1838. They defined ownership and wasteland in such manner that any land left uncultivated for a season could be called wasteland and taken over without compensation (Barpujari, 1996: 254-258).

Besides, most communities of the region, particularly in the Hills were CPR dependent but the law was individual-based. So while they acquired the CPRs in the plains without compensation, they needed the Hill areas less for land than for trade to popularise the finished products of Industrial Revolution (Fernandes and Pereira, 2005). So for practical purposes, the colonialist did not intervene in customary laws and left the administration with traditional tribal institutions. Their main objective was to control their markets. To achieve it, they destroyed or commercialised tribal craft to prevent competition with the Manchester textiles (Bose, 1997: 197 - 201). Thus even while leaving their tradition untouched; they modified it to suit their colonial needs. They introduced changes indirectly to suit their own needs. So the traditional and modern systems remained almost parallel and to some extent affected their traditional land relations (Sinha, 1994: 159-168).

Post-Independence Individual-Community Interface

We have already noted above that from the colonial age, the productive capacities of the tribal economy were destroyed through the onslaught of commercial forces let loose by the British. The Indian State, since independence, has continued this approach in the name of national development. After independence, this individual-community interface has taken the form of the Sixth Schedule or recognition of the customary law through amendments to the Constitution. In the Sixth Schedule areas, the village court or the Autonomous District Council (ADC) deals with civil offences. The ADC exists in two districts of Assam and the whole of Meghalaya. Nagaland never had ADCs but a constitutional amendment in 1963 introducing Article 371-A enabled it to follow its customary law in civil matters. Mizoram followed suit in 1986 with Article 371-G.

Most tribes of Arunachal Pradesh follow their customary laws but the Sixth Schedule does not apply to them. The administrative system evolved under the British continues to be used. Manipur too does not have Scheduled areas but has some laws and district councils governing its Hill areas. Tripura does not have the Sixth Schedule but district councils have been introduced in response to unrest (Barooah, 2002: 99-100).

Introduced as a protective measure, the Sixth Schedule has been superimposed on their tradition. It recognises community ownership and does not allow non-tribals to acquire land in these areas. However, the administration that is in charge of these areas has an individual orientation. So knowledgeable persons say that even in these areas, land alienation is rampant both to tribals and from tribals to non-tribals. Its main reason is that though on paper any alienation needs the consent of the community, in practice the administration treats the *gaonburah* (village leader) as the owner and negotiates land deals only with him. Secondly, the State bodies introduce commercial crops for which they give subsidies and financial institutions give loans only to individuals, understood as heads of families. In most cases they are men.

That lays the foundation of land alienation. Within the tribe it takes the form of land sale or mortgaging to others from the same community, thus sharpening the class divide among them. It has even given rise to absentee landlordism. With the intensification of the commercial processes and globalisation, such alienation is likely to grow leading to greater hardships to CPR dependants. Outside the tribe, it involves non-tribals taking over land either through mortgage or through encroachment (Fernandes and Pereira, 2005: 126-127).

Effects of the Interface

In the paragraphs below, the Garo tribal community of Meghalaya where Sixth Schedule is in operation is taken for discussion to assess the impact of formal land laws on the tribal land laws.

A study of changing land relations (Fernandes and Pereira, 2005: 118-122) shows that 79 of the 100 families studied in East Garo Hills had *patta*s. This shows the process of individualisation is strong among the Garos. In contrast, the *jhum* practicing Akas of West Kameng district of Arunachal Pradesh who are close to their tradition and govern themselves according to customary law without being under the Sixth Schedule, lack the very concept of land ownership and only have the tradition of usufruct right over the CPRs (Fernandes and Bharali, 2002: 7-8). Of the 43 families studied among the Aka, 37 gave no information on land ownership, because most of them still use the CPRs in the *jhum* season. After it, the land reverts to the community. Six others have started occupying community land and getting *patta*s (Fernandes and Pereira, 2005: 118-122). It is possible because they do not have the Sixth Schedule so the CPRs are not recognised. So elite among the Aka are slowly shifting to individual land ownership. The Angami of Nagaland had well protected villages with neatly managed systems of forest conservation and sustaining of natural resources. But, there is evidence to show that a new form of tenancy is appearing for the first time and changing the traditional pattern (D'Souza and Kekhrieseno, 2002). We can give more such examples but the ones given above show a certain trend.

The author of this chapter met some knowledgeable persons and elders in Garo villages across three Garo Hill districts. During his field trips, he found many examples of ill effects of such an interface (Pereira, 2009). In the Garo Hills, for example, the tradition was of community ownership. Their matrilineal system is built on land inheritance through the female line. By issuing *pattas*, the modern institutions recognise man as the landholder and that affects the very foundation of the matrilineal system. In the early 1990s, the administration encouraged the people to plant rubber. The Garos took to horticulture in a big way. The financial institutions and banks give loans only to *patta* holders. Those without the *pattas* are not given subsidy and financial help.

Since land held in common is not considered as collateral, the Garos, who practiced a communal land ownership system in the form of *a.king,* could not avail themselves of loans from banks. Some interviewees, who had usufruct rights in *a.king* land, recounted instances when banks had refused them loans because they did not have the *patta*. 'A *patta* is needed to get loans from the banks. They reject our application for loans, if a *patta* is not produced. I know some people who got disappointed because banks refused to grant them loan on the pretext they do not have a *patta*'.[4]

A Garo elder from Tura had this to say about banks demanding land holding document or *patta* to grant loans:

> The government agencies and banks are granting loans for rubber cultivation but to utilise these loans we need be *patta* holders. *Patta* becomes a necessity in order to get the loans. So we go to our *nokmas* to request for a piece of land and he allots a piece of land and issues a no-objection certificate. With this, we go to the District Council who issues the *patta* to us. Once we are holders of the *patta*, the banks give us loan.[5]

Even the ADC that should have safeguarded the *a.king* land supported this approach and issued *pattas* liberally to the CPRs thus depriving the poor of livelihood. One of the *nokmas* described the way ADCs have encouraged individual ownership of land :

> The *patta* system is introduced by the ADC in order to implement a tax regime. There was no tax system in the past. The ADC for financial benefits introduced this system. It has affected my powers as a *nokma*. Now, I have become a part of this system, because I have to write

> no-objection certificates. I refuse to give a no-objection certificate, but there are *nokmas* who issue such documents and this has affected the *a.king* land system. The ADC, which should have protected the *a.king* system of land administration, is actively involved in its destruction.[6]

The transfer of *a.king* land to any individual or even to the State goes against the Garo customary practices (Marak, 2000: 185-186). In this case, the administration recognised the individual owner as man and considered him the head of the family. This goes against the Garo custom of women inheriting land.

The above discussion on the interface of formal laws with the Garo customary laws showed how the inroads made by the formal laws adversely affects the land ownership system of the Garo. The first trend is a contradiction arising between two systems and the ill-effects of imposing the individual-based laws and economy on the community-based informal societies. Such an imposition results in an encounter of unequals. The individual-based administration encourages the processes leading to a *patta* that is alien to their culture. It recognises CPRs only in the Sixth Schedule areas. Even in these areas official inputs are individual-based. It is such modernisation without protective measures that turns land that was their livelihood and the centre of their culture and identity into a commodity to be sold or leased to the highest bidder. Their communities begin to lose the sacredness attached to it in their tradition and a new worldview emerges that they are not familiar with, as seen among others, in the fact that much of the mortgaging and sale is within the community. One of its results is class formation in their egalitarian societies. Imposition of such modernisation forces, the tribal and other traditional communities to switch over to new lifestyle based on different set of norms. It results in their socio-economic and cultural degradation and depletion of natural resources.

Globalisation Leading to Further Weakening of Tribal Land Laws

The forces of globalisation have further weakened the hold of tribal customary laws on their practitioners and forest conservation. According to Amin, globalisation results in the further integration of the informal economy into the formal one on the terms of the latter (Amin,1999: 23-25). The market forces make land that is the livelihood of tribal communities into a commodity. This results in impoverishment. Globalisation in its present form strengthens the individual land laws and results in monopolisation of natural resources in the hands of few.

In the case of the Garo, the *patta* system has led to class formation. According to the Garo customary law, the Garos held land in common; there were in-built checks and balances to thwart anyone's attempt at owning huge tracts of land. The *nokma* with the help of the *mahari*[7] made sure that land was equally distributed among the clan members and others living in the *a.king*. But the *patta* system seems to have worked in favour of the elite among the Garo and helped them accumulate an enormous amount of land.

Among the Garo, this new phenomenon of some wealthy Garos owning land in many *a.kings*. The 'Achik culture' forbade Garos from owning land in more than one *a.king*. The infiltration of the forces of globalisation has opened up prospects for individuals to own any amount of land in more than one *a.king*, thus opening the doors for accumulation of land in one hand. The phènomenon of elite amassing land, the emergence of rich and poor, and class formation have become a reality in most tribal communities of North East India.

In the context of North East India, of greater importance are the major dams that are being planned (Vagholikar and Das, 2011). The thrust in them is towards private companies building for their own profit. Over a hundred dams are being planned, some are at advanced stages of implementation. Most of them are planned in areas like Arunachal Pradesh, where the tradition is CPR based but without the legal base of the Sixth Schedule. Such move may further weaken the customary laws.

Response to the Interface: Some Considerations

In the sections above, the interface of formal law with tribal land law in Garo Hills Districts of Meghalaya was discussed. The Garos are in the threshold of transition as far as their land ownership system goes. It has been already noted that the Garos have embraced the *patta* system in a big way. However, there is a minority among them, who are concerned about the erosion of their cultural heritage due to the change in land ownership system. In this section, a brief analysis will follow on certain issues that have cropped up while discussing factors that have led to the weakening of the Garo land laws.

Future of *a.king* Land

From the above discussion on the Garo land laws, it was clear that these laws are tied to the concept of *a.king* land. Some Garos hold that the *a.king* land has to be preserved in some form or the other. Are *a.king* land system and *patta* system diametrically opposed land holding systems? Are communal and individual ownership of land antithetical? Are they closely intertwined? Is there middle ground where both forms of land ownership systems exist in a social organisation? Some authors have tried to grapple with this complex idea. According to Nongkynrih:

> In theory, tribal practices do not permit the conversion of community land into private. In practice plots allocated for residential purposes or economic activities get converted over generations into the private property of families or individuals that make permanent improvements on them. Families enjoy the right to sell off the improvement made on the land. In doing so, they also transfer to another owner the land on which improvements have been made (Nongkynrih, 2008:34).

Nongkynrih argues that there might be prospects for communal lands to get converted to private land. The rules of communal ownership need not be so suffocating as to prevent an individual from owning land. If an individual continuously uses a piece of land and invests in the land, s(he) might gradually get proprietary rights. Thus it might not be correct to put these systems of land ownership into watertight compartments.

Is there a way for the Garos to make space for both systems of land ownership? The data from the sample clearly shows that the *patta* system has come to stay in Garo Hills. From the responses of interviewees, it is clear that there is overwhelming support for individual land ownership. People from cross-sections of society seem to have benefitted from the introduction of the *patta* system.

'Everybody prefers the *patta* system. By issuing a non-objection certificate, the *nokma* gets money from people. The District Council gets revenue from the land tax. And people can get loans from financial agencies once they have *pattas*. Everybody seems to be benefiting from this development.'[8]

But there are also voices of caution. These voices are not exactly against the *patta* system, but against the way the new system is introduced, sidetracking and destroying the *a.king* system. As one teacher puts it,

> The *patta* system is inevitable and overwhelming. With population growth and modernisation, the traditional system is slowly giving way to the new and the modern. What matters most perhaps is the type or process of transition from the old to the new. In this transition are we throwing away our rich Garo heritage? This question has to be kept in mind. There is no point in holding on to the obsolete practices, but those which are part and parcel of our culture, those elements which define our very identity, have to be safeguarded.[9]

Is there a way of introducing the *patta* system which does minimal damage to the Garo culture? The quote above seems to be accepting the benefits of *patta* system but cautions that it should not result in weakening the Garo culture. It has been noted already that the defining elements of the Garo culture are matrilineal descent, *a.king* land, and the *nokma* system. How can these core elements be preserved in the context of change, which is largely desired?

The *a.king* system has in-built measures which stopped its members from accumulating huge tracts of land. Can there be protective measures put in place in the *patta* system, so as to avoid the monopolisation of resources in the hands of a few and to the impoverishment of many? There was a suggestion made in this direction:

> To my mind, *a.king* land should remain and *patta* can be granted to individuals. But there should be certain ceiling, say 15 or 20 *bighas*[10] as the upper limit. Any plot of land where an individual is living and cultivating crops should be given a *patta*. This document is important for them to get loans. They should be allowed the proper owner of

> that land. This sense of security is important for any long-term investment. But this does not mean that all the *a.king* land should be given as *patta*.[11]

The above quote suggests a multipronged approach to deal with the introduction of the *patta* system. It makes space both for communal and individual land. The *a.king* and *patta* system can exist simultaneously. A certain portion of land can be retained as *a.king* land, and the rest of the land can be distributed to individuals, who can obtain a *patta* from the ADC. Such an approach allows the Garos to profit from both systems of land ownership. On the one hand, the Garo believes, cultural practices, and institutions are preserved. On the other hand, by obtaining *pattas* families and individuals can make use of the benefits accrued to individual ownership.

The quote also a suggests to regulate distribution of land. That a *patta* can be granted but with a ceiling imposed seems to be a measure which can result in the equitable distribution of land. This can prevent individuals from amassing huge amount of land.

Can *a.king* be Recognised as Collateral?

The financial institutions in Garo Hills have been refusing to grant loans to Garos on the pretext that they do not have an individual land ownership document or *patta*. In a land tenure system, where individual ownership has no place, it seems not fair to deny financial assistance to people, because they do not have adequate collateral. To overcome this systemic hurdle, some Garo intellectuals have suggested the District Council should intervene and pass law making members of an *a.king* eligible to receive loans from banks. Let this law make it necessary that a no objection certificate (NOC) from the *nokma* is mandatory for an individual to receive loans from financial agencies.

> Let the *nokma* be the person who gives no objection certificate for loans. Now, this has to be done in consultation with the *mahari*. So only in case of genuine need, they will issue the no objection certificate. So not all and sundry will get a chance to take a loan from banks. Only responsible persons and families who can repay loan will get this no objection certificate.[12]

The practice of a village chief issuing a NOC to an individual seeking loan from banks is already in practice among the Khasi community in the State of Meghalaya. One of the interviewees mentioned that '....in Khasi villages when people apply for loans, the headman writes a recommendation letter. The bank issues loans to them. So we are suggesting that the bank should accept the *nokma's* recommendation letter and grant loans to Garos.'[13]

The Role of ADC Contested

The role of the ADC was held up to critical scrutiny by some interviewees in the in-depth interview. The Sixth Schedule of the Indian Constitution is a protective measure to safeguard the social practices and self-governing institutions of tribal communities. The role of the ADC as articulated in the Sixth Schedule is to preserve and reform the native social practices while at the same time introducing them to liberal democratic institutions.

Some felt that the ADC should have intervened to protect the Garo culture. It had many opportunities to uphold the Garo culture, which is founded on *a.king* land. An interviewee mentioned, 'So much of our culture and customs are closely related to the *a.king* land. It is the District Council which should have taken the initiative to preserve such lands.'[14.] This interviewee seems to lament the limited role played by the ADC to get involved in defending and preserving the Garo culture.

Some interviewees went further in critiquing the role of the ADC and blamed it for becoming actively involved in the destruction of the *a.king* land ownership system. They hold that the ADC has no right to issue *pattas* to the *a.king* land.

In fact, if you see the whole system, the District Council has no authority to issue *pattas*. No one is challenging this. The property belongs to the community or to the *nokma* who is the custodian of the property of the community. The community can allow members of the *a.king* to cultivate and use. But the ADC has no power whatsoever to issue *pattas* for the *a.king* land, which is the land of the *nokma*. Now by issuing the *pattas*, the District Council has dealt a heavy blow to the *a.king* land, thus undermining the Garo culture.[15]

The *a.king* is the property of a particular *mahari* under the custodianship of a *nokma*. By issuing *pattas* to *a.kings* that come under the purview of *nokmas* the ADC seems to have crossed its boundary and has done great injustice to *nokma* system. A Garo advocate went to the extent of saying that the ADC can be sued in the courts.

Of course, the District Council can be taken to court. There is good ground for bringing suit against the ADC. Till now, no one has challenged the District Council, and hence the issue of *pattas* is going unabated. As far as I understand, the ADC is acting against the provisions of the Sixth Schedule. Instead of protecting the communal property rights, it is violating them.[16]

Was this provision of the Sixth Schedule an intentional governmental measure for assimilating tribal institutions? Some authors have held that the very purpose of the Sixth Schedule was to integrate somewhat different tribal institutions into the State system (Stuligross, 1999). A critique of the intent and rationale behind this provision of the Sixth Schedule could be a topic for deeper analysis in another article.

Conclusion

The tribal communities faced with a set of values and laws founded on an individualistic ethos which apparently goes against the collective and egalitarian philosophy they have practiced. The land laws introduced by the British and later, by the government of India, have gradually but significantly weakened the tribal land laws. These have negatively impacted the forest conservation system and the biodiversity rich North East India. In searching for solution, one had to lay emphasis on a process of modernisation and development that takes into account the rich cultural and social traditions and customary land laws knit around land and its utilisation among tribal communities of North East India.

The first Prime Minister of India, Pt. Jawaharlal Nehru, while enunciating the principles to guide the tribal policies of Indian government, underlined the importance of respecting cultures of tribal people.[17] The first of the five principles that he proposed – principles popularly known as the *Panchsheel* or five principles - asserts that "People should develop along the lines of their own genius and we should avoid imposing anything on them. (Elwin, 1988: xi)". The fourth principle of *Panchsheel* beckons the administrators to make use of the indigenous institutions in administering tribal areas: "We should work through their social and cultural institutions (*Ibid.*)". The State has neglected this advice of Nehru in introducing modern inputs in the tribal communities of North East India.

In finding solutions, one has to begin by questioning eminent domain and by re-valourising the communities that have preserved well-organised land ownership systems and the land laws that guided them. Their concept of land as livelihood has to be the starting point. In other words, one has to begin with what is familiar to the traditional communities i.e. with their customary laws and value system. Many of these laws and values have to be modified to suit a better understanding of equity. The practices have to be adapted to suit the present state of resource use. The traditional communities as well as representatives of the formal system will have to be restrained to achieve it.

Notes

1. *Nokma* is the husband of the heiress of a group of villages called *a.king*. He is the village head and custodian of the village land. He plays a leading role in village administration, especially in resolving disputes and allotting the land to individual families for cultivation.
2. Land, usually a group of villages, is held by a particular motherhood or *machong*. This land is under the custody of the head of the *machong* called the "nokma".
3. The Garo Hills district was part of the State of Assam until 1970. On January 12 , 1970, the State of Meghalaya was carved out of Assam. In the State of Meghalaya, the Garo Hills is a Sixth Schedule District and thus, as per provisions of the said Schedule of the Constitution of India, it is administered by the Garo Hills Autonomous District Council. The Autonomous District Councils (ADC) in Meghalaya was set up in 1952. Thus, the administration in these districts comes under the parallel jurisdictions of both the State and the ADC.
4. The interview with Mr. Nongjeng Ch. Marak took place at his residence in Araimile, Tura, East Garo Hills District, on November 5, 2006 between 4.15 to 5.10 pm.

5. Mr. Llewellyn R Marak is a Garo elder from Tura. This interview took place on November 16, 2007 in his residence between 4.15 and 5.05 pm.
6. Mr. Kollaram T. Sangma is an *a.king nokma* of Bawigre, Jengjal, West Garo Hills district, Meghalaya. The interview with him took place at his residence in Bawigre on October 22, 2006 between 7.15 and 8.45 am.
7. This is the entire set of blood relation belonging to a *machong*. Some authors call such a group "village lineage". When a conflict takes place between two individuals, a *mahari mela* or meeting is called to resolve the conflict.
8. Mr. Alphonsius R. Marak is a youth leader in William Nagar, East Garo Hills district. This interview took place in his house at William Nagar, on November 16, 2006, between 10.05 and 10.45 am.
9. Mrs. Barbara S. Sangma is a lecturer in Don Bosco College, Tura, Meghalaya. The interview with her took place in the college between 10.30 and 11.15 am.
10. One *bigha* is equal to one-third of an acre.
11. Mrs. Miriam D. Shira is a former Minister of Transport and Health, Government of Meghalaya. The interview with her took place at her residence in Tura on October 18, 2006 between 4.45 and 5.35 pm.
12. Mr. Gypson R. Marak is an advocate at District Commissioner's Court, Tura. The interview with him took place in his residence in Dokogre, Tura, on November 12, 2006 between 5.05 and 5.55 pm.
13. Mr. Skylance G. Momin, is a retired Inspector-General of Police of the State of Meghalaya. Currently, he is the President of Council of *Nokma* of West Garo Hills District. The interview with him took place in the office of the Council of *Nokma*, Ringre, Tura, on November 6, 2006 between 11.45 am and 12.35 pm.
14. Mr. Salison R. Marak is a village elder in Siju, South Garo Hills District. The interview with him took place at

his residence in Siju on November 2, 2009 between 4.50 and 5.45 pm. The interpreter was Mr. John A. Sangma.

15. This interview took place on November 10, 2006 between 5.30 and 6.15 am, in the residence of the interviewee in Tura. The interviewee wished to remain anonymous.
16. See note 12.
17. Prime Minister Pt. Jawaharlal Nehru was sensitive to the distinctive lifestyle and culture of tribal communities in India.

References

Agarwal, Bina. 1995. *A Field of One's Own: Gender and Land Rights in South Asia*. Melbourne: Cambridge University Press.

Amin, Samir. 1999. 'Globalisation Yesterday and Today', In Walter Fernandes and Anupama Dutta (Eds): *Colonialism to Globalisation: Five Centuries After Vasco da Gama*. Vol. 1: Main Issues around Colonialism and Globalisation, pp. 22-26, New Delhi: Indian Social Institute.

Barooah, Jeuti. 2002. 'Property and women's inheritance rights in the tribal areas of the Northeast,' In Walter Fernandes and Sanjay Barbora (Eds): *Changing Women's Status in India: Focus on the Northeast*, pp. 99-113, Guwahati: North Eastern Social Research Centre.

Barpujari, H. K. 1996. *Assam in the Days of the Company 1826-1858*. Shillong: North Eastern Hill University.

Bose, M.L. 1997. *A History of Arunachal Pradesh*. New Delhi: Concept Publishers.

D'Souza Alphonsus and Christina Kekhrieseno. 2002. *Social Change in North East India: A Comparative Study of Three Tribes (mimeo)*. Jakhama: St Joseph's College.

Deruyttere, Anne. 1997. 'Indigenous peoples and sustainable development: The role of the Inter-American Development Bank,' *IDB Publications* 39878, Inter-American Development Bank.

Dzüvichü, Bernice. 2003. *Customary Laws of the Angami Nagas*. Unpublished PhD Thesis, Department of Anthropology, Delhi University, Delhi.

Elwin, Verrier. 1988. *A Philosophy for NEFA*. Itanagar: Directorate of Research, Government of Arunachal Pradesh.

Fernandes, Walter and Gita Bharali. 2002. *The Socio-Economic Situation of Some Tribes of Bishnupur and Palizi*. Guwahati: North Eastern Social Research Centre (mimeo).

Fernandes, Walter and Melville Pereira. 2005. *Changing Land Relations and Ethnic Conflicts: The Case of North Eastern India*. Guwahati: North Eastern Social Research Centre.

Fernandes, Walter and Sanjay Barbora. 2002. *Modernisation and Women's Status in the Eastern India: A Comparative Study of Six Tribes*. Guwahati: North Eastern Social Research Centre (mimeo).

Fernandes, Walter. 1998. 'The impact of liberalisation on the tribals in India', *Vikalp*, 4, 2: 81-103.

Jha, J.C. 1996. *Aspects of Indentured Inland Emigration to North-East India 1859- 1918,* New Delhi: Indus Publishers.

Kerkhoff, Elisabet and Eklabya Sharma. 2006. *Debating Shifting Cultivation in the Eastern Himalayas*.Kathmandu: ICIMOD and IFAD.

Marak, L.R. Julius. 2000. *Garo Customary Laws and Practices*. New Delhi: Akansha Publishing House.

Menon, Manju, Neeraaj Vagholikar, Kanchi Kohli and Ashish Fernandes. 2003. 'Large dams in the Northeast: A bright future?' *The Ecologist Asia* 11 (n. 1, Jan-March), pp. 3-8.

Nongkynrih, A. K.2008. 'Privatisation of the communal land of the tribes in North East India: Sociological viewpoint', In Walter Fernandes and Sanjay Barbora (Eds): *Land, People and Politics: Contest Over Tribal Land in Northeast India,* pp. 16-37. Guwahati: North Eastern Social Research Centre and IWGIA.

Pereira, Melvil. 2009. *Customary Law and State Formation in Northeast India: A Comparative Study of the Angami of Nagaland and the Garo of Meghalaya*. Unpublished PhD

Thesis, Centre for Political Studies, Jawaharlal Nehru University, Delhi.

Ramanathan, Usha. 1999. 'Public purpose: Points for discussion,' In Walter Fernandes (Ed): *The Land Acquisition (Amendment) Bill 1998: For Liberalisation or for the Poor?* , pp. 19-24, New Delhi: Indian Social Institute.

Sangma, Milton. 1981. *History and Culture of the Garos.* New Delhi: P.K. Jain for Books Today.

Sinha, A.C. 1994. *North-Eastern Frontiers of India: Structural Imperatives and Aspects of Change,* New Delhi: Indus Publishing House.

Stuligross, D. 1999. 'Autonomous Councils in Northeast India: Theory and Practice', *Alternatives,* 24, 4: 497-525.

Vagholikar, N. and P J Das. 2011. *Damming the North East India.* Kalpavriksh, Aranyak and Action Aid India. Pune, Guwahati and New Delhi.

6
Forest Villages in Assam

– *Chandrajyoti Sonowal*

Forest and Tribal Interface in India

In India, any discourse on forest and forestry programme reminds the interrelation between forest and the tribal population. The traditional symbiotic relationship between traditional tribal societies and forest has revealed that the forest dwellers create a culture where forests are treated as a renewable means of subsistence. In return, the forest provides livelihood to people living in and around. Numerous instances have been found among different tribal people of the country who use forest as source of fodder and also a means of earning by collecting economically valuable things (Ray Burman, 1988; Hembram, 1988). Researchers indicate that there is a strong tie between the social system of the tribals and the forests. The scholars also reveal that the tribal culture protects and regenerate the surrounding forests by means of traditional socio-cultural processes like imposing taboo, planting certain varieties of plants, etc. Thus, the traditional practices of the tribal forest dwellers have been constructive towards forest management.

Forest Villages Defined

The creation of forest villages was a part of forest management in the early part of last century. The practice of scientific forestry in India had begun sometimes in 1884. The British government had to meet the supply of raw material for railway expansion and revenue to support the British Imperial Government. The need for exploitation of forest resources required maintaining a regular supply of labourer. As far back as 1856, Mr. D. Brandis, the first Inspector-General of Forest of Colonial India, conceived the idea of pressing the shifting cultivation, as practiced by Karens, initiated a system called *taungya,* where local people were allowed to raise crop in forest, cut and burn forest to raise level of ashes, whereby teak plantation could be initiated.

In India, the practice was followed mainly in the areas where the local people refused to lend labour for government sylvicultural programmes. Initially, the forest labourers were treated as serfs by the government as they were forced to render free service for forest work for a number of days in a year as earmarked. This service is called "*begar*" (Sonowal, 1997). Later, the situation changed slightly as the migrant labourers were provided homesteads and one hector of land in lieu of services rendered to the forest department. These settlements came to be known as forest villages. Thus, by definition, forest villages does not mean the villages located in the forest, but means such villages or colony of collies or labourers established by the Forest Department for maintenance of assured supply of labour required in forest works done departmentally (Sinha, 1987). In this process, either existing habitations in the forest were declared as forest villages or people were brought from outside to establish them.

Individuals in forest villages were permitted to construct small temporary huts and raise some food crops to supplement the earning. The land thus utilised legally continues to remain 'reserved' forest and the villages were expected to be shifted when there was no work. There are evidences especially from Madhya Pradesh and Gujarat (Prasad and Jahagirdar, 1993) that some revenue villages were transferred to form forest villages. With the enforcement of Constitution on 26th January, 1950 '*begar*' and other forms of forced labour stood prohibited and punishable in accordance with law. The condition did not change in many places. It was only in the year 1969 when such system was first challenged in Kerala. Later on, it was advocated that the tribals living in forest villages should be given the right to inherit but such land should be inalienable. The decision of the Ministry of Agriculture (1984) suggests the State should confer long term heritable but inalienable right to tribals in forest villages.

The specific problems of the forest villages as pointed out by a scholar like Jahagirdar (1993) as follows :

(a) Inhabitants of the forest villages do not enjoy tenancy right on the land which they cleared once and there is always fear of eviction by the forest department.

(b) Being the inhabitants of remote forest area and as untouched by revenue department, they hardly come to the development administration of block.

(c) Unable to get financial assistance from institutional sources as they have no recognised right on land and other properties.

Forest Villages in Assam

The root of forest villages lies in the *Taungya* system, which was current in Myanmar. In this system, local people were allowed to clear forest and burn them to ashes and grow crops on it. Repeated burning of vegetation led to amass of ashes on the ground suitable for teak plantation. These labourers were given permission to raise crops in such clear land. In the same way, teak plantations were initiated in Assam in the year 1901 in Longai Reserved Forest in Sylhet district and the first forest village was established. The success story of this village encouraged the department to establish forest villages in land suitable for wet rice cultivation within the reserved forest. In the process, by the year 1902-03, 15 forest villages came up and the number increased up to 145 by 1913-14.

As a starting point, three districts were selected for the functioning of forest villages. These were Cachar, Goalpara and Kamrup having 8, 15 and 12 forest villages respectively in each district. The forest department of Assam has a record of 450 forest villages and 49 *taungyas* in total in the State. The inhabitant of the forest villages consist of tribes, scheduled castes and other unspecified communities according to census as well as Forest Department records. According to 2001 census, the total population in these forest villages is 5,36,157. Among them 38 per cent are Scheduled Tribes, 8.00 per cent are Scheduled Castes and 54 per cent are other communities. If we take 1994 Forest Department record as base line the increase of population till 2001 among these categories ST 94 per cent, SC 114 per cent and others 217 per cent (Sonowal, 2007).

The settlers in forest villages had to enter into an agreement with the Secretary of State for India in Council (or the party of the first part). Some of the crucial terms of the agreement were as follows :

(i) The settler (or the party of the second part) shall hold the land specified as service *Jagir* only so long as he performs the duties and observes the prescribed conditions. The land shall be held rent free.

(ii) The land shall be held as service *Jagir* and shall not be alienable and shall be liable to resumption.

(iii) The Forest Department has the first claim to the labour of the settler on payment.

(iv) The settler will not accept any employment which is likely to interfere with the prior claim of Forest Department.

(v) The settler shall be liable to summary ejectment without compensation by the order of DFO for any breach of terms and conditions of this agreement.

In Assam over and above these points, the following rules were also added :

(vi) An allotment up to 12 *Bighas* of land may be given to such resident for homestead or *bari* (garden), but no *rupit* (wet cultivation) land will be allowed to him. No concession shall be allowed in respect of and revenue for the land occupied, but the DFO shall consult the DC in each case as to what would be an appropriate rate of charge, bearing in mind not only the character of the land but the use to which it is put.

The political history of the State shows that in several tribal dominated areas the forest covers were opened for immigrants who were basically non-tribals, coming mainly from present day Bangladesh, by the then administrative authorities. The imposition of Reserved Forest Act curtailed the power and authority of the tribal people on their traditional domains. Thus in Assam, heterogeneous population groups are found in the forest villages.

The Issue of Conversion

In pursuance of the recommendation of the Ministry of Agriculture in 1984, giving the status of revenue villages to the forest villages and ownership rights over land to the dwellers in forest villages, the government decided to convert forest villages into revenue villages so that the normal development programmes could be extended to the concerned tribals. However, in spite of the recommendation made by the Working Group on the Development of Scheduled Tribes during seventh plan (1985-90), and the concern expressed in the National Forestry Policy (1988), the process of conversion had been at a snail's pace.

Development of Forest Village

GOI release on June 7, 2010 indicates that even after initiatives taken for conversion of Forest Villages, there are still 2,474 forest villages/ habitations in the country, spread over 12 States. The Ministry of Tribal Affairs allotted development grants as 'Central Assistance' towards the development of forest villages in Assam including other 11 States in the country. Between the year 2005-06 and 2008-09 the amount of Central Assistance released was Rs 10572.05 Lakhs for 498 forest villages (including *Taungiya*). The Tribal Development/ Welfare Department of the State Government is to monitor the progress and the timely implementation of projects for the development of forest villages, carried out by Forest Development Agencies (FDAs). The Ministry of Environment and Forests monitors the progress on receipt of the State Government and the concerned Principal Chief Conservator of Forests. Utilisation of funds is monitored through submission of the utilisation certificates.

Joint Forest Management and Forest Village Development

Joint Forest Management (JFM) is a concept of developing partnership between fringe forest user groups and the Forest Department (FD) on the basis of mutual trust and jointly defined roles and responsibilities with regard to forest protection and development. Bhagat (1999) termed it a concept, which is based on the principle of rights of local communities in forests. Raju (1999) saw it as a mechanism to manage the forest that is owned by the State but appropriated by local communities. Datta (1999) identified it as an approach involving the evolution of a very complex property rights regime to generate a sustainable interface between the Forest Department (FD) and the local community. According to Saxena (1999), it is a possible way through which the interests of people and of long term sustainability are harmonised in a mutually supporting manner.

The crucial discourse on JFM, therefore, has to be critical in nature and had to look into its diverse components. Thus, JFM needs to be seen in the context of the many policy arenas and the maze of institutions, which affect the forests. The actual and potential role of forest goods and services in people's livelihood is directly related to what's happening with forest reserves, protected areas, 'non-timber forest product' (NTFP) use, farm forestry, the forest-product industry and the extent to which policy and institutions can influence all of these.

Ministry of Tribal Affairs, government of India has been implementing the programme of forest village development in Assam through FDAs by constituting Joint Forest Management Committee (JFMC) in 373 forest villages. The activities under the programme include community welfare works and income generation activities for the forest dwellers. The activities of these JFMCs are in the line of National Afforestation Programme (NAP) as they are also run by the forest department of the State under selected FDAs. It was found that there are list of 352 number of forest villages who have Joint Forest Management Committee formed under the auspices of forest department and Ministry of Tribal Affairs (MoTA). A detailed study was conducted in some forest villages to understand the problems, prospects and emerging issues of implantation of JFM programme. Some selected issues have been placed here for the readers.

Roles of Incentives in JFM

Since forest resources became a State property and the authority of forest dependent communities over such resources were undone or curtailed, such communities had lost interests in regeneration and protection of resources to a great extent. Obviously, to reallocate their concern towards regeneration and management such people need some sort of incentives. These may be material, socio-cultural or emotional aspects people deal with. Incentives can be understood by breaking the problems down, and considering three kinds of incentives that people typically face. Broadly, these incentives may be described and categorised in the following ways :

Table 6.1: Characteristics of Incentives in JFM

Incentives related to characteristics of the resource base	Incentives related to the characteristics of the community	Characteristics of rules in place
Resource may be naturally grown and value of resources to a particular community may be varied	To keep away unauthorised harvesters, community may have intended or unintended shared religious beliefs	There may be some rules to punish or disincentify violators
Resources like forest may be planted or invested individually or commonly	There may be shared moral obligation not to harm or destroy produces	The nature and scope of implementation of such rules can emerge as incentive
Resources may be accessed or harvested easily by unauthorised entity	There may be belief in spirit, forest deities, curse for miscreants	The cost factor of implementing rules may influence incentives
Resources may be fully protected		Sometimes, rules may not be implemented at all
Cost of protection may be very high or low		There may be incentives to obey the rules

Some of the ideas have been taken from "Grafting institutional arrangements for community forestry". FAO, Forest Department (Corporate Document Repository).

Incentives Related to Resource Base

A detailed study in the field has revealed dependency on forest resources among the selected villagers vary considerably. Tribal dominated villages having larger attached areas are found more fundamental necessity relevant to livelihood. Basically, these people have been extracting fuel and fodder from forest for own use and to some extent some NTFP for cash income. Thus any forest regeneration scheme promising better return in terms of immediate utilisation works as an incentive and attracts people towards forestry work. Thus absence of dependency on forest resources results in lukewarm response to forestry work, where people with higher dependency on forest resources are seen more involved in forestry work under JFM schemes.

It is interesting to note that forest dependency as an incentive cannot alone sustain people's involvement. The nature of forestry schemes is directly related to people's long-terms and short-term needs. It has been revealed that such schemes are planned at administrative level and imposed on village people undermining immediate needs. People in villages have hardly shown interest in long-term benefits of investment. Thus, in the absence of immediate output, people use to treat schemes mostly as an additional opportunity of wage-earning nearby villages. Thus people's moral and emotional attachment to such schemes was greatly missing. Such emerging perceptions have good deal of impact on management and protection of plantation sites. As these activities are imposed from outside, they remain alien to the traditional custom of communities. Therefore, socio-cultural and moral obligation hardly includes protect against unauthorised entities. The only option remains is the administrative rules framed by forest department. But when the offenses are held at community basis or amounts to rivalry among adjacent villages and communities, it is very difficult to implement such rules to punish the guilty. Constant vigil to plantation sites is the only option which again is a costly business in terms of money and physical labour. Being a common pool, people do not take the issue as prime concern at individual level amounting to negligence and resources loss. It has been revealed that a massive loss of investment in post plantation period occurred in most of the JFMCs.

It is very important to identify the characteristics of resources and the resource management incentives. Trees and bushes, whether in a forest, on fields, or in gardens are resources. These resources work as a 'Production Plant' or factories. They can generate various goods and services. Goods like fuel wood, construction materials, food for humans and animals; and services such as providing shade, protection against soil erosion, enhancing water conservation, producing green manure, cleaning air, habitat for wild life etc.

There may be two primary characteristics of output from resources in creating incentives for how resources are managed:

Feasibility of exclusion: It implies how easy or difficult to keep others away from the access to one's valued resources. This easy or difficulty may imply in terms of keeping vigil, cost of vigil in terms of cost and physical prevention etc.

Nature of consumption: It implies whether the consumption of the output is subtractive or joint. Consumption is subtractive when one person consumes a good for a particular purpose, with the result that another person cannot use the same good. Person A has subtracted all or part of the good from the total available and this prevents Person B from using that same good. The consumption of many forest goods is subtractive. The consumption of leaves and fruit is also subtractive. If one animal consumes the leaves of a certain bush, no other animal or person will be able to eat them.

The nature of consumption, like the feasibility of exclusion, creates incentives and disincentives that influence the way people act toward resources. In general, individuals are likely to feel a stronger incentive to protect resources from which they gain subtractive benefits. When the benefits are joint, and often less tangible, people may feel less of a personal stake in the resource, thinking that "someone else will take care of the problem." Since a larger community benefits from a resource that has joint benefits, protection of that resource may require organisation at the community level. It is often harder to organise the maintenance of such windbreak than to persuade people to water privately owned trees from which they will enjoy subtractive benefits.

Table 6.2: Relation between feasibility of exclusion and nature of consumption

		Nature of Consumption	
		Subtractive	**Joint**
	EASY	Cut and stored fuel wood and building poles, forest product medicines, trees in fenced gardens.	Nature parks where entrance fee is charged for hiking, camping, tourism and wildlife viewing.

		Common Pool Goods and Services	Public Goods and Services
FEASIBILITY OF EXCLUSION	DIFFICULT	Browse on trees/bushes and fruits fallen from trees in unfenced fields and woods, wildlife, fish in streams and lakes.	Air quality, environmental duality, shade, protection of biological diversity, protection that trees provide against wind,: water erosion.

(Adapted from Ostrom and Ostrom, 1977).

Incentives Related to Community Characteristics

The community characteristics are found to be divergent in terms of utilisation of forest resources. It was found that the socio-cultural aspects of tribal people are very much related to forest, whereas the non-tribal communities have hardly shown any such attachment. The tribal communities have certain taboos in venturing through forest at different period of the year. They also have taboo in extracting certain forest resources at certain point of time. They maintain some sacred grooves in forest from where they are not supposed to collect benefits. Most of their deities live in the forest and on the tree tops. Thus their involvement in forest activities is mainly subsistence in nature and lots of socio-cultural rules are imposed to regulate their interaction with forest and forest resources. Contrary to such aspects, the non-tribal population usually use forest beyond their subsistence base need, mainly for commercial purpose or for making benefit.

Besides, ethnic composition in the villages may influence the involvement in forestry activities concerning diverse interests of people in forest resources. Moreover, socio-economic status of the population, may be across ethnic composition may create yet another diversity in interest. In such situation, the rules made, moral codes of conduct laid down by communities may differ and come into conflict with each other making the running of JFM programme difficult. While congenial condition among the communities creates positive incentives, a problematic condition among the communities may attract negative incentive for JFM programme.

Rules and Resource Management Incentives

Once a community decides to engage in a JFM (or any collective activity), creation of rules or enforcement of rules is inevitable for the governance of trees and forest resources. These rules help keep management of forest resources so created in order and create incentives for people engage–by protecting valued resources from unauthorised persons. Rules may be formal and informal. Formal rules comprise the codified laws and regulations issued by a legislative process or formal decree. Non-formal rules, on the other hand, are generally unwritten often deriving from custom or practices. They are more likely to exist at village or community level. Rules become meaningful only on the basis of their being working and non-working. Rules are considered to be either working or non-working depending on whether they actually affect what people do.

In this particular case, the Forest department is the primary institution framing and implementing entire schemes. The formation of JFMC is also at the behest of forest department. Thus, at village or community level, the entire process was neither felt nor experienced need to generate forest resources by involving in JFM activities. This basic socio-cultural components and moral issues were hardly attached to these institutions. In recent FDA activities, such issues have been tried to resolve by an intensive collaboration between forest department and local communities. Immediate incentive and compensation in the form of EPA and short term outputs like fodder, compost, has been tried to generate and cater community participation in forest management and regeneration.

Besides, State level data input, a total of 15 forest villages and five revenue villages were selected for in-depth study. The following tables have been prepared on the basis of some selective responses from a part of the forest villages studied. These tables indicate incentives and people's involvement in JFM activities. In all these tables the positive incentives have been indicated by a "+" sign and the negative incentives are indicated by a "–" sign. By positive, here it means the incentives that help increase people's involvement in forestry works, and contrarily, negative means factors that lead to lack of interest in participating in such activities. Finally, positive trends have been calculated to show the strength of these incentives in JFM programme. It is revealed that higher positive scores indicate better expected results in JFM activities.

Table 6.3 enumerates the incentive related to the characteristics of the resource base of the selected villages. The criteria have been prepared on the basis of the discussion made elsewhere in this writing. A total of seven characters have been identified to assess the nature of incentives attached to resource base of the forest villages. As mentioned above, the characters have been identified as either positive or negative keeping an eye on the influence in full participation of JFM activities. The table indicates only 33 per cent positive indication in terms of incentive in this domain giving a grim picture of the effectiveness of JFM activities in forest villages in Assam.

Table 6.3: Incentive related to the characteristics of the resource base

Resour ce Characters	*Villages*										*Total*			*Positive trends %*
	Torani	*Ritumi holi*	*Burh idihi ng*	*Bisgh oriya*	*Saru sajai*	*Lokhar a*	*Gorb hanga*	*Topato li*	*Jaip ur*	*Boh otp ur*	+	-		
Forest Resources in JFM are naturally grown (Y es +, No-)	-	-	-	-	-	-	-	-	-	-	0	10	0.0	
Value of forest Resources to dif ferent people: (Same +, Dif ferent -)	-	+	+	+	-	+	+	+	-	+	7	3	70.0	
Resources may be accessed or harvested by unauthorized entity: (dif ficult +, Easily -)	-	+	+	-	-	+	+	+	-	+	6	4	60.0	
Resources are Subtractive: (Yes -, No +)	-	-	-	-	-	-	-	-	-	-	0	10	0.0	
Resources may be well protected: (Yes +, No -)	+	-	-	-	+	+	-	+	-	+	5	5	50.0	
Invested Resources need protection: (Yes -, No +)	-	-	+	-	-	-	+	-	-	-	2	8	20.0	
Cost of Protection very high: (Yes -, N0 +)	-	-	-	-	-	+	-	+	-	+	3	7	30.0	
Total +/-	1/6	2/5	3/4	1/6	1/6	4/3	4/3	4/3	0/7	4/3	23 (33%)	47 (67%)	33.0	

In the same way Table 6.4 indicates rather a better positive incentives in terms of community characters that help people meaningful involvement.

Table 6.4: Incentives related to the characteristics of the community

Characteristics of the Community	*Villages*										*Total*		*Positive trends %*
	Torani	*Ritumi holi*	*Burh idihi ng*	*Bisgho riya*	*Saru sajai*	*Lokhar a*	*Gorb hang a*	*Topato li*	*Jaipur*	*Boh otp ur*	+	-	
Have religious beliefs that debar : Plucking of immature fruits (Y es +, No -)	-	-	-	+	+	-	+	+	+	+	6	4	60
Have religious beliefs that debar : Collection of fodder at individual will (Yes +, No -)	-	-	-	-	+	+	+	+	+	-	5	5	50
Have Social sanction against entering community resource base before collective ceremonial observances (Yes +, No -)	-	-	-	-	-	+	+	+	+	+	5	5	50
Have Moral Obligation against destroying or harvesting community resources (Y es +, No -)	+	+	-	-	-	+	+	+	+	+	7	3	70
People fear of bad influence of supernatural beings in case of unauthorised harvesting of resources (Yes +, No =)	-	-	-	-	-	-	+	+	+	+	4	6	40
Total (+/-)	**1/4**	**1/4**	**0/5**	**1/4**	**2/3**	**3/2**	**5/0**	**5/0**	**5/0**	**4/1**	**27 (54%)**	**23 (45%)**	**54**

Table 6.5 : Characteristics of Rules in place

Characteristics of the Community	Villages										Total		Positive trends %
	Toranii	Ritumiholi	Burhidihing	Bisghoriya	Sarusajai	Lokhara	Gorbhanga	Topatoli	Jaipur	Bohotpur	+	-	
Institutional Rules are explained in case of JFM activities: (Yes +, No -)	+	+	+	+	-	+	+	+	+	-	8	2	80
Disadvantaged groups find places in the defined functional Rules: (yes +, No -)	-	-	-	+	+	+	+	+	-	+	6	4	60
Rules gives special advantages to the disadvantaged groups (Yes +, No -)	-	-	+	+	+	-	-	-	-	+	4	6	40
Rules are followed in Selecting plant varieties (Yes +, No -)	-	-	-	-	-	+	-	+	-	+	3	7	30
Rules are followed in convening meetings (Yes +, No -)	-	-	+	-	-	-	-	-	+	-	2	8	20
Rules are followed in fund allocation issues (Yes +, No -)	-	-	-	-	-	-	-	-	+	-	1	9	10
Rules are followed in allotting jobs and benefits (Yes +, No -)	-	-	-	-	-	-	-	-	-	-	0	10	0
Rules are functional in terms of breach of rules (yes +, No-)	-	-	-	-	+	-	-	-	+	+	3	7	30
Decision taken in presence of majority members (Yes +, No -)	-	-	-	-	-	-	-	-	-	+	1	9	10
Accounts and other financial matters are kept transparent: (Yes +, No -)	-	-	-	-	-	-	+	-	-	-	1	9	10
Total (+/-)	1/9	1/9	3/7	3/7	3/7	3/7	3/7	3/7	4/6	5/5	29	71	29

Table 6.5: shows a rather hopeless picture regarding positive incentives in following the administrative rules related to JFM in forest villages

Table 6.6 : Incentive profile of villages in JFM.

Villages	*Resour ces Characters*		*Community Characters*		*Rules Characters*		*Total*		*Positive Trend %*
	(+)	(-)	(+)	(-)	(+)	(-)	(+)	(-)	
Torani	1	6	1	4	1	9	3	19	14
Ritumiholi	2	5	1	4	1	9	4	18	19
Bisghoriya	1	6	1	4	3	7	5	17	24
Burhidihing	3	4	0	5	3	7	6	16	29
Sarusajai	1	6	2	3	3	7	6	16	29
Jaipur	0	7	5	0	4	6	9	13	43
Lokhara	4	3	3	2	3	7	10	12	48
Gorbhanga	4	3	5	0	3	7	12	10	57
Topatoli	4	3	5	0	3	7	12	10	57
Bohotpur	4	3	4	1	5	5	13	9	62
Total	**24**	**46**	**27**	**23**	**29**	**71**	**80 (38%)**	**140 (62%)**	

Table 6.6 shows the summary of incentive profiles of the forest villages studied. It shows that Bohotpur village, an all tribal inhabited village possesses 62 per cent positive characters closely followed by Topatoli and Garbhanga forest villages. Torani has the least positive trends followed by Ritumiholi forest village. In these villages tribal people are not a majority. But though Bisghoriya is an all tribal inhabited village, due to its location far away from forest resources it indicates mostly negative incentives. The overall positive trend among these selected forest villages is only 38.00 per cent indicating a rather discouraging picture of JFM programme which has been implemented for the development of the forest villagers.

Contrary to previous forest management policies, JFM came up as ray of hope for State as well as for forest fringe communities. There has been a good deal of instances of successful JFM programmes where the interest of State and the communities were served to a great extent. Many other cases show relatively and sometimes entirely unsuccessful results. Researchers have primarily put the blame on the policy planners for such failure. It has been observed that the objective of Forest Department rests on two principles – fulfilled the set target to bring under plantation map and increase cover. In doing so, the department very often undermined the necessity of identifying genuine requirement like the need of selected communities to re-generate forest and/or community's requirement or interest in forestry work. To fulfill the target, it is found the department imposes the programme on certain village communities to initiate JFM. This amounts to an involvement of certain section of selected community with definite interest – mostly the interest of meeting immediate need for wage earning and for some to appropriate opportunities coming to doorsteps. In this entire process, there was hardly any preliminary study on nature and extent of people's dependency on forest, nature and extent of utilisation of forest resources and probable positive impact of activities on people concern, and people's interest, genuinely, to get benefit from forest products in changing socio-economic situation.

This certainly attracts the issue of participation of forest fringe communities in JFM activities. The discussion made so far clearly indicates the nature and extent of participation of people in JFM depends on various factors like incentives-based on resources, community characters, and rules in place along with the requirement and opportunity cost of participation of people involving in JFM. The study tried to cover as much as possible, the related factors influencing people's meaningful participation in JFM activities. The study reveals people's culture in terms of relation with forest makes some determining impact on forestry work participation and forest management. For example, tribal communities, who are traditionally attached to forest in the socio-cultural and socio-economic terms, are seen to be more inclined towards forest management. But, it is also a fact that the resourcefulness or the quality of forest also influence as to what way people get attached traditionally to forest. Changing requirement of people in contemporary period has s great deal of influence on people's behaviour towards forest management and forest protection. The forest no longer remained the primary source of livelihood. They have to look for non-forest based and non-farm activities to earn a living. Forest produces like NTFP in most cases does not come at par with such occupations. Thus importance of forest in terms of livelihood support has decreased to a great extent among the people. For want of money, forest resources have been extracted in an unsustainable way. Above all, forest regeneration and forest protection did not emerge as a priority or obligation for the part of communities because forests are owned by state and there is no guarantee that investment (of any type) made by people will pay them back as there is no such arrangement in place to assure. Thus alienation between forest and forest fringe communities developed over a period of time. In such a situation, introduction of JFM has been visualised by most of the communities as another opportunity to easy and immediate earning by rendering physical labour. For most of the people interviewed, pay back from re-generated and planted forest is a distant dream. The study also highlights many other facts like way of decision making, fund allocation and fund management, nature of distribution of benefits like wage labour and influential entities in the process JFM programme. The drawbacks and loopholes in the entire process have to be addressed for meaningful result from JFM.

Implementation of Forest Rights Act

Special provision has been kept for the welfare of the forest villages under the newly initiated Forest Rights Act (2006) in India.

It has been expected that under this Act, the forest villagers will get land rights and rights over forest they are attached to. The study reveals that Forest Rights Committees and *Gram Sabhas* have been constituted in those villages (except in Bodoland Territorial Council Areas) and the forest department and department of tribal welfare have briefed the people about the procedures of placing claims for rights on land in forest villages. It was seen that no clear instruction was given to the people as how to prepare the tentative maps of land they claim. It was further ambiguous what part of non-cultivated land under forest department can be claimed by the forest villagers for common rights or community rights. Because, in all the studied forest villages no such forest land was available. Lands are divided as cultivable land and reserved forest. Due to such ambiguity preparing claims was very slow and faulty. The Forest Rights Committees were asked to make the list of people of every existing family in forest village on generation basis so that a third generation heir could be traced. The FRA has been translated into local language (Assamese) and was given to respective *Gram Sabhas* and FRCs.

There has been clear denial from the part of forest official sitting at the top position in the State regarding this issue. The Chief Conservator of Forest (Territorial) in Guwahati commented that conversion of forest villages into revenue villages attracts a huge amount of money to be spent according to the Forest Conservation Act 1980. He informed that a land area equal to that occupied by forest villagers (to be converted to revenue village) had to be acquired for aforestation to compensate the loss of forest land in the process of conversion. This was quite impossible in terms of feasibility relating to money, manpower and administrative procedures. The forest officers at Divisional Forest Offices of the State simply pushed the ball to the court of tribal welfare department. They are of the opinion that according to the FRA the land has been allotted to the people permanently and the development of people are now the concerns of the said department. In this regard the report of MoEF/MoTA Committee on FRA 2010 can be cited here. During the interaction with department and WPTA officials, it came to the notice that their attitude towards approach to FRA and its implementation is highly bureaucratic and shows lack of serious commitment. The sturdy confrontation on the part of the department in opposition to the Act was well observable. Most of the officials see the rural forest dwelling population as non-dependent of forest historically. It was also noticed that they primarily view this Act as meant for forest villagers only.

Other Development Aspects

A detailed analysis of socio-economic and political administrative aspects reveals that in terms of infrastructure facilities including transport and communication, school, water supply and electric supply, health and sanitation, the forest villages have been lagging behind the revenue villages. In terms of economic pursuits, the revenue villages are comparatively in better position. It was seen that in revenue villages, people were engaged in more diversified income generation activities, ultimately resulting in more income opportunities. Utilisation of forest resources for income generation was present in some villages. This depends on the proximity of villages to the forest and its resourcefulness they are close by.

In some forest villages, the rate and level of literacy was found to be very low. Higher education was quite low in forest villages, especially among females. Remoteness to school is one of the major factors leading to such situation. Very few forest villagers were found to be engaged in government or other jobs. But overall literacy status of revenue villages (except one) was not very promising. The strategic position of forest village like proximity to road and communication facilities, market place has positive bearing on the better condition of the forest villages. One more fact is that the educated and well off people in forest villages tend to shift to nearby urban locality for better life style and comfort. Once they get a job or settle in business, they tend to migrate to urban places leaving behind the deteriorated families in the village.

There is hardly any trace of development activities initiated by the department or the Tribal Welfare department in these studied villages. Grants for one-room huts under *Indira Awas Yojna* have reached these forest villages as lot of families have received such grants. Compared to revenue villages very little or no other development grants have been received by the forest villages. In some villages, tube-wells were distributed by department for drinking water. As a traditional rule, the department tends to install ring wells in forest villages. There are evidences of such half-made effort, where rings are still lying in the villages.

In terms of basic livelihood, life style and amenities there are not much difference between forest village and revenue villages, if they are situated close by. A brief investigation leads to the fact that most of the forest villages are not isolated from the vicinity of revenue villages. Usually, the forest villages are established aside the reserved forest for better connectivity and are close by already existed revenue villages. Being the tribal and rural population usually these people from revenue villages as well as forest villages follow same sort of economic pursuits, tread through same environment, economic and socio-political. Thus, any sharp distinction has not been noticed between two categories of the villages. Most importantly, now there is no restriction for inflow of development initiatives from Panchayats, Development blocks and other development agencies to the forest village. But, the problem lies with the representation of forest villages in such agencies. Forest villages hardly have any recognised body to represent in Panchayat and other development bodies to claim for development initiatives. It is learnt that the officials of these development authorities still have the sense of negligence, otherness towards forest villagers as there is another authority, the forest department, as the mentor of the forest villages.

Formation of JFMC in forest villages were the result of initiatives taken up by the forest department for want of implementation of development programmes for which grants were allotted by the Ministry of Tribal Affairs, Government of India. It was found that villagers were benefited in terms of common utilities through the entry point activities under which village roads were constructed; community halls, schools and other important entities were erected in the village. But, it was found that the plantation work had not shown promising benefits to the villages in terms of income generation in future. Most of the plantation sites are either partially destroyed or not coming up to the expectation. The very idea of community participation, as per the NAP objective, has failed to a great extent. This is because; the study shows the people join the scheme as wage labourer. They did not have decision-making power. They did not have any idea about fund allocation, benefits incurred, plan and future of work.

Fund allocation, operation and distribution are entirely a matter of forest department. In most of the cases, the JFMC president is reduced to a signing entity in the cheque book to draw the money by the member-secretary of the JFMC, who happens to be the Forester of the concerned forest beat office. In most of the cases, such programmes became a scheme for providing wages for villagers and wastage of precious money meant for development of forest villagers, especially the tribal population in forest villages.

Conclusion

The problems of forest villages, especially the villages inhabited by tribal peoples, remained unnoticed to the policy planners as well as to researchers and social scientists of the region. Issues like compulsory physical labour, draconian terms and conditions for labour exploitation, lack of land ownership, and lack of infrastructure and development initiatives compelled the forest villagers to lag behind their non-forest villager counterparts to a great extent. The forest department of the State did not pay due attention for the development of the people. Despite the recent initiatives towards development of forest villages, it has been evident that such activities are not properly planned and efficiently implemented and largely undermines the needs of the people for whom these are made. It can be hoped that with academic input and empirical data base anthropologist will be able to help out these people linking the facts with plans and programmes.

References

Hembram, P. C. 1988, *Sari-Sarna*. New Delhi: Mittal Publications.

Ostrom, V. and E. Ostrom, 1977, 'Public goods and public choices'. In E.S. Savas (Ed): *Alternatives for Delivering Public Services: Towards Improved Performance*, pp. 7-49. Boulder, Westview Press.

Prasad R.R. and M.P. Jahagirdar. 1993, *Tribal Situation in Forest Villages: Changing Subsistence Strategies and Adaptation.* New Delhi: Discovery Publishing House.

Raju, G. 1999, *Joint Forest Management: Design of People's Institutions for Empowerment,* Vol. 123 of Working paper, Institute of Rural Management, Anand, India.

Roy Burman, B. K. 1988, 'Development of forestry in harmony with the interest of the tribals', *Background Paper for Indian Forest Service Training Programme at TISS*, Bombay, Nov. pp. 21-26.

Saxena, N. C. 1999, *Forest Policy in India, Policy and Joint Forest Management* Series-1, World Wide Fund for Nature-India.

Sinha, S.P. 1987, 'Forest village in Bihar: An analysis of their present status', p. 297. In S.P.Sinha (Ed.): *Tribals and Forests*. Government of Bihar, Welfare Department, BTWRI, Ranchi.

Sonowal, C.J. 1997, 'Forest villages in Assam: Continued Ghettoisation'. *Economic and Political Weekly*. Vol. 32, No 39, September 27 - October 3.

Sonowal, C.J. 2007. 'Demographic transition of tribal people in forest villages of Assam'. *Study of Tribes and Tribals*, 5, 1: 47 - 58.

Sonowal, C.J., *Problems of Youth in Forest Villages of Assam: A Study in Dibrugarh District*. (Unpublished Project Report, TISS, Mumbai).

7

The Great Leap of Zeme Nagas : A Study in the Evolution of Religions

– *Michael R. Kolb*

Introduction

The final chapter, 'Towards a Theoretical Proposition,' of Babul Roy's *Zeme Naga : From Polytheism to Monotheism* (2002), seeks to provide insight into the unusual cultural movement of the Zeme people. This 'great leap' began from the basis of a religious culture that embraced a multitude of spirits that the Zemes held directly responsible for many things that happen in human life. A healer and prophet, Jadonang, a member of the Kabui tribe, closely related to Zemes, founded what would become the Heraka movement. Jadonang's disciple Rani Gaidinliu effected the later development and consolidation of the movement, with present-day outlines, solidifying by 1970 (Roy, 2013). Through this movement, a large number of non-Christian Zemes became monotheists, or at minimum, the monolators.

Roy asserts that this change consisted of several facets. Primary among them was the gradual establishment of relatively minor god, Tingkao-Raa-Gong, as a chief deity among seven traditional gods and the abandonment of interest in other, evil spirits which until that time had been the center of propitiatory sacrifice (Roy, 2011: 278). Additionally, traditional celebrations were discarded or shortened. This was made more complicated by the onset of Christian missionary efforts among the Zemes at roughly the same time. With the first Zeme Christian convert confessing as late as 1910, Christian growth in the area was slowed because of active opposition by Gaidinliu's Heraka movement (Longkumer, 2011: 195). The Heraka movement also moved more strongly toward monotheism with the chief deity now known as Tangwang.

The result is a variety of beliefs among Zemes in the Dima Hasao District. A very small number hold to old ways of close attention to propitiation of lesser, often malicious spirits—a tradition known as *Perese* (the old faith) or *Paupaise* (the great-grandfather's faith). With that small exception, the Zeme people are divided between Christians and Herakas, with roughly 40.00 per cent, or 8,000 Zemes following Heraka. Moreover, political activity by Gaidinliu and the strength of the Heraka faith has helped unite the Zemes with two other Naga tribes, the Liangmai and Rongmei/Kabui to form the Zeliangrong people, though this unification movement started apparently from other sources (Roy, 2002).

While admitting to some influence of Hindu and Christian thought Jadonang and Gaidinliu, Roy presents this movement towards monotheism as unique case of an "indigenous religion transformation" (pp. 282) and, as such a unique case offering privileged insights into the process. Despite this, he remains vague about the actual mechanism that spurs and enacts this type of religious revolution. While accepting that elements of religions are products of "psycho-social stimuli and of different historical contexts", Roy seems to reject the notion that their development can be grouped in any evolutionary pattern. He proposes that polytheism contains elements of monotheism that "may emerge" and, further, that this emergence demands "the intervention of an individual (i.e., a prophet) or an organised body for its establishment" (pp. 282). Indeed, Roy elsewhere indicates that the question of how "the present-day Heraka religion and religious reform movement emerge from traditional Naga animism...[has] not yet been properly answered...(Roy, 2013).

In the end, then, Roy provides only a scant outline of an explanation for the emergence of monotheism among the Zemes, a phenomenon that invites further inquiry. More intriguingly, the inquiry must address a failure of monotheism emergence. This seemingly extreme demand lies in the presence of the neighbouring Dimasa people, among whom monotheism did not in any way emerge.

The Dimasas, in fact, share the same physical environment as the Zemes, today's Dima Hasao District of Assam in North-East India; due to specific cultural differences, Zemes settle on hilltops, while Dimasas inhabit river valleys. Economies of societies in the early part of the 20th century were identical, based on subsistence swidden (slash-and-burn, *jhumming*) agriculture. The societies seem to have been somewhat parallel religiously as well, with both embracing religious culture often described as "animistic," honouring a mixture of a few deities and innumerable spirits of often malevolent intent. Roy even argues the two societies share gods (Roy, 2011: 162) Both have pantheons of gods (the Zemes eight, the Dimasas seven), two of whom appear identical and borrowed: *Sibrai* and *Banglaraja* of the Dimasa; *Suprai* and *Banglawang* of the Zemes, this latter *Banglaraja / Banglawang* deity having similar priority in the myths of cultures, but in both cases has passed from important worship and sacrifices. The societies share a strong exogamous clan-based social organisation, though the Dimasa have the unusual aspect of paternal and maternal clan lineages. One might exaggerate that Dimasas might be considered Zemes of the valley, the Zemes, Dimasas on the hilltop; so extreme a mash-up is, of course, inaccurate and unhelpful, but the similarities are more than merely superficial. Yet among the Zemes, monotheism developed; among the Dimasas, as will be seen, monotheism, at least in its Christian form, was actively resisted and continues to be. How to account this in terms of social theory?

Attempting to give the answer to such question is presumptuous in the extreme. Rather, the following possible social influences will be explored: (1) millennial movements near and far; (2) theories of the evolution of societies and the parallel evolution of religion; (3) intellectualist approaches to the religious cultures of small pre-literate societies; (4) specific factors within Zeme and Dimasa societies that promoted or retarded a jump to monotheism.

Millennial Prophets

Roy (2011: 231) denies "any connection whatsoever" between the Jadonang and an earlier Dimasa prophetic figure, Sambhudan Phonglo. In terms of direct influence, this is almost certainly the case. Despite this disjunction, both prophets arose in a milieu that provided fertile soil for such phenomena, the encounter with colonial powers. Soppitt provides a jaundiced summary of Phonglo's origin :

> Sombadan…set himself up as a curer of ills, and invited people to visit him, offering them for a consideration to free them of ailments. His fame soon spread, and people travelled long distances, in some cases from remote villages in the plains, to

> see him, bringing buffaloes, goats, and fowls. At the end of a few months, however, finding that he could not work the miracles that he professed to, his patients began to fall off. Seeing that his reputation was on the wane, Sombadan now gave out that that he was inspired by the gods, and in the course of short time succeeded in collecting a band of fanatics, all professing to be equally inspired (Soppitt, 1885: 13).

> Sambhudan claimed to have rediscovered ancient writing, and bestow on his followers immunity from bullets (Roy, 2011: 230), and lead short-lived rebellion in 1882 before being killed in an encounter with British forces (Soppitt, 1885).

Jadonang's career was quite short, starting as a traditional healer among Kabui people. Roy, apparently quoting from the report of British political agent, provides Jadonang's testimony. He received messages in dreams from the "Bhuwan god" to build a temple so "that there would be prosperity and good health for everyone if I did so, although it is not our custom to build temples" (Roy, 2011: 232). The image of The God was "Bisnu," apparently an alternative name for the Hindu Vishnu, an unknown consort of that god, and a bull of Shiva, having heard of these from a foreigner, a non-Kabui *fakir*. Jadonang strongly denied any agitation towards war with the hated Kukis, though in his dream he saw people who had been killed in previous Naga-Kuki war.

For comparison, it is instructive to look at the origins of the Ghost Dance that swept the western plains of United States at roughly the same time, culminating in the Wounded Knee Massacre 1890. The original prophecy was made by the Paiute prophet Tavibo, who went to the sacred mountain of the Paiutes to commune with God in 1869 :

> He returned with a prophesy and a dance. The world was going to be destroyed, then and then renewed. The dead would return, game would be abundant; the Indians would live in the old way once more. Non-believers would be damned. One report on his doctrines indicated that the white race would be destroyed; another said the Indians would become white, an idea possibly derived from Mormon teachings about the Lamanites (McCann, 1966: 26).

This effort was a complete failure, and was abandoned even by the Paiutes by 1875. The prophecy and dance was revived by

Tavibo's son, Wovoka. Because of his father's legacy, Wovoka was a man of power among the Paiutes.

During an Eclipse

Wovoka fell into a coma. He dreamed he was speaking to God in heaven... Yet, it was an Indian heaven where Indians lived an infinitely better version of the old life. God told Wovoka that if the people followed his commandments, they would join their ancestors in this Indian Utopia... while a tide of new earth covered across the old and pushed the whites back across the eastern sea. On the new land, the Indians would find their ancestors resurrected from the dead (pp. 32).

Rather than belabor the obvious common features of the three prophets, it is best to turn attention to the ground breaking work of Joel W. Martin on Native American messianic movements (Martin, 1991). Martin alleges that almost all of the writing on these movements denies the possibility that Native Americans could creatively encounter historical events. The accepted tragic narrative of doomed and fading tribal ways continues to devalue Native Americans, and a fresh and more accurate look establishes native peoples as innovative and resilient. "In contrast to deprivation theory, this approach affirms the full humanity of Native Americans by assuming that they were actors in history rather than merely victims" (pp. 684).

Native American encounters with settlers (and often their slaves) constituted a "new world" for the tribal people as well, a world to which they proved quite adept at adapting. This often consisted of both reaching back into parts of tribal culture that had fallen into disuse and adopting ideas and ideals from the new culture they encountered. Recalling the work of Victor Turner, Martin proposes millennial movements—wherever they might occur—to be best imaged as communal rites of passage:

> If the traditional rite of passage is connected to crises in the human life-cycle, the millenarian movement is connected to phases of history that impose great changes upon people. Both rites of passage and millenarian movements enable the participants to reduce internal differences and increase solidarity (communitas).

Such "renewals" or "passages" often involve dramatic separation from the old life, as when during puberty rituals, young man's forsake childhood ways. Longkumer (2011) notes that many of Heraka's early followers "preached against working in the fields because grains would fall from the sky or said that the Zeme need not attend school, as knowledge could be acquired by using a book as a pillow" (pp. 196). Jadonang's actions, singular even when unencumbered by the blackening of his critics, seem directed towards these ends, specifically, a renewal of his people's culture to creatively encounter the "new world" of colonial Manipur.

Jadonang's reforms to a great extent both rid his followers of the need to propitiate the myriad of spirits traditionally appeased and rigorously reduced the number of days spent in *tinga* celebrations during which no work was allowed. Of great interest is his introduction of an annual pilgrimage to Bhubal Cave in eastern Cachar district. Roy astutely notes that an emergence from a cave is a vital part of the creation story of the Zeilangrong tribes as well as being a well-known practice in Hindu piety. We see here the mixing of traditions again in the effort to deal creatively with the "new world" while remaining rooted in traditional culture.

Religious Evolution

Rodney Stark and William Sims Bainbridge have noted that "any adequate theory of relationship between the nature of societies and the nature of gods must place major emphasis on change. Neither societies nor gods simply pop into existence. When we examine societies and their gods, we must ask how both developed rather than treating them as static entities" (Stark and Bainbridge, 1987: 55). The effort to determine exact correlation between various characteristics of society and broad categories of religious styles—particularly the development from polytheism to monotheism—has been marked more by ardor than success.

Robert Bellah proposes a schema of five stages of religious evolution (Bellah, 1964), later slightly modified in his discussion of the Axial Revolution (Bellah, 2011). Because of the specific focus of the later work, the earlier one, "Religious Evolution," provides a more accessible entry to this discussion. While eschewing any judgment with respect to truth, beauty, or adequacy of any of the religious phases, Bellah notes that they correspond closely to social realities. The stages that are of interest to this study are the second and third, the "archaic religion" and "historical religion."

Archaic religion is the phase traditionally held by small societies of the type seen in the hills of the North-East India. Having developed from "primitive" phase, an archaic society sees the emergence of a cult of personified gods and spirits to whom sacrifice is offered often by a formal priesthood. A key aspect of archaic faiths is that they remain monistic, focused on the here and now which the sole and entire arena of reality is: fertility, avoidance of disease, and bountiful crops are generally some of the main areas of concern. Thus, while the religious action remains one of sacrifice to spiritual beings, who, because these are always unpredictable in their response, remain a great challenge to assay.

Religious organisation closely parallels social organisation—clan gods, village gods and the like—but can become quite complex as a society's stratification increases, with divine beings taking on similar hierarchies, and even having a high god emerge that reflects emerging warlords and larger chiefdoms. Social structures and practices are seen as grounded in divine order, an order that helps ensure social conformity. Yet this socio-religious synthesis is always ready to develop into another world-picture. Throughout the ancient world, the "...breakdown of internal order led to messianic expectations of the coming of a savior king in such distant areas as Egypt on one hand and Chou-period China on the other" (Bellah, 1964: 366).

"Historic" religions, Bellah claims, are distinguished by their transcendental concerns. No longer are concerns so strongly centered on this world, and uncovering of other worldly focus—heaven, enlightenment, *nirvana,* liberation—greatly relativises this-worldly ideals. Religious action moves from a sacrificial emphasis to whatever might attain the world to come, often expressed in universal moral ideals and practices by which the devout are somehow set apart. Priesthoods and prophecy flourish, the latter finding reason to criticise both peasants and kings from their transcendent stance; "... political acts could be judged in terms of standards that the political authorities could not fully control. ((Bellah, 1964: 368).

While Bellah's formulation has a "feel" of accuracy, empirical validation has remained elusive; finding correlation between "high gods" and social states has proven difficult. Swanson (1960) found monotheism was related to the number of hierarchically organised sovereign groups: family, village, and clan did not, by and large support a high god; a greater number of strata—chiefs, kings, bureaucrats—did. Underhill (1975) related strong monotheism to economic and political complexity, and faulted Swanson for mistaking sovereign groups for this economic reality. The discussion included social stratification, societal, size and various other theories.

A large cross-cultural study by Sanderson and Roberts (2008) finds that Samson's sovereign groups correlate significantly, but not strongly with a High God; other previously offered correlations failed to register. The study also measured religious evolution, divided into four categories: shamanic with only individual cultic practices; communal, which add communal institutions and calendric rites; polytheistic, with specialised priesthoods and numerous gods, often in a hierarchy; and monotheistic, which is much like the previous, but with worship focused on a single god.

Communal religions are most common in agricultural societies, particularly those employing shifting cultivation; monotheism was limited to societies of intensive plow agriculture or pastoral herding. Sanderson and Roberts attribute this to creation of enough surplus wealth to support an elaborate priesthood. A second indicator was writing: 93 per cent of societies with a communal style of religion were non-literate, as were two-thirds of the polytheistic societies. The big flip was movement to monotheism, of which 87 per cent were found in literate societies (pp. 460). Monotheism is also a characteristic of large societies, rarely occurring in societies of less than 100,000 souls. This finding was corroborated by Roes, who found size to be a significant factor, though not social stratification (Roes, 1995). The shift from communal to polytheistic faiths seemed to be made possible by intensive agriculture. The researchers conclude with an admission that more studies are needed, particularly in the movement from communal to polytheistic faiths.

These findings specify those reflections of Bellah, who asserts :

> In this framework, the baseline from which all later development begins is characterised by a social structure rooted almost entirely in kinship and neighbourhood. What is characteristic of such baseline societies, which we might—though the term is not without ambiguities—call tribal societies, is that all aspects of life are organised

> through kinship and local group association. There is no differentiated political system or economic system. Hierarchy is not missing but is organised almost exclusively through age and sex differences. Economic life is carried on largely through kinship and neighbourhood reciprocity. Religion is embedded in the ongoing social life of the people and is largely oriented to immediate needs, which led Weber to characterise it as magic. (Bellah, 1999: n.p.)

The "communal" style of religious culture best fits with the subsistence farming, simple clan-based societies found among the hill societies of the North-East India.

All of this indicates that a move to strict monotheism by Jadonang would have been nearly impossible, if for no other reason the lack of surplus income and social structure to support such a leap. What he did approach was polytheism of Bisnu/Tingkao-Raa-Gong leading the other traditional Zeme gods and excluding the multitude of nasty spirits, not from existence but from attention. Zeme society was too poor, too illiterate, and too small to expect anything else. In light of this, the real anomaly is the move by his successor Gaidinliu to proclaim monotheism in a society that seems incapable of supporting it.

Intellectualist Influences

Robin Horton, writing on West African small societies, offers an answer to this incongruence. As first pointed out by Arkodhan Longkumer (2011), Horton argues that small societies tend to hold dear small gods. Though there is often a high god concerned with creation and perhaps morality somewhere in the society's pantheon, though rarely is that god an object of much worship or sacrifice. In expanding relationship beyond traditional social limits, e.g., in regularly encountering other groups, that high god comes to the fore. To oversimplify a bit, for a wider world, a bigger god is necessary. Horton offers the example of the Aro society, an Ibo people of Nigeria, whose worship centered on local spirits and gods until their emergence as a major trading group that created a sphere of peace and order. With this expansion came development in worship of a supreme being, whom they claimed provided them their success. This development, Horton notes, was in the absence of any Muslim or Christian missionary activity (Horton, 1975a:

228). In a word, then, at least in the African context, we know that, in general, the lesser gods provide an interpretation of the special features of the microcosm formed by a limited population maintaining intensive social interaction within a limited territorial area, whilst the high god provides an interpretation of the world seen as a whole. Taking this as given, I suggest that the extent to which any population actively worships its high god is partly determined by the degree of its active contact with the wider world outside the microcosm (Horton, 1962: 139).

Another area of interest in Horton's position is his discussion of the essentially "closed" nature of traditional societies. While affirming that members of these societies are equal in rationality to any other human being, they in general face lack of options. There is no choice except to agree and accept what everybody else accepts. There is no scope for questioning established beliefs. Horton continues:

A second important consequence of lack of awareness of alternatives is vividly illustrated by the reaction of an Ijo man to a missionary who told him to throw away his old gods. He said: 'Does your God really want us to climb to the top of a tall palm tree, then take off our hands and let ourselves fall?' Where the established tenets have an absolute and exclusive validity for those who hold them, any challenge to them is a threat of chaos, of the cosmic abyss, and therefore evokes intense anxiety (Horton, 1975b).

With such powerful intellectual status quo, small societies are profoundly conservative. Despite slow and constant change in societies, new ideas, often resisted and even thought insane, rarely affect reflection and absorption by an individual or the society as a whole.

Dimasas and Zemes : Two Responses

With this in mind, it is possible to at least offer for consideration some factors that contributed to the resistance of Dimasa society to religious innovation and the acceptance of change among the Zeme Nagas of Assam.

The Dimasas strongly resisted missionary efforts. There is a tale, perhaps true, that around the year 1910 the Dimasa community gathered all Christian Bibles and tracts together and burnt them in a huge bonfire. The missionaries themselves were luckily a step too quick and so avoided a similar fate (Palonchandra Warisa, Personal Communication, 2008). This continues despite a ten years' presence of Catholic-sponsored schools in the Dima Hasao District, conversions to Catholicism have been scant at best. The society is slightly Hinduised, not least because of the formal conversion of their king to caste Hinduism in the early nineteenth century. In general, they continue the communal style of religious culture as described earlier.

From the influence traced above, and particularly Horton's reflection on the closed nature of traditional societies, the Dimasa response can be seen as normative. Two factors, one more religious, one more cultural (insofar as that distinction is possible in traditional societies) seem to encourage this conservatism.

First, Dimasa worship, beyond propitiatory offerings to spirits, has communal offerings to members of the pantheon, and this in three different ways. First, entire clans meet annually to worship the clan god, seeking protection of clan; second, the entire Dimasa homeland is divided into *khels,* areas under the protection of a god, who is also honoured annually by men of district (Danda, 1978). In addition, there exists a less regular gathering of the entire community, attended, officially at least, by men of the community. These three styles of *puja* exert strong centripetal tendencies on the society, serving as regular enhancement of *communitas.*

A second major influence is the tradition of double descent among Dimasas. Exogamy is a strict rule on both sides of young person's family. It is impossible, short of expulsion from the community, to marry anyone of a parent's patriclan (*sengphong*) or matriclan (*jadi*). Marriage laws thus yield an unusually thick web of familial relationship that like the regular rituals for clan, region, and entire society that expand internal horizons beyond local villages—but no farther than the whole society—produce strong internal bonds and, in a complimentary way, strongly reinforce cultural insularity.

Thus the Heraka movement remains an outlier. Monotheism is rarely introduced as part of a millennial movement because such movements typically seek to conserve what is best in old cultures. Presumably many monotheistic "prophets" have arisen, and presumably almost all have been rejected by the closed, conservative societies they addressed. The Zemes of Assam experienced recent war with the Kukis, British taxation and other oppression and doubtless other destabilising realities, but destabilisation seems never by itself to have effected a change in religious focus. Certainly, it did not in the Zemes' similar Dimasa neighbours. What made the Zeme people different?

Three possible influences emerge. First, Jadonang was, in the end, not proposing a complete break with the past. His change of focus from a spirit-and-gods reality to a pantheon of traditional Zeme gods headed by Bisnu / Tingkao-Raa-Gong; a pantheon that would prevent the depredations of the nasty spirits, though a large step did not demand of the people a revolutionary rethinking of reality.

Second, the Zemes were entering the early stages of literacy. Presumably, Christian missions to the Zemes embraced the standard package of evangelisation, health care, and education. If, as Longkumer (2011) notes, the first Zeme Christian was baptised in 1910, a much larger number of Zemes must have received schooling and so become literate prior to that date. Telling, too, is a Jadonang's own effort to write prayers in his self-invented script, an interesting combination of imitating the new while simultaneously rejecting it, adapting to bring it in line with the society's cultural heritage. In any case, as the findings of Sanderson and Roberts show, the presence of literacy greatly facilitates religious change of the type seen here.

Thirdly, change was in the air, and central to that change was an expansion of horizons. Christianity had penetrated the Naga Hills earlier, with the first Baptist congregation founded December 23, 1872 (Moses on Mission, 2008). The success of these efforts was limited at best. Roy notes that " until 1920's Nagas were hundred per cent animists (i.e. tribal religion followers)..." (Roy, 2011: 18); only during that decade did the number of Naga Christians begin their rapid rise. In a sense then, we are faced with an additional question, though one that I would posit is intimately related. What happened to Naga tribes in general, including Jadonang's Kabui / Rongmeis?

The most obvious answer is the creation of the Naga Club in 1918. Most significantly, the organisation was founded by Nagas from the various tribes who had served as porters in Europe during

World War I. This constituted a double expansion for those who so served. First, it provided a rare occasion for members of different "Naga" tribes to encounter one another (admittedly under ghastly conditions) and so come to know and understand fellow hill men who were previously ancient enemies. Second, it exposed the veterans to people and cultures of an even larger world: England, Europe, and the West in general. Following Horton, their military service could well have broken through the closed nature of their societies, could have led to their own "microcosmic" gods seem suddenly inadequate, and so initiated a movement towards instating a high god, whether or not such figure was previously present in their cultures.

Seen in this light, the Christian missions were in the right place at the right time. Their proclamation of a universal god filled this need as well: only after the return from Europe and the formation of the Naga Club to espouse Naga identity did the missions begin to be successful. Further, it is most reasonable to suspect that, given the Club's agenda of uniting the Naga tribes, their outreach embraced at least the leadership of the Rongmei, Liangmai, and Zeme tribes, and so forcing a wedge through the cultures' strong boundaries and forcing the encounter of new ideas. This was the ground, recently opened, newly expanding in horizons, in which Jadonang and later Gaidinliu led their movement towards monotheism.

This effort at understanding the rapid conversion of Zeme Nagas to Heraka and Christianity ignores other well-documented political and social realities. In his concise treatment, Thong (2010) argues that for Nagas, the choice of Christianity was, to a degree, a form of political resistance. Their act of conversion, which was to identify them with erstwhile Christian western colonisers, was in part an opposition to their immediate non-Christian coloniser, that is, India (pp. 599). Yet, he also asserts that "trauma of near total cultural and psychological breakdown, which finally led to a religious movement into Christianity" (pp. 603). While the present effort did not deal with these factors that Thong sees as crucial, those concrete historical events must be considered in any full assessment.

Conclusion

Jadonang was eventually implicated in the murder of four people, though in testimony was far from the scene of the crime. A strong sentiment remains that he was framed and the victim of judicial murder by the British Raj, who thus hoped to eliminate a source of rebelliousness among the cultures of Manipur.

Gaidinliu, Jadonang's disciple, quite quickly assumed leadership of the movement. She, too, was eventually tried and jailed for being an accomplice in Jadonang's alleged crime. A visit in her imprisonment by Pt. Jawarhal Nehru, seeking alliance with any opponent of British rule raised her profile, particularly when the fervent democrat Nehru bestowed the title of "Rani" (queen) upon her. Neither she nor her disciples apparently ever eschewed the moniker. Does it press too hard to comment that monotheism appears most comfortable in a monarchy, and so monarchy, at least of the Heraka, surfaced?

Under the leadership of Gaidinliu, the Heraka faith continued reforms of traditional *Paupise*, moving towards a firmer monotheism. Political involvement continued with Gaidinliu and some followers going underground during the 1960's. Gaidinliu eventually moved Heraka under the wing of the *Viswa Hindu Parishad*, probably to gather further legitimacy in its struggle with Christianity that continued to make significant inroads among the Zemes and, of course, other "Naga" societies. While this is often presented as the Heraka movement being "co-opted" by the Hindutva movement, it can as easily be seen as a canny leader dealing with the exigencies at hand. Who was using whom? Gaidinliu died in 1970. By this time, Heraka had established itself as a monotheistic faith, vying with Christianity for the devotion of the Zeme Nagas of today's Dima Hasao District.

Needless to say, it is impossible to say with any assurance the specific dynamics of the Zemes' leap to monotheism, either Christian or Herakan. The factors outlined in this short presentation I would submit, form influences that in the cases of Dimasa and Zeme societies either hindered or promoted the seemingly insane notion "letting go of the branch" of an accepted cultural heritage and so "falling from the palm tree." If nothing else, it is hoped this analysis might cause some further reflection on the ability of small societies of the North-East India to deal with the "new worlds" they face in ways that are unique, and in ways worth investigating for resilience and creativity.

Almost one hundred years ago, awareness was dawning about the complexity changes in religious direction. Ruth Shonle, in still a fascinating account of Christian missionary efforts among the Esquimeaux people of Greenland, observed:

> While this lack of appreciation of cultural organisation has been somewhat modified by the work of anthropologists, there is still prevalent a notion that people will discard in its entirety its traditional culture and whole-heartedly accept a dissimilar culture. A study of actual situations seems to indicate that instead of complete substitution of a new culture for an old, the process consists of the mutilation of the old culture to permit elements of the new to enter, the result being a fusion of the two into a third type of culture (Shonle, 1924: 262).

As with early Christian efforts among the Nagas, gods of the far north were identified with Satan and his minions. Customs were regarded as heathenism and so eradicated, either by force or through bribery. The Esquimeaux were brought to a "foreign religion, connected in no way with the traditional values and codes of behavior of the tribe....But the result was not, as the missionaries had hoped, the remaking of the Indians into European Christians" (pp. 267).Instead, the Esquimeaux approach Christianity through the structure of their cultural conceptions, creating a very uneasy third way.

Insofar as Jadonang and Gaidinliu perceived an invasion of culture by the Christian missionaries, their effort to resist by re-enlivening and restating traditional faith in similar third way represents a hope and a means to ingeniously deal with challenges they and their community faced.

References

Bellah, Robert. 1964. '*Religious evolution*'. *American Sociological Review*, 29, 3, 358-374. http://www.jstor.org/stable/2091480.

Bellah, Robert. 1999. 'Max Weber and world-denying love: A look at the historical sociology of religion'. *Journal of the American Academy of Religion*, 67,2: 277-304. http://www.robertbellah.com/articles_3.htm.

Bellah, Robert. 2011. *Religion in Human Evolution: From the Paleolithic to the Axial Age*. Cambridge, Massachusetts: The Belknap Press.

Danda, Dipali G. 1978. *Among the Dimasa of Assam: An Ethnographic Study*. New Delhi: Sterling.

Horton, Robin. 1962. 'The high god: A comment on Father O'Connell's paper'. *Man*, 62: 137-140. http://www.jstor.org/stable/2796883

Horton, Robin. 1975a. 'On the rationality of African conversion'. Part I. Africa. *Journal of the International African Institute*, 45, 3:18.

Horton, Robin. 1975b. 'On the rationality of African conversion'. Part II. Africa: *Journal of the International African Institute*, 45,4:28.

Longkumer, Arkotong. 2011. 'Cleanlinessis next to godliness: Religious change, hygiene and the renewal of Heraka villiages in Assam'. *Contributions to Indian Sociology*, 45, 2: 189-216. doi:10.1177/006996671104500202.

Martin, Joel W. 1991. 'Before and beyond the Sioux Ghost Dance: Native American prophetic movements and the study of religion'. *Journal of the American Academy of Religion*, 59, 4: 677-701. http://www.jstor.org/stable/1465529

McCann, Jr., and D. Frank . 1966. 'The Ghost Dance, last hope of the western tribes'. Montana *The Magazine of Western History*, 16, 1:25-34. http://www.jstor.org/stable/4517018

Moses on Mission. 2008, 'Edwin Clark - Missionary to Naga India'. Retrieved 21/10/2013, from http://mosesonmissions.wordpress.com/2008/11/29/edwin-clark-missionary-to-naga-of-india/

Roes, Frans L. 1995. 'The size of societies, stratification, and belief in high gods supportive of human morality'. *Politics and the Life Sciences*, 14, 1: 73-77. http://www.jstor.org/stable/4236100

Roy, Babul. 2002. 'Descent groupings, belief system, and social structure among the Dimasa Kacharies of Assam'. *Man in India*, 82, 1-2:73-99.

Roy, Babul. 2011. *Zeme Naga: From Polytheism to Monotheism*. New Delhi: Serials Publications.

Roy, Babul. 2013. 'Mapping the Heraka identity: Are we engaged truly?' *Economic and Political Weekly*, XLVIII,40. http://www.epw.in/discussion/mapping-heraka-identity.html

Sanderson, Stephen K. and Wesley K. Roberts, 2008. 'The evolutionary forms of religious life: A cross-cultural, quantitative analysis'. *American Anthropologist*, 110,4: 454-466. doi:10.1111/j.1548-1433.2008.00078.x

Shonle, Ruth. 1924. 'The christianising process among preliterate peoples'. *The Journal of Religion,* 4,3: 261-280. http://www.jstor.org/stable/1195619

Soppitt, C. A. 1885. *An Historical and Descriptive Account of the Kachari Tribes in The North Cachar Hills.* Shillong: Conyngham Francis.

Stark, Rodney, and William Sims Bainbridge, 1987. *A Theory of Religion.* New Brunswick, NJ: Rutgers University Press.

Swanson, Guy E. 1960. *The Birth of the Gods: The Origin of Primitive Beliefs.* Ann Arbor, Michigan: University of Michigan Press.

Thong, Tezenlo. 2010. 'Thy kingdom come: The impact of colonisation and proselytisation on religion among the Nagas'. *Journal of Asian and African Studies,* 45, 595-609. http://jas.sagepub.com/content/45/6/595 doi:10.1177/0021909610373915

Underhill, Ralph. 1975. 'Economic and political antecedents of monotheism: A cross-cultural study'. *American Journal of Sociology,* 80, 4: 841-861. http://www.jstor.org/stable/2777195

8

Youth Organisations in the Ri Bhoi District of Meghalaya

– *Geetika Ranjan* and *Yashisenla Longkumer*

O TALK not to me of a name great in story;
The days of our youth are the days of our glory;
And the myrtle and ivy of sweet two-and-twenty
Are worth all your laurels, though ever so plenty.
(Lord Byron : 1875)

Youth, the very word sketches a picture in the mind-a picture that exudes with exuberance, enthusiasm and energy but is also fraught with frustration, fury and frenzy. The studies on youth have gained pertinence in the fast changing, jet speeding life of today. Youth constitute roughly 1.2 billion of the world's more than six billion people. While the cliché "youth are the leaders of tomorrow" has become a universal adage in numerous ceremonial occasions, they are often not taken as seriously as these words are intended to imply (Singh, 2008–editorial). Dickens thought on the era of the French Revolution (1859), "It was the best of times, it was the worst of times, it was the age of wisdom, it was the age of foolishness, it was the epoch of belief...", resonates the picture of the present as well. The present time is rife with progress, parity and pleasure, but it is also snared in penury and pathos. Development and degeneration are moving hand in hand. Ideals, values and principles are being revisited and redefined with the youth standing on their crossroads. In general parlance, unlike childhood which is far away from the thought of immediate worry of being on one's feet and unlike middle age which has crossed the challenge and has 'settled', the youth grapples with the juxtaposition of desire , dreams, despair and dilemma. There is a need for such agencies which channelise the energy of the youth in an organised way and train them to become empowered individuals. The youth organisations in many societies come up to cater to this requirement.

The present study based on fieldwork brings to the fore the

role of the youth organisations in the life of the Khasi youth in Umden area, Ri Bhoi district, Meghalaya. The Draft, Meghalaya State Youth Policy , 2012 mentions Meghalaya as the home to India's largest and fastest growing youth population which constitutes one-fourth of the total population. It takes into account the state's youth in the age group 15-25 years. Thrusting the Youth Policy of the state to three Es – Empowerment, Employment and Engagement, the policy spells out the need of the hour to make youth participative, proactive and productive. Interestingly, there is no consensus on the definition of 'youth' and there are diverse views regarding who constitutes a 'youth'. The United Nations defines 'youth' as those persons between the ages 15 to 24 years. The National Youth Policy of India 2003 brackets those in the age group of 13 to 35 years as 'youth'. The State Youth Policy of Meghalaya intends to cover all youth in the state within the age group of 13 to 30 years. Oxford Dictionary defines, 'youth' as the period between childhood and adult stage". It is a stage in life when a person is young, especially the time before a person becomes an adult (Hornby, 2001). Psychologically, it refers to the stretch of time in between childhood and adulthood. Characteristically, youths at this stage of growth and development are biologically known to be full of libidinal energy and ideas and are also numerically known to outnumber the middle-aged and the aged (Omede, 2012).

Anthropological research attempts to understand 'youth' as an emic concept – how a people themselves define 'youth'. This is pertinent as it manifests how individuals in a culture perceive the meaning of the word 'youth'. This is particularly significant in cultures, where the understanding of people about age is not necessarily about numbers. Many people in such areas have no idea and do not attribute any importance to the number of years. While conducting fieldwork in a Uttaranchal village when I asked a woman about her age she said – '*likh lo pacchhis saal* (write twenty five years). When I asked her the age of her eldest son, she pondered and said – *likh lo bees saal* (write twenty years). Anthropological training helps in making an assessment of relative age by cross-checking with relevant episodes in the history of that culture. In the Umden area, some youth organisations consider those in the age group of 15-35 years as 'youth'. For some youth organisations as well as for the senior (those having grown up children as well as for the elderly population) the stage of youth starts with one around 15-16 years and lasts up till s(he) considers one 'young at heart'.

Umden area brings under its canopy nine villages—Umden Nungthluh, Umden khasi, Umden Manipur, Umden Langphador, Umden Umpyrdong, Umden Diwon, Umden Lumding, Umden Nongthneng and Umden Kyntonphynram. There are 198 in all households with a population of 3,046 out of which the youth population was 677. Going by the general perspective of the people as well as the age criteria taken by most of the youth organisations in the area, among the people of Umden the category of youth comprises men and women, who are in the age group of 15 to 35 years.

Nongpoh is the administrative centre of the district and Umden area is about twenty kilometers in the interiors from Nongpoh. Bhoi is a sub group of Khasi, one of the major indigenous tribes of Meghalaya. They follow matrilineal system and speak their local dialect, Karew, commonly known as the Bhoi dialect. Large majority of the Bhoi have converted to Christianity, while a few continue to follow their traditional Khasi religion – Ka Niam Mawsam.

The influence of church is paramount on the people of Umden. They report that with the arrival of christian missionaries in the eight decade of the 19th century many Khasi converted to Christianity. The dominant youth organisations in Umden are those which base themselves on the principles of the church. At Umden, the Bhois belong to different Christian denominations. Large majority of them are Catholics, followed by the Presbyterians, Church of Christ, Church of God- Ecclesia., Church of God (Meghalaya-Assam). These different denominations under Christianity profess independent ideology, yet they all uphold the same principles and values about human life. Church plays a pivotal role in emphasising the importance of education for the development of a grounded personality and society at large. The literacy rate at Umden which is 84.5 (85.2 for men and 83.8 for women) speaks volumes about impetus given to education by the Church.

A study on the youth organisation in a tribe reminds one of the youth dormitories in various tribal communities of India. With the coming of various processes of change such as urbanisation and industrialisation, the importance of youth dormitories is diminishing but they were 'the' erstwhile organisations where the youth was groomed in the ethos of his/her culture.

Advent of Christianity, particularly in the area of northeast brought with it a fresh wave of missionary activities. What we witnessed at Umden is that an ideal life revolves around the axis of faith in Christianity. How far the ideal and the real are enmeshed or polarised is another issue of discourse but nevertheless the importance of church in the lives of the people can be garnered from views of the people. Faith in the church is a way of life for them. The Youth Organisations are very popular in Umden. Every youth is a member of some youth organisation or the other.

Religion as a social institution has tremendous potential to unite people as well as to divide them. It can inspire and it can ignite. It can herald a new era and it can also signal the end. These results of paradoxical nature are created by the interpreters of the religious tenets rather than the tenets themselves. Thus religion can be a tool of construction and destruction the onus lies in the hand. Youth organisations in Umden are based on one denomination of Christianity or the other. This chapter highlights the role of these organisations in serving as platforms and pathways of driving home to the youth the importance of human values.

Seng Samla Katholic Lumsenai Parish, Umden (SSKLPU)

This youth organisation was formed in the year 2006 by the parish Council Members. Seng means 'organisation' and 'samla' means 'youth'. A very popular youth organisation, it has around 500 members from twenty one villages in the Bhoi area. It has members in the age group of 15 to 35 years. The members elect the executive committee members and the latter are expected to be the torch bearers for the others in the organisations and are expected to have high morals, be sincere in faith and are driven by the mission to work towards the social good. The executive committee members are elected for tenure of two years. The chief office bearers of the organisation are the – President, General Secretary, Education Secretary, Sport Secretary, and Secretary to the Pastor. Apart from these, there is a sister and a father from the church who acts as their advisors.

The motto of this organisation is, "Do Knerlakti" which means "Give a helping hand" . The organisation has lofty aims like, to bring the youth together in a bond as brothers and sisters; to encourage love and cooperation amongst each other; to spend more time of their youth in spreading the gospel; to help the needy and bring them closer to the church; to encourage the youngsters to be good leaders in church as well as in the society and to give them the platform to express their talent.

Various activities are carried out by SSKLPU. It conducts an annual youth convention every year. This is organised in the third week of January week from Friday to Sunday with a new theme every year. This year the theme was, "Do Suh Dhiet Bat Nangkhain Ha Ka Gingngiet Takabanang Hau Khrist" meaning to grow deeply in faith through Christ. The organisation organises various activities like Bible quiz, debates, extempore speech; cultural shows through which the members showcase unique talents. Apart from the annual convention, they also organise other activities like holding youth conferences in which they award student who secure a 1st division in class 10 and those who excel in sports outside the state. The organisation leaders explained that the purpose of organising these activities is to instill in the minds of youth the value that talent, hard work and sincerity is always rewarded.

SSKLPU at Umden also organises youth programmes in other villages every three month. They usually go on a Saturday, stay overnight and return on Sunday. There they meet-go to the house of the people, listen to their problems, encourage and pray for them.

In the month of August, the organisation organises a sports meet every alternate year in which basketball, football and other sport matches are organised.

Christian Endeavour Society, Umden

This youth organisation is based on Presbyterian denomination and the Presbyterian youth are its members. This is an old organisation in the area established on January 22nd, 1933 with the motto "Na Ka Bynta u Khrist Bad Ka Balang" meaning "for the Christ and the church". It is one of the biggest youth organisations in Umden area having about 250-300 members from Umden alone. The office bearers hold tenure of two years. They may be re-elected. Interestingly, to be eligible to be its member, one should be minimum 15 years of age but there is no upper limit (unlike 35 years as in the case of SSKLPU). One can continue to be its member till the age 'one still feels young and active'. In fact, some of its members are even married and as they have more experience and wisdom on their side, they are usually appointed as office bearers so that they can lead the youth in a better way.

In comparison to the other youth organisations in the area, this organisation has the largest number of women members. The respondents explained that being an old youth organisation in the area , it carries a lot of prestige and weight of tradition, and parents prefer to attach their daughters to that. Many women members' mothers and grandmothers were also the members of this organisation in their youth. However although married men mostly continue to remain members of this organisation, women members give up their membership after marriage.

Any young person who joins this organisation is administered the following oath: This is the pledge between the Catholic Endeavour Society members and God :

1. I promise to do good things pleasing in his sight and would do whatever He wants me to do to the best I can.
2. It is my duty to have a close relation with God by reading His words, praying and by doing what is good.
3. I will try to gain lost souls for the extension of His kingdom.
4. I will try to promote the fraternity in our society through Christ.

Catholic Endeavour society upholds the spirit of having peaceful relations with the other church denominations. They have a yearly calendar of events to be organised under its aegis. However in order to address the matter of immediate concern, they call short notice meetings as well.

One yearly event is the youth week which is organised in the first week of October. Apart from organising various programmes like Bible quiz, extempore, games and sports, crusades are also carried out. They also organise a singing festival where the various divided groups sing and enjoy. On this occasion, they also invite Church elders to address the youth on the tenets of faith. On the last day of the week, all including the young and the old attend the service.

During Christmas, the Society goes for field trips, picnics, excursions etc. They also visit the non-believers, orphanages and destitute homes to encourage the poor and old and pray for them. They gift those Bibles, blankets, umbrellas and other items of daily need.

The organisation lays great emphasis on the spirit of offering helping hand in time of both celebration and mourning. Many of the members are enthusiastically engaged in giving their assistance during Christmas, New Year, wedding and death. They help in decoration, cleaning, cooking and also pray for the people they help. They clean the church every Sunday morning. The social committee of the society organises mass social work once in a year where the youth of the organisation take up the cleanliness drive in the village.

The Christian Endeavour Society is not as strict a SSKLPU in terms of dealing with its inactive members. SSKLPU members do not attend the marriage of a member, who is not regular to the church and who does not take any interest in church activities. In a way, they socially boycot the person. The Christian Endeavour society does not take such an extreme stand. They continue to encourage the inactive members to come closer to the church through the Society. However, the church based youth organisations come heavily on a member who violates any church rule. Trespassing the moral code is met with excommunication from the main church body. Thereafter, the excommunicated person loses membership of the concerned youth organisation. For example, pregnancy before marriage calls for ex- communication of the person from the church and from the youth organisation thereafter.

Seng Samla Katholic Umden Phyllum, Jingia Seng Samla Church God (Assam-Meghalaya), Church of God (Ecclesia), Catholic Church, Lumding are other church based youth organisations in the Umden area. They share their basic guidelines and activities in common. The differing point is their adherence to the tenets of a particular church denomination (Catholic, Presbyterian and others).

Seng Samla Shnong Diwon (SSSD)

This organisation was established on May 20, 2002 with the motto "*Jingstad Ngin Tynkai Lawei Ban Phyrnai*" which means, "We Save Knowledge to brighten our Future". It was earlier known as Seng Samla Pule Diwon (SSPD), 'pule' meaning 'students' but the name was changed to 'Shnong' in 2007 because many members in the organisation were not students or had ceased to be so. The name of the organisation was changed from Seng Samla Pule Diwon to Seng Samla Shnong Diwon so that those young people who are not students can be a part of it. Members in this organisation are in the age-group 15-35 years. After marriage, a person cannot remain a member of the organisation.

This organisation aims to work against the evils in the society such as the youth addiction to drugs and alcohol. It organises frequent camps to drive home to the young the ills of drug abuse and alcoholism. As reported by elders in the society, the instances of rape have increased over time. SSSD makes a conscious effort to sensitise the youth who are its members as well as the others in the area towards women in society.

SSSD is a strong pressure group on the political leadership at the village level as well as the District Council. While conducting field work, a latent air of tension was felt between the organisation's leaders and the Headman. When it comes to the relation with the headman, it was found that it wasn't cordial. The president of SSSD said the headman of Diwon is helpful and the organisation performs after his permission. They informed they cooperate with him in maintaining law and order in the village. The Headman's response was quite different. He said there was a clear lack of co-operation and trust between the youth organisation and him. Youth take part in maintaining law and order as individuals rather than as an organisation. Such an organisation might exist but it is not in the knowledge of the Village Durbar. As research went ahead, it was understood that some active members were regularly questioning the working of village durbar and this was not going down too well with the headman and other members.

Seng Samla Shnong Nongthluh (SSSN), Umden

This organisation was found to be less active. Written records of its establishment are lost and the earliest recorded list of members was that of 1999-2002. The executive members are holding various offices since 2008. According to the rules and regulations of the organisation the tenure of office bearers is three years but this is not often adhered to. The main reason given by the office bearers was that the youth are not willing to shoulder the responsibility and there was lack of well-educated and responsible youth in the village. Executive and General meetings are conducted but its members do not take those seriously. The members do not carry many activities, except for some usual help during Christmas, weddings, social works like cleaning the road side and youth meet where the organisation form a part of village defense party. They also guard the village during festive seasons when the rates of alcoholism and other anti- social activities are rampant.

Ri-Bhoi Youth Development and Social Organisation (RBYDS)

This organisation is led by the motto, "*Tylli Ngin Iang Lawei Ban Tei*" which means "together we stand to build a better tomorrow".

Apart from looking into the welfare of village by catering same functions as other youth organisations in the area, this organisation endeavours to work towards infrastructure development and sensitise the people on ecological protection. In Umden circle, they are encouraging and helping the farmers to take KCC loan from the State Bank of India. The people of Umden were not aware of this provision for the farmers, so this youth organisation also organised an awareness programmes with the help of the State Bank on December 14, 2011. Apart from this case, the RBYDS, also organises awareness camps on other subsidies and benefits being given by the government. They also organise football tournaments in honour of their former king Nursing Syiem.

The youth organisations collected funds in different ways – by selling broomsticks and offering labour for random chores, by making an annual collection of rupees ten from each of its members and by asking the money from the local MLA. The funds are utilised to organise activities and also for charitable purposes to help the needy.

The perspectives of different sections of the society were sought. The office bearers and members of youth organisations, the parents and relatives of the members as well as the leaders of the village political system were interviewed. The study points out youth organisations play an important role in the lives of youth as well as in the society at large. Joining a youth organisation looks like a natural consequence of growing up. Every youth in the village is a member of such organisation or the other. They serve as platforms which regularly reinstate the importance of adhering to human values of compassion and righteousness and of practicing 'good life'. Human values of philanthropy are reinforced by youth organisations and in this way the human tradition of compassion for others is kept alive in this fast paced world where extreme individualism sidelined the importance of shared humanity. Many elders in the area believed that youth organisations channelise the youth energy in right direction. They express their apprehension that if the youth organisations are not there, the youth in the area would go more astray, with alcoholism and drug abuse. India's northeast is an area on continuous challenge for insiders and outsiders. Sanjeeb Baruah points out that most of the writings on northeast India discuss the issues of its underdevelopment and difficult integration with the so called mainstream (2004). Burning issues such as the ongoing conflict on the Inner Line Permit, the Tenancy Bill has brought the youth unrest in Meghalaya to the forefront. Elders in the Umden area explain that church-based youth organisations play an important role in driving young members home, the necessity to believe things with rationale and patience rather than giving way to mob mentality and taking law in their hands. The moral values upheld by the church-based youth organisations may find different degrees of adherence on the part of members, with some making a sincere effort to put the guidance into practice while some others looking at tenets as 'nice words to hear than to follow on paper'. Yet its supporters of a cross section of people of different age groups and gender, opine even constant hearing of the 'nice words' does play some role in 'cleansing' the conscience. By organising song, dance and Bible quiz competitions, the organisations provide a much needed platform for expression of aesthetic desires and abilities of youth. Annual activities around keep them fruitfully engaged. One is reminded of Ronald Goldman (1969) work, 'Angry Adolescents' in which citing a case he explains that adolescents become delinquent when their energy is not catered in a fruitful direction. Having no platform for leisure can be dangerous. At Umden, the youth members shared that Umden being a rural area away from the excitement of a city life, they remain idle with not much to do. They look forward to events organised by youth organisations in which they get an opportunity to showcase talent. The present study takes into account the emic and etic perspectives of understanding the role of youth organisations in the area. Draft Meghalaya State Policy mentions as one of its main objectives, to "Strengthen culture of patriotism among young people and help them become responsible citizens who care for their families and communities wherein they live and instill a sense of national unity and social cohesion among the young people while recognising and respecting diversities–in religion, language, culture, ethnicity, lifestyle and habitat–in the State" (2011: 4). The church-based youth organisations at Umden are much respected and wield major influence on the people and have the power to bring them together transcending. However, it has been observed that this is not a priority with the church-based organisations. The youth organisations based on churches of different denominations, like Catholic and Presbyterian, are more driven to elevate themselves in the eyes of people compete with each in one up-manship. The different organisations in the area seldom come together for common cause. There is no apparent rift in between, but neither there is any effort on their part to stand as an ideal symbol of unity and integration. In fact, it appears that the missionary zeal focuses on increasing numbers in the organisation. Other youth organisations such as SSSD, SSSU and RBYDS are playing an active role as pressure groups on the local polity. They monitor the implementation of developmental schemes particularly those dealing with village infrastructure development like construction and maintenance of schools, roads and water supply. Emerging leadership could be seen in the working of these organisations. It was also observed that there is underlying tension between village political body, the Dorbar Snong and SSSD, SSSU and RBYDS. This is due to the latter's role as watch guard of the working of the Durbar. The Durbar comprising village leaders consider them as "time waste", who have members who "have nothing better to do".

Conclusion

Most of the youth organisations in the Umden area of Ri Bhoi district of Meghalaya play an active role in the life of youth as well as in the area in general. There are some which are almost defunct. Interpersonal differences between the leaders and members of organisation as well as within the leaders themselves do exist. Yet the members try to resolve and tide over those. Youth organisations are platforms for recreation, healthy competition and regular reckoning with moral values that they uphold. There are many among older generation of the Khasis who look back fondly and with nostalgia to the time when they were youth organisation leaders and members. Some of them find the present organisations having lost the purity and simplicity which existed in the bygone days. Yet they continue to support these which they consider as representations of their culture and also as pedestals to groom the personality of youth.

References

Baruah, Sanjeeb 2007. *Durable Disorder: Understanding the Politics of Northeast India*. India, Oxford University Press.

Byron, George Gordon Lord. 1875. *All for Love in The Golden Treasury*. London : Macmillan.

Dickens, Charles 1859. *A Tale of Two Cities*. London: Chapman Hall.

Goldman, Ronald. 1969. *Angry Adolescents*. London: Routledge and Kegan.

Hornby, A.S. 2000. *Oxford Advanced Learner's Dictionary of Current English* (6th Ed.). New York: Oxford University Press.

Omede, Jacob. 2012. 'Youths unrest and vices in Nigeria: Value and moral education'. *Research Journal in Organisational Psychology and Educational Studies* 1, 6: 313-318

Singh, Anand. 2008. *Youth and Migration* (Editorial). New Delhi, Kamla-Raj Publication.

The Draft, Meghalaya State Youth Policy, 2012.

9
Family and Marriage among Sherpas of Sikkim

– Manis Kumar Raha

Marriage and family are universal and found in all human societies of the world. Some of these are very 'backward' found in the very inaccessible or semi-inaccessible areas like forest and mountains. Some of these are most advanced ones find located in the most modern metropolitan cities. While 'the family is a social group characterised by common residence, economic co-operations and reproduction (Murdock, 1949:1), the definition of marriage as given by many anthropologists, sociologists and others, do not suit to different forms of marriage present in different human societies in different parts of the world. Most of the definitions are inadequate (Raha, 2007:21-23). Leach is quite skeptical about any 'universal' definition of marriage (1961:107). Needham has doubt about the possibility of having any such definition of marriage that covers different forms and types of marriage (1974:44). Same is the view of Sarana (1969:159-161). Even about her own definition of marriage, Gough admitted, "I do not argue that all societies must necessarily be found to have marriage by my definition" (1989:226). Considering the inadequacy of such definitions of marriage, I have attempted to define marriage, and hope this definition covers all forms and types of marriage like monogamy, polygyny, polyandry, polygynandry, group marriage etc., and even same sex marriage. The definition of marriage given by the present author goes as follows:

Marriage is a socially approved relationship of one or more persons with one or more persons involving residential cohabitation, socio-economic co-operation and reciprocal rights and obligation between partners entering into the union (Raha, 1996, 2007:23).

The above definition of mine justifiably includes monogamy (marriage of one man with one woman), polygyny (marriage of one man with more than one woman), polyandry (marriage of more than one man than one woman), group marriage (marriage of a group of men with a group of women) and even woman-woman or man-man marriage. And again with the different forms of marriage, different types of families are formed. So, we find in different human societies in different parts of the world, different types of families like monogamous, polygynous, polyandrous families etc.

Now in the light of the above discussion I have analysed and discussed below these two important institutions (family and marriage) of the Sherpas of Sikkim.

The Sherpas are treated as scheduled tribe as the Bhutias are, a Scheduled tribe in Sikkim and the Bhutias include the Sherpa. In Sikkim, the Bhutias are also known as the Khampas, came from Kham province of Tibet (Bhatt and Bhargava, 2005:37). The term Bhutia is derived from the original habitat 'Bhot' in Tibet. "The Bhutias originally migrated from Tibet, had been known in Sikkim since thirteenth century onwards as "Lhopo" or "Lhopas" which means "the dwellers of the southward" and the earliest inhabitants of "The Greater Sikkim" (Subba, 2008:267).

The Bhutias, who live in different places, are also known by the name of that place. For example, those who lived in Drukul of Bhutan, are known as the Drukpas, those who came from the Chambi valley, are known as the Chumbipas. The Dhopthapas were the inhabitants of a place in southern part of Tibet and the Tromopas or Do-mu-pas were the residents of Do-mu. Again those who came from Lachung valley are called the Lachungpas. Some of the Lachungpas migrated to Lachung from Hah valley. The inhabitants of Lachen valley, who came here from Hah valley, are known as the Lachenpas (Subba, 2008:267; Subba, 1999:140-142).

As already said the Sherpas are treated as the scheduled tribe in Sikkim as they are included in the broad group, Bhutia which is a scheduled tribe of Sikkim. The Bhutias also include the Chumbipa, Dopthapa, Dukpa, Kagatey, Tibetan, Tromopa and the Yolmo besides the Sherpa, as mentioned in the *Annual Report* 2008-09, of Ministry of Tribal Affairs, Government of India (pp.56). These groups are included in the broad group of Bhutia, so they are treated as the scheduled tribes.

As regards population of the Sherpa of Sikkim, it may be said that they have not been separately enumerated in 2001 census. The Bhutia have been enumerated, and we have to remain satisfied with their population so far as this census is concerned. According to 2001 census, the total Bhutia population in Sikkim was 70,308 of which 35,770 (50.88 per cent) are males and 34,538 (49.12 per cent) were females. They formed 13 per cent of the total populations (5, 40,851) and 63.11 per cent of the total scheduled tribe population (1, 11,405) of Sikkim. Again, out of the total Bhutia population, 62,662 (89.12 per cent) lived in rural areas and 7.646 (10.88 per cent) were in urban sector. The Bhutias are found in some other areas like Nepal, Bhutan and Darjeeling of West Bengal. In West Bengal the Sherpas are included in the broad category of 'Bhutia'.

In Sikkim, the Sherpas are found to live in all the four districts. The name, Sherpa is derived from the world Sharva meaning the people 'living in the east'. Before the Sherpas were so highly publicised by mountaineering expeditions, they introduced themselves to other societies by the term *Shar Khombo,* i.e., the inhabitants of Shar Khumbu (Bista, 1976:160). According to Gangopadhyay, 'the word Sherpa is derived from the word *Sharya,* meaning east and *pa* meaning residents / people' (1993:155). Mitra also thinks that the word *Shar-va* meaning 'people of the east' is the word from which the Sherpas derived their name. Bisht and Bankoti have similar opinion about the origin of the name (2004:1483). Furer –Haimendorf also thinks that the name Sherpa is derived from the Tibetan word *Shar-pa* (easterner). But it is not clear in what manner this term came to be associated with this particular group (1964:1). According to him the Sherpas were southerners rather than easterners from the Tibetan point of view (*ibid*: 2). It is believed the Sherpas penetrated Himalayan region on the south of Sagarmatha nearly 600 years ago. They started migrating through the Nangpa la (Bisht and Bankoti, 2004:1483).

In fact, the Sherpas are the original inhabitants of the frontier district in the Tsing-hai-sechwan province in Eastern Tibet. From there, they came to Nepal. Some of them migrated to Sikkim and Darjeeling (Subba, 2008:279).

In Sikkim, we studied two villages from south district inhabited by Sherpas. In these villages, a total of 692 Sherpas live. Out of this total population, 363 (52.46 per cent) are males and 329 (47.54

per cent) females. Out of this total of 692 Sherpas, 340 Sherpas live in one of our studied village, Sherpagaon. The remaining 352 Sherpas reside at the other studied village, Sherpahat. At Sherpagaon village out of the total 340 Sherpas 192 (56.47 per cent) are males and 148 (43.53 per cent) are females. On the other hand, at Sherpahat village out of 359 Sherpas 171 (48.58 per cent) are males and 181 (51.42 per cent) females.

The Sherpas of two villages are basically agriculturists; some are labourers and daily wagers. A few of them help mountaineers in their expeditions. While some of them are service holders, some others look after their own business (Coomar and Raha, 1999: 195-196; Coomer and Raha, 2013:37; Raha, 2011: 80-82).

The Sherpa society of two villages is divided into a number of exogamous clans (*rii*) some of these clans are sub-divided into sub-clans. One of the main functions of the clan organisation of the Sherpas is to regulate marriage (Coomar and Raha, 2013:37).

The Sherpas have their settlements on the slopes of mountain and valleys. Their cultivable lands are situated either on the hill slopes or on the valleys, and they practice terrace cultivation.

In Sikkim, the Sherpas are basically Buddhists. Buddhism is interwoven intimately with their life and activities. They belong to Nymgma-pa sect of 'Buddhism' (Raha, 2006:81). They worship a number of deities and spirits and celebrate a number of festivals.

The Sherpas in Sikkim have their own traditional council. The main functions of this council are to look after the customary rules of the society and dissolve the disputes between members of the society. However, the activities and influence of this traditional council has much been reduced in the present day.

Family

Like the families of all ethnic groups, the families of the Sherpas have varied number. Therefore, the average number per family among the Sherpas is also variable (Coomar and Raha, 1997: 249-253).

In our studied villages in the south district of Sikkim there are altogether 124 families. Out of them, the village Sherpagaon has 64 (51.61 per cent) and the other village, Sherpahat has 60 (48.39 per cent) families.

Table 9.1: Sherpa families and average number of members per family in Sikkim

Villages	*Family*		*Total Members*		*Average Members*
	No	*%*	*No*	*%*	
Sherpagaon	64	51.61	340	49.13	5.31
Sherpahat	60	48.39	352	50.87	5.87
Total	**124**	**100.00**	**692**	**100.00**	**5.58**

Again we see from Table 9.1 that in these 124 Sherpa families a total of 692 members live. These 692 members are again distributed in the Sherpa families of two villages. A little less than half (49.13 per cent) inhabit in 64 Sherpa families of the village Sherpagaon and a little more than half (352 or 50.87 per cent) are living in 60 Sherpa families of the village, Sherpahat.

At Sherpagaon village, the Sherpa families have members varying from one to fourteen members. The highest number of families (21.88 per cent) have four members. The next higher strength goes to families with three and five members, each having strength of 17.19 per cent. The lowest strength goes to families with thirteen and fourteen members, each having one family (1.56 per cent each).

The other village, Sherpahat has family varying from one to thirteen members. Like the first village, Sherpagaon the highest number of families in this village, Sherpahat have four members (18.33 per cent). Families with five and six members have the next higher number of families (15.00 per cent each). Families with one, ten, eleven and thirteen members have the lowest strength (each with 3.33 per cent) in this regard.

Table 9.2: Family size and average number of members in different family sizes

Size of Family	*Sherpagaon*			*Sherpahat*		
	No.	*%*	*Average Members*	*No.*	*%*	*Average Members*
1 to 3 (small)	16	25.00	2.56	13	21.67	2.23
4 to 6 (medium)	31	48.44	4.74	29	48.33	4.93
7 to 9 (large)	13	20.31	7.77	7	11.67	7.43
10+ (very large)	4	6.25	12.75	11	18.33	11.64
Total	**64**	**100.00**	**5.31**	**60**	**100.00**	**5.87**

From Table 9.2, it is apparent that among the Sherpas of Sherpagaon, the medium size families (4 to 6 members) have earned the highest share (48.44 per cent) of the total Sherpa families of this village. The average number per small size families have the next higher strength (25.00 per cent) with average number per family being 2.56. The very large families have the lowest strength (6.25 per cent) but the highest average number (12.75) per family.

At Sherpahat village of Sikkim, in a similar way, medium size families of the Sherpas have the highest share (48.33 per cent). These families have on an average number of per family is 4.93, a little higher than that of the Sherpa of Sherpagaon village. The small size families among the Sherpas of this village have the next higher strength (21.67 per cent) with an average number per family being 2.23. In this village, the large size families have the lowest share (11.67 per cent). But the Sherpas of Sherpahat village has significant strength (18.33 per cent) of very large size of families.

Now when we look at the relationship or kinship ties between the members of particular family, we find they are differently related; and so the Sherpa families of two villages of Sikkim have different types and sizes, changes sometimes with the marriage, birth, death, separation, divorce or departure of some members in a family.

On analysis of data of two villages, Sherpagaon and Sherpahat of South District, Sikkim, we find the nuclear families have the highest strength. Out of a 64 families of Sherpagaon village, 39 (60.94 per cent) are nuclear type. This village has seventeen (26.56 per cent) extended families and eight (12.50 per cent) broken families.

At Sherpahat village, the Sherpas have majority (32 or 53.33 per cent) families as nuclear type. But, this village has a little more number of broken families (10 or 16.67 per cent).

If we further examine the size and type of the families, we see at Sherpagaon village, the nuclear type has secured the highest strength in small and medium size Sherpa families (68.75 per cent and 67.74 per cent respectively). But in the large size families nuclear and extended types have equal strength.

At Sherpahat village as in Sherpagaon village, the nuclear types of families among them have the highest number of small

(61.54 per cent) and medium (68.77 per cent) size families. But the extended families are highest in large and very large (77.77 per cent) sizes of the families of this village.

In human societies, a family is constituted of members belonging to different generations. The same is the case with the Sherpa society of Sikkim. In the families of the Sherpas, members of ego's generation are in some cases, found to inhabit with those of ascending or descending or both generations. While some families are made of members of one generation, in some other families members of different generations do live together.

Table 9.3: Generation-wise gradation of Sherpa families of two villages of Sikkim

Generation wise Gradation of Sherpa families	*Sherpagaon*		*Sherpa hat*		*Total*	
	No.	%	No.	%	No.	%
I	1	1.56	2	3.33	3	2.42
II	2	3.13	5	8.33	7	5.65
III	-	-	2	3.33	2	1.61
IV	8	12.50	15	25.00	23	18.55
V	53	82.81	36	60.00	89	71.77
Total	**64**	**100.0**	**60**	**99.99**	**124**	**100.0**

For the sake of our study, we have divided the families into the following five grades on the basis of the presence of members belonging to different generations.

Grade – I: Families composed of members of Ego's generations, Ego's first ascending generation and Ego's first descending generations.

Grade – II: Families consist of members from Ego's generation only.

Grade – III: Families constituted of members from Ego's generation and Ego's second descending generation.

Grade – IV: Families made of the members of Ego's generation, Ego's first ascending generation and Ego's second descending generation.

Grade – V: Families composed of members belonging to Ego's generation and Ego's first descending generation.

Now from Table 9.3, it is found that at Sherpagaon village overwhelming majority of families belong to Grade-V (82.81 per cent). The next higher strength goes to Grade-IV (12.50 per cent). Grade-I has the lowest number of families (1.56 per cent). This village does not have any Grade-III family.

At Sherpahat village, the picture is almost the same. Grade-V has the highest number of families (60.00 per cent), but not as high as that of Sherpagaon village. As usual, Grade-IV has the next higher number of the Sherpa families of Sherpahat village (25.00 per cent) which is double the strength of Grade-IV families of Sherpagaon village. In this village, both Grade-I and Grade-III have the lowest number of families, each with 3.33 per cent.

When we find the strength of the families of villages combined together, we find among the individual villages, Grade-V has the highest strength (71.77 per cent). Grade-IV has the next higher number (18.55 per cent), Grade-III has the lowest number of families (1.61 per cent).

Subba (2008) in connection with the family of Sikkim Sherpa finds the family among these is patrilocal and the descent is reckoned through male line. Among these nuclear, stem, nascent and broken families are found. The nuclear families are very common. It is mostly monogamous with patrilocal post-marital residence.

Bisht and Bankoti (2004) have revealed that among the Sherpas of Sikkim, nuclear type is the most common type of family. Gangopadhyay (1993) has found nuclear family as the common type of family among them.

In connection with their families of Darjeeling District, West Bengal, Coomer and Raha have found them mostly live in families with four to six members. The medium sized families are most preferred which cover over half of the Sherpa population of two villages studied. The nuclear type of families is the societal profile and covers majority of Sherpa people. It can well be asserted that the mountainous terrainous habitat of the Sherpas can sustain only small and medium sized families having two to three or four to six members at the maximum. Most of the families have members of ego's first ascending generation. They have the highest frequency of married males as heads belonging to the age group of 30-44 years (1997: 252-253).

So, we notice the Sherpas of Darjeeling and Sikkim, have many similarities in family organisations.

Marriage

Marriage is a universal phenomenon. It is found to be practiced in all human societies. So, it is prevalent in the Sherpa society of Sikkim. Though the institution of marriage exists among Sikkim Sherpa, still a good number of them are found unmarried, because of the tender age, acute illness, deformity, lunacy, the Sherpas marry after certain age. So, those below that age, remain unmarried till they attain marriageable age.

Table 9.4: Marital status of the Sherpas of two villages of Sikkim

Marital	*Sherpagaon*						*Sherpahat*					
	Male		*Female*		*Total*		*Male*		*Female*		*Total*	
	No.	%	No.	%	No.	%	No.	%	No.	%	No.	%
Unmarried		64.58	77	52.03		59.12		59.65		59.12		59.38
Married	60	31.25	59	39.86	119	35.00	60	35.09	62	34.25		34.66
Widowed	7	3.65	11	7.43	18	5.29	8	4.68	10	5.53	18	5.11
Divorced	1	0.52	1	0.68	2	0.59	1	0.58	2	1.10	3	0.85
Total		**100.0**		**100.0**		**100.0**		**100.0**		**100.0**		**100.0**

Apart from the age restrictions, many other factors as mentioned earlier compel some Sherpa to remain unmarried. However, we shall see their marital status (Table 9.4).

Among the Sherpas of Sherpagaon village, majority of males and females are unmarried (64.58 per cent and 52.03 per cent respectively). But, the frequency of married Sherpas of two villages is below 40.00 per cent (31.25 per cent for males and 39.86 per cent for females), the number of widowed and divorced persons is quite low though widows are outnumber widowers.

Almost similar is the marital status of Sherpas of Sherpahat village. Here the number of unmarried is more than half (59.65 per cent) for male and 59.12 per cent for female Sherpas). The widowed Sherpas stand below 6.00 per cent and the divorced ones were insignificant.

The Sherpas of Sikkim in general, follow endogamy. Usually they prefer to marry in their own community. But, because they live in close neighbourhood of different groups like different Nepali castes, Lepcha, Bhutia and others, some of them have married non-Sherpas. Out of 75 married Sherpa couples of Sherpagaon village, 94.67 per cent have married Sherpas (Sherpa-Sherpa marriage). But, the remaining 5.33 per cent Sherpa males have married non-Sherpa women like the Bhutia and the Nepali (Sherpa-non-Sherpa marriage). In this village, there is only one case where a non-Sherpa (Nepali) male has married a Sherpa woman (non-Sherpa-Sherpa marriage).

As we come down to other village, that is, Sherpahat of Sikkim, we find out of 81 Sherpa married couples, 87.65 per cent males have married Sherpa women (Sherpa-Sherpa marriage). But, in the remaining ten cases–the Sherpa males have taken non-Sherpa women as wives (Sherpa-non-Sherpa marriage). The non-Sherpa women, whom the Sherpas have taken as wives, belong to Lepcha, Bhutia and the Nepali. In this village, there are three cases of non-Sherpa males (one Bhutia and two Nepali) to have married the Sherpa women (non Sherpa-Sherpa marriage).

In both the villages, the Sherpa-non-Sherpa and non- Sherpa-Sherpa couples live in the Sherpa society in the close neighbourhood of the Sherpa-Sherpa couples.

The Sherpas of both villages follow clan (*rii*) exogamy, very strictly. No one is allowed to marry in his or her own clan. The same clan marriage is considered by Sherpa as the worst kind of sin. One will be ex-communicated if so in one's own clan. From the two villages we have not got a single Sherpa who has married in his or her own clan (*rii*).

The Sherpas are in general monogamous though polygyny is also permissible. But, in our studied villages of Sikkim, the married Sherpas have gone for monogamy. We could not trace even one case of polygynous marriage among them during our field work. Again through Furer-Haimendorf (1964:68-74) found polyandry among the Sherpas of Nepal, but failed to locate one case of polyandrous marriage among them in two studied villages. The Sherpas do not allow any of their women marry polyandrously though they admitted such form of marriage in the past, but its frequency was quite low.

Among the Sherpas of studied villages, the largest number of males have married for the first time, when they belonged to the age-group, 20 to 24 years. The largest number of Sherpa females have married when they were in the age-group of 15 to 19 years. A good number of males are also found to have married when they were in the age-group of 15 to 19 and 25 to 29 years. A significant number of Sherpa females married when they were in the age - group up to 14 and 20 to 24 years.

So, we find the largest number of males marry soon after they cross twenty years of age, while the largest number of females marry in their teens. Thus, it is not that they always prefer to wed when they were quite adult.

Among the Sherpas of Sikkim, as we have seen marital residence is normally patrilocal. In some cases of course, the husband after marriage takes his wife in his newly constructed house instead of taking to his father's house. In some other cases after short stay, he goes to his newly constructed house with newly wed wife for permanent stay. In such cases, the residence is neolocal.

In connection with the marriage of Sikkim Sherpas, Subba believes them follow clan exogamy. Among marriage by negotiation and elopement, are prevalent. According to him, the Sikkim Sherpas prefer adult marriage, and monogamy is the norm of the society (2008:286).

Bisht and Bankoti (2004) have found Sikkim Sherpas practicing clan *(rii)* exogamy. Marriage is permitted 'within the sub-divisions *(pin)* of the same division, *rii*. Among them arranged marriage is the norm though some cases of marriage by elopement are met with (2004:1490).

Gangopadhyay (1993) has noticed the Sherpas of Sikkim normally practice monogamy. They follow the rule of exogamy in the clan and sub-clan levels. Among them, marriage by negotiation is the norm, except some cases of marriage by elopement (1993:156).

We thus, see the two institutions family, and marriage are very important in the life of Sikkim Sherpa as the same institutions are very important in all human societies of the world.

References

Bhatt, S. C. and G. K. Bhargava. 2005. *Land and People of Indian States and Union Territories*. Delhi; Kalpaz Publications.

Bisht, N.S. and T. S. Bankoti. 2004. *Encyclopaedic Ethnography of the Himalayan Tribes*. Delhi; Global Vision Publishing House.

Bista, D.B. 1976. *People of Nepal*. Kathmandu; Ratna Pustak Bhandar.

Coomar, P.C. and M. K. Raha. 1997. 'Family among the Sherpa of West Bengal'. In K.C.Mahanta (Ed): *Peoples of the Himalayas: Ecology, Culture, Development and Change*. Delhi; Kamala Raj Enterprise.

Coomar, P.C. and M.K. Raha. 1999. 'Women in the Sherpa society of the Himalayas'. In R. Indira and D. K. Behera (Eds): *Gender and Society in India*, Vol. II, New Delhi; Manak Publications (P) Ltd.

Coomar, P.C. and M.K. Raha. 2013. 'The Sherpas of Sikkim and their land'. In Sarthak Sengupta (Ed): *Tribal Panorama of North East India*. New Delhi; Gyan Publishing House.

Furer – Haimendorf, C. von. 1984. *The Sherpas Transformed: Social Change in a Buddhist Society of Nepal*. New Delhi; Sterling Publishers Pvt. Ltd.

Furer-Haimendorf, C. von. 1964 *The Sherpas of Nepal: Buddhists Highlanders*. Calcutta; Oxford Book Co.

Gangopadhyay, S. 1993. 'Sherpa'. In K.S. Singh (Ed): *People of India: Sikkim*, Vol. XXXIX, Calcutta; Seagull Books.

Gough, K.E. 1959. 'The Nayars and the definition of marriage'. *Journal of the Royal Anthropological Institute*, Vol. 89. Also in M.K. Raha (Ed): *Polyandry in India*. New Delhi; Gyan Publishing House.

Leach, E. R. 1961. 'Polyandry, inheritance and definition of marriage with special reference to Sinhalese customary law'. In E. R. Leach (Ed): *Rethinking Anthropology*. London; The Anthlone Press.

Mitra, A. 2008. 'Sherpa'. In K.S. Singh (Ed): *People of India: West Bengal*. Vol. XXXXIII, Calcutta; Seagull Books.

Murdock, G.P. 1965. *Social Structure*. New York; The Macmillan Co.

Needham, R. 1971. 'Remarks on the analysis of kinship and marriage'. In R. Needham (Ed): *Rethinking Kinship and Marriage*. A.S.A, Monograph No II, London; Tavistock Publications.

Orter, S.B. 1979. *Sherpas through their Rituals*. New Delhi; Vikash Publishing House.

Raha, M. K. 1995-1996. *Polyandry in the global context. Presidential address*, Anthropology and Archaeology Section, 83 Indian Science Congress.

Raha, M. K. and P. C. Coomar. 2001.'Some aspects of the Sherpa religion'. In S. Sengupta (Ed): *Tribes of Eastern Himalayas*. New Delhi; Mittal Publications.

Raha, M.K. 2006. 'Buddhism (Lamaism) among the Sherpas of Sikkim'. In S. Dutta and B. Tripathy (Eds): *Buddhism in North East India*. New Delhi; Indus Publishing Co.

Raha, M.K. 2007. 'Marriage in India with special reference to Arunachal Pradesh'. In Tamo Mibang and M. C. Behera (Eds): *Marriage in Tribal Societies - Cultural Dynamics and Social Realities*. New Delhi; Bookwell.

Raha, M.K. 2011. 'Pattern of livelihood, ecological involvement and survival strategy: The case of the Sherpa of Darjeeling district'. In M. Desai and S. Mitra (Eds): *Clouds, Stone and the Mind*. Kolkata; K. P. Bagchi and Co.

Sarana, G. 1969. " Some observation on the definition of marriage'. *Ethnos*. 33:

Subba, J. R. 1999. *The Limboos of the Eastern Himalayas with Special Reference to Sikkim*. Gangtok; SYMS.

Subba, S. R. 2008. *History, Culture and Customs of Sikkim*. New Delhi; Gyan Publishing House.

10
Intra and Inter-State Variation of Height and Weight in North-Eastern States of India

– *Papiya Roy, Suparna Som, Manoranjan Pal* and *Premananda Bharati*

Introduction

North Eastern India is endowed with vast resources like forest, biological diversity, hydro-electricity, but still, this region is not much developed. This region comprises eight States, namely Arunachal Pradesh, Manipur, Meghalaya, Mizoram, Nagaland, Sikkim, Tripura and Assam. India comprises variety of ethnic population, such as - scheduled tribes, scheduled castes, other backward classes and general castes people (Som *et al.*, 2013). The most important characteristics of North East India are that the States, except Tripura and Assam, are predominantly tribal dominated. The tribes constitute around 50 per cent of the total population of the region. However, percentage of scheduled tribe to general population in the State of Assam is enumerated to be 24.66 (Baruah *et al.*, 2012), i.e., about one-fourth of the general population.

It is known that human population vary in height and weight (Evelth and Tanner, 1990), but as the tribes of North East India occupy different habitat, it is expected that heights and weights will vary more in this region. Studies reveal that height may vary between populations due to genetic factors but within a population the differences are mainly due to socio-economic, nutritional and health factors (Som *et al.*, 2013). Both height and weight is known to be positively dependent on age and sex. BMI depends on both height and weight, so it depends on genetic and environmental factors (Bharati *et al.*, 2010).

Human development may be divided into two major phases– early phase and later phase. Early phase includes childhood and adolescent, while the later phase includes adulthood and old age. The increase in heights and abilities start from early phase of life and becomes very slow at later phase. The increases in size or height stops somewhere in the age group 21-23 years in case of Indian population, but the abilities continue to develop as people continue adapting to the environment (Baltes *et al.*, 1998). Weight, however, can increase or decrease at any stage of life except possibly at very old age.

North Eastern region was neglected for a long period of time, but recently some welfare schemes have been introduced by Central and State governments for the development of the region and these are the main reasons for short-term nutritional gain reflected in their heights and weights.

The main objective of the study is to find out :

(a) The variation of height and weight over different States,

(b) The variation of height and weight among different ethnic groups and lastly,

(c) The variation of height and weight among different religious groups.

Materials and Methods

For this study, data were collected from the third National Family Health Survey (NFHS-III) of 2005-06. The survey was coordinated by the International Institute of Population Sciences (IIPS) in collaboration with the Ministry of Health and Family Welfare. The total sample size is 30,467 in which 10,698 are male and 19,779 are female.

For males, heights were classified as very short (<149.99 cm), short (150.00 cm – 159.99 cm), below medium (160.00 cm – 163.99 cm), medium (164.00 cm - 166.99 cm), above medium (167.00 cm – 169.99 cm), and tall (>170.00 cm). For females the classification was very short (<145.00 cm), short (145.00 cm – 149.99 cm), medium (150.00 cm – 154.99 cm), tall (155.00 cm – 159.99 cm), and very tall (>160.00 cm). A more simplified way of classifying height in both groups is to categorise height into three categories, (i) above medium, (ii) medium and (iii) below medium (Singh *et al.*, 1994; 1997). For BMI, it is classified according to WHO (1995) classification, (i) underweight (<18.5), (ii) normal (18.5- 24.9), (iii) overweight (25.0-29.9) and (iv) obese (>30.0). This classification is same for both males and females.

For statistical analysis and making of tables, SPSS version 12.0 was used.

Results

The State-wise variation of mean heights and weights are shown in Table 10.1. The highest and the lowest mean height among males are observed in the States of Manipur (163.21±5.97) and Meghalaya (157.31±7.09) respectively. In case of female, the corresponding States are Nagaland (152.69±5.47) and Meghalaya (148.87±5.99) respectively. When we take weight into consideration, the highest and the lowest mean values for males are found in the States of Mizoram (56.49±8.37) and Tripura (51.32±8.72) respectively. In case of female, the highest and the lowest mean weights are 50.80 kg (±8.29) in Sikkim and 46.42 kg. (±8.72) in Meghalaya, respectively. The highest mean BMI is observed in case of male is in the States of Sikkim (21.93±3.04) and the lowest mean BMI is observed in the States of Tripura (19.64±2.90). In case of female, the highest mean BMI is in Sikkim (22.25±3.41) and the lowest mean BMI is in Tripura (20.17±4.23).

Table 10.1: State-wise Distribution of Height, Weight and BMI in North East India

State	*Gender*	*Height*			*Weight*		*BMI*	
		No.	Mean	SD	Mean	SD	Mean	SD
Sikkim	Male	745	159.8	7.40	56.01	8.53	21.93	3.04
	Female	209	151.1	5.72	50.80	8.29	22.25	3.41
Arunachal	Male	653	161.3	6.39	54.59	8.22	21.05	3.97
	Female	158	150.7	5.53	48.20	7.77	21.17	2.91
Nagaland	Male	361	162.6	6.31	55.64	8.23	21.01	2.66
	Female	378	152.6	5.47	49.15	7.65	21.05	2.90
Manipur	Male	345	163.2	5.97	56.36	9.15	21.14	3.25
	Female	394	152.0	5.15	49.99	8.22	21.60	3.22
Mizoram	Male	628	162.0	6.22	56.49	8.37	21.48	2.68
	Female	176	151.6	5.17	48.92	7.77	21.22	2.88
Tripura	Male	637	161.5	6.01	51.32	8.72	19.64	2.90
	Female	185	149.7	5.71	45.22	8.91	20.17	4.23
Meghalaya	Male	595	157.3	7.09	52.33	7.28	21.14	2.54
	Female	188	148.8	5.99	46.69	6.64	21.20	4.09
Assam	Male	1169	163.0	6.91	53.16	9.42	19.93	2.91
	Female	287	150.8	5.67	46.42	8.72	20.42	4.01

Table 10.2 shows the variation in height, weight and BMI over different regions for male and female adult populations. It shows that in comparison with the other regions, North East India has the lowest mean height for males (162.23±6.54), but mean weight (55.20±8.78) and mean BMI (20.96±3.04) are not the extreme values. In case of female, the mean height is 151.23±5.64, mean weight is 48.39±8.24 and the mean BMI is 21.15±3.50.

Table 10.2: Region-wise distribution of Height, Weight and BMI in India

Region		*Height*			*Weight*		*BMI*	
		No.	Mean	SD	Mean	SD	Mean	SD
Northern	Male	7249	166.56	7.02	57.75	11.30	20.79	3.81
	Female	20278	154.06	5.92	50.83	10.79	21.40	4.31
North	Male	11499	162.23	6.54	55.20	8.78	20.96	3.04
	Female	19779	151.23	5.64	48.39	8.24	21.15	3.50
Eastern	Male	5708	163.31	6.58	54.07	10.11	20.21	3.19
	Female	16788	150.75	5.57	46.15	9.40	20.30	4.09
Central	Male	13880	164.50	6.75	54.75	10.71	20.19	3.59
	Female	21314	151.72	5.78	47.11	9.65	20.45	4.04
Western	Male	9739	165.15	6.99	56.35	11.68	20.62	3.95
	Female	14228	152.24	5.98	48.72	10.88	21.05	4.84
Southern	Male	16852	165.14	6.90	57.57	11.95	21.09	4.23
	Female	20876	152.53	6.08	50.55	11.54	21.75	5.03

Table 10.3 shows the ethnic group-wise differences in both males and females. Results show that in case of male, the highest mean height (163.23±6.34) and the highest mean weight (55.80±9.80) are observed in other caste groups, i.e., the caste groups other than SC, ST and OBC. The lowest mean height (161.54±6.27), mean weight (53.64±9.22) and the mean BMI are all observed among scheduled castes. But the highest mean BMI (21.15±2.51) is found among the scheduled tribes. In case of females again, the lowest mean height (149.98±5.78), mean weight (46.50±8.89) and the mean BMI (20.67±3.95) are observed among the scheduled castes. Also, the highest mean height (151.40±5.62),

mean weight (48.70±7.32) and mean BMI (21.24±3.09) are all observed among the Scheduled Tribes.

Table 10.3: Population-wise distribution of mean Height, Weight and BMI in North East India

Population	*Gender*		*Height*		*Weight*		*BMI*	
		No.	*Mean*	*SD*	*Mean*	*SD*	*Mean*	*SD*
SC	Male	1070	161.54	6.27	53.64	9.2	20.52	3.05
	Female	1914	149.98	5.78	46.50	8.8	20.67	3.95
ST	Male	4864	161.68	6.54	55.37	7.9	21.15	2.51
	Female	9310	151.40	5.62	48.70	7.3	21.24	3.09
OBC	Male	1940	162.55	6.65	55.12	8.5	20.84	2.85
	Female	3191	151.32	5.82	48.46	8.7	21.18	3.96
None of them	Male	2814	163.23	6.34	55.80	9.80	20.97	3.88
	Female	5364	151.32	5.45	48.50	9.0	21.15	3.69

Table 10.4 shows the variation of male and female–heights and weights by different religious groups. It shows that, in case of male, the highest mean height (162.74 ± 6.57) is among Hindu religious groups but the highest mean weight (56.27 ± 8.43) and the highest mean BMI (21.53 ± 2.74) are observed in other religious groups which include Sikh, Buddhist /Neo-Buddhist, Jain, Jewish, Parsi / Zoroastrian/ etc., though the mean height (161.56 ± 6.71) is the lowest in this religious groups. The lowest mean weight (53.28 ± 8.59) and the lowest mean BMI (20.25 ± 2.87) are observed in Muslim religious groups. In case of females, the highest mean height (151.60 ± 5.58) is observed among Christians and the lowest mean height (150.61± 5.29) is observed in the Muslim religious groups. The highest mean weight (49.64 ± 7.74) and the mean BMI (21.83 ± 3.03) are observed in other religious groups. The lowest mean weight (45.98 ± 8.40) and the lowest mean BMI (20.23 ± 3.31) are observed in Muslim religious groups.

Table 10.4 : Religious group-wise distribution of mean Height, Weight and BMI in North East India

Religion	*Gender*	*Height*			*Weight*		*BMI*	
		No.	*Mean*	*SD*	*Mean*	*SD*	*Mean*	*SD*
Hindu	Male	4720	162.7	6.57	55.44	9.59	20.94	3.57
	Female	9053	151.0	5.72	48.35	8.96	21.18	3.95
Muslim	Male	1096	162.1	6.39	53.28	8.59	20.25	2.87
	Female	1254	150.6	5.29	45.98	8.40	20.23	3.31
Christian	Male	4672	161.8	6.47	55.19	7.94	21.02	2.48
	Female	7876	151.6	5.58	48.58	7.31	21.13	3.01
Others	Male	1011	161.5	6.71	56.27	8.43	21.53	2.74
	Female	1565	150.6	5.57	49.64	7.74	21.83	3.03

Tables 10.5A and 10.5B show the variations of male–female height and weight in accordance with various religious groups. It shows that the highest mean height (162.74 ± 6.57) of male is among Hindu religious group, but the highest mean weight (56.27 ± 8.43) and the highest mean BMI (21.53 ± 2.74) are observed in other religious groups which includes Sikh, Buddhist / Neo-Buddhist, Jain, Jewish, Parsi/ Zoroastrian, though the mean height (161.56 ± 6.71) is the lowest in this religious groups. The lowest mean weight (53.28 ± 8.59) and the lowest mean BMI (20.25 ± 2.87) is observed in Muslim religious groups. In case of females, the highest mean height (151.60 ± 5.58) is observed among Christians and the lowest mean height (150.61 ± 5.29) is observed among the Muslims. The highest mean weight (49.64 ± 7.74) and the mean BMI (21.83 ± 3.03) are observed in other religious groups. The lowest mean weight (45.98 ± 8.40) and the lowest mean BMI (20.23 ± 3.31) are again observed in Muslims. It thus shows that the male and female height, weight and BMI values have significant differences among the ethnic and religious groups.

Table 10.5A: Religious group-wise differences in male Height, Weight and BMI

Religion	*Height*				*Weight*				*BMI*			
	No.	*Mean*	*SD*	*Anova*	*No.*	*Mean*	*SD*	*Anova*	*No.*	*Mean*	*SD*	*Anova*
Hindu	4720	162.74	6.57	17.706**	4720	55.44	9.59	23.857**	4720	20.94	3.57	32.886**
Muslim	1096	162.10	6.39		1096	53.28	8.59		1096	20.25	2.87	
Christian	4672	161.89	6.47		4672	55.19	7.94		4672	21.02	2.48	
Others	1011	161.56	6.71		1011	56.27	8.43		1011	21.53	2.74	

Table 10.5B: Religious group-wise differences in female Height, Weight and BMI

Riligion	*Height*				*Weight*				*BMI*			
	No.	*Mean*	*SD*	*Anova*	*No.*	*Mean*	*SD*	*Anova*	*No.*	*Mean*	*SD*	*Anova*
Hindu	9053	151.09	5.72	23.267**	9053	48.35	8.96	49.448**	9053	21.18	3.95	49.079**
Muslim	1254	150.61	5.29		1254	45.98	8.40		1254	20.23	3.31	
Christian	7876	151.60	5.58		7876	48.58	7.31		7876	21.13	3.01	

*–F value; **–Significant in 1 per cent level

We now turn to the results of ANOVA as shown in Table 10.6. As expected, between-State variances are much more than within-State variances. When these are compared between genders, it is seen that between-State variances are more among females, where as within State variances are more among males except for BMI. The ratios of between-State variances to within-State variances (F-values) differ much across height, weight and BMI. These ratios are more for females, which is clearly seen from Table 10.6. Only among males the F ratio is maximum for height. For females, the maximum value of the ratio is observed for weight. Thus, we may conclude that compared to within-States, the females differ more on weight among-States and males differ more on height.

Table 10.6: ANOVA of Height, Weight and BMI across States in North East India

Gender	*Variable*	*Between State Variance*	*Within State Variance*	*F (df, d)*	*Sig.*
Male	Height	3473.869	40.679	85.397 (7, 11502)	0.000
	Weight	3777.709	74.813	50.495 (7, 11502)	0.000
	BMI	485.186	8.950	54.212 (7, 11502)	0.000
Female	Height	3913.535	30.501	128.307 (7, 21153)	0.000
	Weight	10714.067	65.097	164.587 (7, 21153)	0.000
	BMI	1216.715	11.856	102.620 (7, 21153)	0.000

Discussion

The height-weight variation of male and female adult population of North Eastern India by its various ethnic and religious groups is presented here. Results show the lowest mean height for male is observed in Meghalaya, whereas the lowest mean weight and BMI are seen both in Tripura. The highest mean height, weight and BMI for men are seen in Manipur, Mizoram and Sikkim, respectively. In case of female population, the lowest mean height, weight and BMI are observed in Meghalaya, Assam and Sikkim respectively.

The adult male population of Meghalaya and Sikkim are short in stature and the rest are in the below medium group. In case of females, Tripura and Meghalaya show the higher incidence of short stature inhabitants and the rest belongs to the medium stature group. In case of BMI, all the States show good nutritional status on the average and the values are more than 18.5 and it is also observed here that the health status show a better result in females than males.

Ethnic group-wise differences show that the 'other' caste group has the highest mean height and weight in males only and scheduled tribal groups show the highest mean BMI in case of male and the highest mean height, weight and BMI for females. Scheduled caste groups show the lowest mean height, weight and BMI in both male and female groups.

The highest mean height for male is in Hindu religious groups, and for females it is the Christian groups. The 'other' religious groups show the highest mean weight and BMI in both males and females. 'Other' religious groups also show the lowest mean height in males. The Muslims show the lowest mean height in females and the lowest mean weight and BMI in both males and females. Thus Muslim population of the region needs maximum attention.

The prevalence of underweight is high in Assam and Tripura and the percentages of overweight or obese people are high in Sikkim and Manipur for both males and females. When compared with other regions in India it is observed that North Eastern India has the lowest mean height, weight and BMI in males and second lowest in females as because North Eastern region has been neglected for long period of time (Shome *et al.*, 2012).

A good nutritional status is observed in Mizoram, Sikkim, Manipur and Nagaland. In these States the differences between rural and urban area are very less than the other States of India (Bharati *et al.*, 2008). It is known that in North East India, the economic development is not as important as indicators of social development like literacy, awareness, gender equality and health are in a satisfactory level compared to other regions in India (Bharati *et al.*, 2012).

References

Baltes P.B., U. Lindenberger and U. M. Staudinger.1998. 'Life-span theory in development psychology'. In R.M. Lerner (Ed.): *Handbook of Child Psychology: Theoretical Models of Human Development,* Vol. 1. 5th edition, Wiley, New York.

Baruah T., D. K. Adak and P. Bharati. 2012. 'An appraisal of health of the tribes in Assam'. In T. Baruah (Ed): *People of Contemporary North-East India.* pp. 49-58. Pratisruti Publication, Guwahati.

Bharati S., D. Mukherjee, M. Pal, S. Som, D.K. Adak, T.S. Vasulu and P. Bharati. 2010. 'Influence of ethnicity, geography and climate on the variation of stature among Indian populations'. *Coll. Antropol.* 34: 1207-1213.

Bharati S., M. Pal, and P. Bharati. 2008. 'Determinants of nutritional status of preschool children in India'. *Journal of Biosocial Science,* 40: 801-814.

Bharati S., M. Pal, D.K. Adak and P. Bharati. 2012. 'Ideology of son preference in North-East India'. In T. Baruah (Ed): *People of Contemporary North-East India*. pp. 84-97. Pratisruti Publication, Guwahati.

Evelth P.B. and J.M. Tanner. 1990. *Worldwide Variation in Human Growth*. 2nd edition, Cambridge University Press, Cambridge.

National Family Health Survey (NFHS 3). 2005. India. IIPS, Mumbai.

Shome S., M. Pal, D.K. Adak and P. Bharati. 2012. 'Adult body mass index (BMI) in the North East States of India'. pp. 9-25. In T. Baruah (Ed): *People of Contemporary North-East India*. Pratisruti Publication, Guwahati.

Som S., S. Ulijaszek, M. Pal, S. Bharati and P. Bharati. 2014. 'Variation in height and BMI of adult Indians'. *Journal of Biosocial Science*, 46: 47-65.

11
Adolescent Nutrition Assessment with Special Reference to North East India

– *Nitish Mondal*

Introduction

The prevalence of under nutrition is considered to be the major public health concern in many developing countries that increases premature mortalities and morbidities in population. The nutritional scenarios of these countries have been changed radically during past two decades due to changes in dietary habits, socio-economic development, lifestyle modification and risks of non-communicable diseases. Currently, India is undergoing a rapid transition in economic, demographic, epidemiologic, nutrition, and sociological fronts (Popkin, 2002; Subramanian *et al.*, 2007; Kapil and Sachdev, 2012). There is an evidence of decline in the prevalence of under nutrition with an increase of overweight-obesity and also associated non-communicable diseases (NCDs), thereby simultaneously increase the occurrence of the double burden of malnutrition (Rao, 2001; Popkin, 2002; Subramanian *et al.*, 2007; Kapil and Sachdev, 2012). Extreme poverty is mainly concentrated in rural areas, while economic growths, have been dynamic in urban areas (Ramachandran, 2007; Subramanian *et al.*, 2007; Antony and Laxmaiah, 2008), but due to immense population size, socio-economic disparities, illiteracy and inadequate access to healthcare facilities, the prevalence of under nutrition is very high in population residing in the rural and sub-urban regions in India (Rao, 2001; Subramanian *et al.*, 2007; NFHS-III, 2005-06; Parasuraman *et al.*, 2009). Moreover, India has shown the highest occurrence of childhood under nutrition in the world (Bamji, 2003), and it has been estimated that more than half of Indian children are undernourished (Measham and Chatterjee, 1999). The nutritional status and health are considered to be the crucial and interlinked indicators of human development that interact with demographic and socio-economic variables in important ways.

The World Health Organisation (WHO) believes that the ultimate objective of nutritional assessment is the improvement of human health (WHO, 1995). Currently, the national policy responses to tackling under nutrition are still primarily restricted to under-nutrition determination in Indian populations (Measham and Chatterjee 1999; Rao, 2001; Kapil and Sachdev, 2012). Several nutritional investigations have reported that the prevalence of under nutrition is still a serious public health concern in Indian populations especially among children and adolescents (e.g., Bose *et al.*, 2007; Medhi *et al.*, 2006; 2007; Mondal and Sen, 2010 a, 2010b; Sen and Mondal, 2012).

Importance in Adolescent Nutrition

The adolescent period is a very important stage in the human lifespan, characterised by an exceptionally rapid growth rate and transition period between childhood to adulthood (e.g., 10-19 years) (WHO, 1995; Bogin, 1999; Parasuraman *et al.*, 2009). Currently, it is estimated that adolescent contributes to the 'Largest ever generation of human history' (1.20 billion) of the total world population and significantly belongs to the largest population cohort of 21.4 per cent individuals aged 10-19 years in India (MHRD, 2000). Furthermore, a very high proportion of adolescent girls get married (28.0 per cent) at an early age of (15-19 years), even before completing their physical growth and at least a quarter of them conceive early (Venkaiah *et al.*, 2002). Recent National Survey data (NFHS-III) showed that a total of 44.5 per cent of women aged 20-24 years were married before age 18 years, 22.6 per cent were married before age of 16 years, and 2.6 per cent were married before age of 13 years in India adolescents (Raj *et al.*, 2009). The nutritional status of the adolescent girls, the future mothers, bear special significance as they contribute significantly to the nutritional status of the population. Moreover, a large proportion of the growing children and adolescents in the developing countries are deprived of appropriate nutrition on account of their poor socio-economic status, ignorance and lack of healthcare and promotional facilities that leads to prolong nutritional deprivation and growth retardation (WHO, 1995; Measham and Chatterjee, 1999; Antony and Laxmaiah, 2008). The existing National data (NFHS-II and III) reveals that very high proportion (56.0 per cent) of the adolescents' women (aged 15-24 years) were suffering from anaemia in India (Parasuraman *et al.*, 2009; Bharati *et al.*, 2012). Therefore, the role of the nutritional assessment investigation should emphasise to identifying the actual magnitude of under-nutrition and their relative risks in population in order to establish appropriate intervention and surveillance programme. Many of the physical and psychological changes that occur are closely related to nutritional well being of adolescents. However, this group has received less importance related to nutritional assessment and promotion to health situation in India. However, a large number of literature review has suggested that the majority of adolescents was suffering from different grades of under-nutrition in India (Singh and Mishra, 2001; Venkaiah *et al.*, 2002; Rao *et al.*, 2006; Deshmukh *et al.*, 2006; Medhi *et al.*, 2006; 2007; Das *et al.*, 2007; Mondal and Sen, 2010b; Banerjee *et al.*, 2011; Singh and Mondal, 2013; Basu *et al.*, 2013).

Anthropometric Assessment of Adolescent Nutrition Status

Anthropometry has become a widely used an easy, non-invasive and inexpensive practical technique of assessing the size and proportion of the human body and nutrition status in clinical and epidemiological studies. The prevalence of under-nutrition among children and adolescents are generally assessed (WHO, 1995, 2007; Nandy *et al.*, 2005; Cole *et al.*, 2007) by using conventional anthropometric indices of stunting (height-for-age), underweight (weight-for-age), wasting (weight-for-height), thinness (Body Mass Index or BMI–for-age) and skin fold-for-age (e.g., triceps and sub-scapular). However, these conventional anthropometric indices (e.g., stunting, underweight and wasting) are grossly underestimate the actual magnitude of under-nutrition in population (Nandy *et al.*, 2005; Sen and Mondal, 2012). The BMI as measured by weight in kilogram (kg) divided by height in meter square (m^2) is a derived surrogate anthropometric measure that has been extensively utilised to determine the prevalence of chronic energy deficiency (CED) and / or overweight-obesity (in adults) and the thinness (e.g., children and adolescents; WHO, 1995, 2007; Cole *et al.*, 2007). The prevalence of stunting is generally assessed below the third percentile or -2SD of the National Centre for Health Statistics (NCHS/WHO, 1983) and BMI-for-age used to assess the thinness or CED status assessment among adolescence (WHO, 1995). Furthermore, the BMI is also adjusted for age to account for changes due to growth and expressed as z-scores (WHO, 1995, 2007). The World Health Organisation has recommended cut-offs are the <5th and the >85th percentile of the Nutritional Health and Nutrition Examination Survey (NHANES) references to assess the thinness and overweight respectively (WHO, 1995). The age and sex specific >85th and >95th percentiles of BMI values have been used as International Standard cut-offs to define overweight and obesity, respectively (Must *et al.,* 1991a; de Onis *et al.,* 2001; WHO, 1995, 2007), whereas an alternative International cut-off of overweight and obesity for children and adolescents (aged 2-18 years) corresponding to an adult BMI of >25.0 kg/m^2 and >30.0 kg/m^2 have also been proposed respectively (Cole *et al.,* 2000). Very recently, International age and sex specific cut-off have also been proposed in order to facilitate the measure of fatness and nutritional status in terms of thinness among children and adolescents for the world population aged 2-18 years (Cole *et al.,* 2007). A detail of the anthropometric measures and cut-off used to determine the adolescent nutrition status is described in the Table 11.1.

Table 11.1: Anthropometric indices and references used to assess adolescent nutrition

Category	*Indices*	*Cut-offs*	*Reference*
Undernutrition	Stunting (low height-for-age)	<3rd percentile or <-2SD	NCHS, 1983; WHO, 2007
		<5th percentile	CDC, 2000
	Thinness (low BMI-for-age)	<5th percentile or <-2SD	WHO, 1995; 2007
		<BMI18.50kg/m^2	Cole *et al.*, 2007, IASO, 2000
Overweight	BMI-for-age	>85 percentile or >BMI 25 kg/m^2	Must *et al.*, 1991a; WHO, 1995
		>85 percentile	Cole *et al.*, 2000
		= 85th and < 95th	CDC, 2000
		>25.00 kg/m^2	IASO, 2010
Obesity	BMI-for-age	>95th percentile or >BMI 30 kg/m^2	Must *et al.*, 1991a; WHO, 1995
		>90th percentile	Cole *et al.*, 2000

		=95th percentile	CDC, 2000
		>30.00 kg/m^2	IASO, 2010
	Triceps-for-age	>90th percentile	Must *et al.*, 1991b; WHO, 1995
	Sub-scapular-for-age	>90th percentile	

Stunting Prevalence

Physical growth pattern in terms of weight and height is considered as an important parameter reflecting the growth and development in a population. The assessment of stunting is usually considered as significant indicator of the health and overall nutritional status of adolescents. The prevalence of stunting due to poor chronic conditions is very common in rural and sub-urban population in India including north eastern region (Venkaiah *et al.*, 2002; Das and Biswas, 2005; Deshmukh *et al.*, 2006; Medhi *et al.*, 2006, 2007; Das *et al.*, 2007; Mondal and Sen, 2010a, 2010b; Banerjee *et al.*, 2011; Sil *et al.*, 2011). Studies on growth patterns have reflected that poor living conditions and environmental variations influence on the physical growth patterns which manifested as linear growth retardation. The growth retardation in height manifested as stunting among the adolescents probably due to long term chronic nutritional deprivation during the early ages (WHO, 1995; Medhi *et al.*, 2007; Mondal and Sen, 2010b). Stunting is an indicator of chronic under-nutrition, the result of prolonged food and nutritional deprivation and/or disease or illness. This index reflects distinct biological processes and is associated with environmental factors, thus their use is necessary for nutritional status and determining appropriate nutritional intervention (WHO, 1995). The prevalence of stunting among girls was 45.0 per cent and that among boys was 20.0 per cent, with an average of 32.5 per cent in both sexes (WHO, 1998). Medhi *et al.*, (2007) reported that 50.1 per cent (in boys) and 43.1 per cent (in girls) were suffering from stunting in Dibrugarh, Assam. Furthermore, the results showed the mean height of tea garden adolescents worker were found to be similar to that of adolescent girls mentioned in National Family Health Survey (NFHS-II) but lower than the adolescents of other States of India (Medhi *et al.*, 2007). The data also indicate that a total of 23.1 per cent of the adolescents (aged 15-19 years) were found to have height <145.0

cm (NFHS-II, 2000). A high prevalence of stunting (52.5 per cent) has also been documented from West Bengal by Das *et al.* (2007). Deshmukh *et al.* (2006) also reported a high prevalence of stunting (50.7 per cent) from rural Wardha. Utilising the data from the National Nutrition Monitoring Bureau (NNMB), Venkaiah *et al.* (2002) reported about 39.0 per cent of the rural adolescents was found to be stunted. A Similar finding (38.5 per cent) also have been reported by Anand *et al.* (1999) from North India. Malhotra and Passi (2007) reported the lower prevalence of stunting to be 29.7 per cent among rural adolescent. Mondal and Sen (2010b) reported the prevalence of stunting was higher among girls (50.1 per cent) than boys (43.1 per cent). Sil *et al.* (2011) reported the prevalence moderate level of stunting (23.7 per cent) among the rural tribal children and adolescents in Tripura State of North East India (Fig. 10.1). A similar study of early adolescents (9-14 years) working in tea garden in Dibrugarh, Assam, North East India (Medhi *et al.*, 2006) showed a very high proportion (53.6 per cent) were suffering from stunting among boys (51.8 per cent) and girls (56.0 per cent). The prevalence of stunting is considered the long-term cumulative health and nutritional inadequacy (WHO, 1995) that considered as a legacy of nutritional deprivation during childhood among Indian adolescents (Medhi *et al.*, 2007; Mondal and Sen, 2010b). It is generally accepted fact that mean height and weight of the Indian adolescence were found mostly <50th percentile as compared to the reference population including North East, India (Medhi *et al.*, 2007; Mondal and Sen, 2010b; Basu *et al.*, 2013). The existing data suggested the prevalence of stunting was found to be greater among girls than boys among adolescent in North East India (Medhi *et al.*, 2006; 2007, Sil *et al.*, 2011). The literature review reveals the prevalence of stunting was found to be very serious (>40.0 per cent; WHO, 1995) and reflects prolonged chronic nutritional deprivation among adolescents including North East India (Rao *et al.*, 2006; Medhi *et al.*, 2006; 2007; Prashant and Shaw, 2009; Madot *et al.*, 2009; Mondal and Sen, 2010b ; Fig. 11.1).

Thinness Prevalence

The World Health Organisation (1995) has recommended the use of thinness as best surrogate anthropometric indicator to determine the prevalence of chronic under-nutrition (CED). It has also been observed in case of thinness that adolescent boys were more affected than adolescent girls (59.4 per cent versus 41.3 per cent) in Assam (Medhi *et al.*, 2007). Similarly, the results of the NFHS-II reported that a considerable proportion (28.7 per cent) of Assam's adolescent girls (aged 15-19 years) was suffering from CED (BMI<18.59 kg/m^2; NFHS-II). Rao *et al.* (2006) utilising the NNMB data reported a similar trend regarding the prevalence of thinness among tribal adolescent boys (63.0 per cent) and girls (42.0 per cent) from nine Indian States. In another study, Venkaiah *et al.* (2002) also reported the prevalence of thinness to be higher in boys (53.1 per cent) than in girls (39.5 per cent). However, Anand *et al.* (1999) reported the prevalence of stunting in the 12-18 years age group to be 37.2 per cent (in girls) and 41.00 per cent (in boys) with an overall prevalence of 38.50 per cent. Low prevalence thinness among adolescent girls (30.60 per cent) has also been reported from North India (Malhotra and Passi, 2007). It is however, generally accepted that there is a high prevalence of thinness among Indian communities with more than 50.0 per cent of adolescents being affected (Das and Biswas, 2005; Deshmukh *et al.*, 2006; Medhi *et al.*, 2007; Parasuraman *et al.*, 2009; Shivaramakrishna *et al.*, 2011). The poor nutritional status of the adolescents, particularly girls have important implications in terms of physical work capacity and adverse reproductive outcomes (WHO, 1995; Mondal and Sen, 2010b). Mondal and Sen (2010b) reported the prevalence of thinness was greater among boys (52.1 per cent) than girls (32.0 per cent) among rural adolescent of Darjeeling, West Bengal. A similar study of early adolescents (9-14 years) working in tea garden in Dibrugarh, Assam, North East India showed a very high proportion (53.9 per cent) were suffering from thinness among boys (51.8 per cent) and girls (56.7 per cent; Medhi *et al.*, 2006). Khongsdier *et al.*, (2005) reported the moderate prevalence of thinness among the Khynriam Khasi (8.56 per cent), War Khasi (27.08 per cent) in Meghalaya and Hmar (12.77 per cent) in Mizoram (adolescents aged 9-16 years) of North East India. Sil *et al.* (2011) reported a moderate (23.7 per cent) prevalence of thinness among the tribal children and adolescents of Tripura, North East India (Fig. 11.1). Very recent study by Singh and Mondal (2013) reported high (25.9 per cent) prevalence of thinness among the tribal Sonowal Kachari boys (28.1 per cent) and girls (23.9 per cent) using recently developed thinness reference of Cole *et al.* (2007). The existing literatures are suggested that the magnitude of thinness or CED prevalence was found to be greater among boys than the girls in Indian adolescents including North East India (Khongsdier *et al.*, 2005; Medhi *et al.*, 2007; Mondal and Sen, 2010b). The greater prevalence of CED among boys than girls indicative of 'Biological fragility' of males as compared to female counterparts (Kraemer, 2000; Khongsdier *et al.*, 2005). The recent National data (NFHS-III, 2005-06) suggested that more than half (58.0 per cent) of adolescent boys and 47.0 per cent of adolescent girls are suffering from thinness compared with 36.0 per cent of men and 41.0 per cent of women age 20-24 among Indian adolescents (Parasuraman *et al.*, 2009). When State wise prevalence of thinness was taken into consideration, the prevalence was found to be lower (<23.0 per cent) in Meghalaya, Mizoram, Manipur, Arunachal Pradesh and Nagaland as compared with the serious situations existed in Assam (men 44.0 per cent and women 40.0 per cent) and Tripura (men 55.0 per cent; women 41.0 per cent) of North East India (NFHS-III: 2005-06; Parasuraman *et al.*, 2009).

Overweight-Obesity Prevalence

The prevalence of overweight and obesity in the developing countries including South-east of Asia have been tripled in last 25 years due to economic development, adoption of western lifestyle and reduction in physical activity. It is evident that the Indian populations are passing through major demographic, socio-economic and nutritional transition phase, where subsistence conditions are being replaced by plentiful food, reduced physical work (Popkin, 2002; Kapil and Sachdev, 2012) and therefore, an understanding of the changing nutritional scenario reflected as overweight and obesity among children, adolescents and adults (Subramanian *et al.*, 2007; Kapil and Sachdev, 2012). Studies have already reported the lower prevalence of overweight and obesity among different Indian populations among adolescents and the magnitudes are even more frequent in higher socio-economic groups and population groups residing in urban than rural inhabitants (de Onis *et al.*, 2001; Chhatwal *et al.*, 2004; Sidhu *et al.*, 2006; Jain *et al.*, 2010; Goyal *et al.*, 2010, 2011; Kapil *et al.*, 2011; Ghosh *et al.*, 2011). Recent data suggested that very marginal segments of the National population (NFHS-III, 2005-06) are found to be overweight in 15-19 years (men 2.4 per cent; women 1.7 per cent) and 20-24 years (men 5.9 per cent; women 4.7 per cent; Parasuraman *et al.*, 2009). Low prevalence of overweight were also reported among rural adolescents from Assam (0.30 per cent ; Medhi *et al.*, 2007) and rural Wardha (2.00 per cent; Deshmukh *et al.*, 2006), rural Darjeeling of West Bengal (0.30 per cent; Mondal and Sen, 2010b), tribal children of Tripura (0.80 per cent ; Sil *et al.*, 2011) and Mishing of Assam, North East India (1.95 per cent; Singh *et al.*, 2001). A marginally higher prevalence of overweight (5.00 per cent) has been reported in Bengali adolescents (de Onis *et al.*, 2001). Goyal *et al.* (2010) reported the prevalence of overweight was found to be 14.3 per cent (in boys) and 9.2 per cent (in girls) among urban adolescents of Ahmadabad. Jain *et al.* (2010) have reported the prevalence of overweight and obesity was found to be 19.7 per cent and 5.3 per cent (in girls) and 18.36 per cent and 10.82 per cent (in boys) among the affluent adolescents of Meerut. A relatively greater prevalence of overweight and obesity have also reported among girls than boys belongs to the tribal Khasi adolescents (aged 11-17 years) of Meghalaya, North East India (Basu *et al.*, 2013). Therefore, it is evident from the existing literature that the prevalence of overweight and obesity is relatively recent phenomena and found less prevalent than the magnitude of stunting and thinness among the Indian adolescent including North East India.

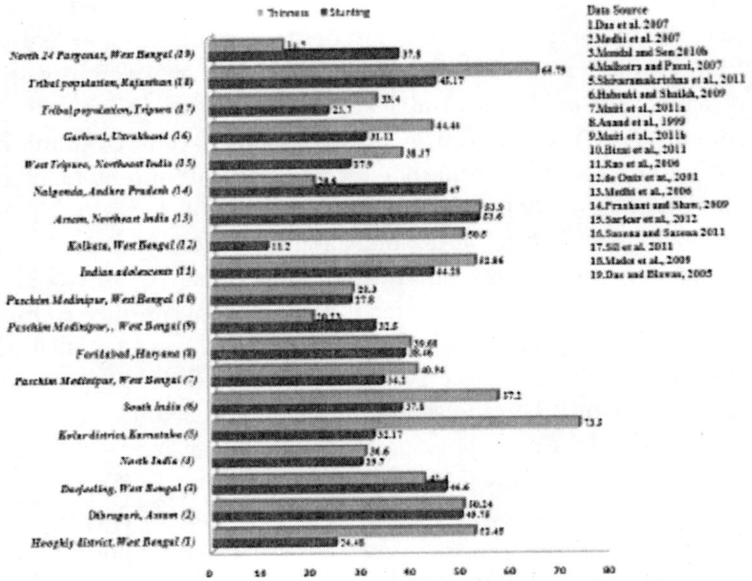

Figure 11.1: **Prevalence of stunting (low height-for-age) and thinness (low BMI-for-age) among Indian adolescents**

Adolescent Nutritional Status

The nutritional studies have typically used the model of determinants of socio-economic status, poverty, heavy workload and lesser access to food in developing countries including India (Rao *et al.,* 2006; Mondal and Sen, 2010b). Generally, the adverse socio-economic conditions have significant influences along with the inadequate dietary consumption probably delay the physical developmental render to meet their optimal growth potential among Indian adolescents (Venkaiah *et al.,* 2002; Rao *et al.,* 2006; Medhi *et al.,* 2007). Studies have highlighted the extent of under nutrition was found to be greater among the lower as compared to higher socio-economic groups (Deshmukh *et al.,* 2006; Medhi *et al.,* 2007). It has been suggested that undernourished individuals showed a minimal catch up growth, if they continued to reside in the same environment that give rise to stunting in the early childhood, although this can be reduced if the environment improves or improvements in living conditions by introducing food supplementation (WHO, 1995; Bogin, 1999). Existing National data suggested that Assam, Arunachal Pradesh, Meghalaya and

Tripura have high prevalence (>40.0 per cent) of childhood under-nutrition (e.g., stunting) amongst north-eastern States of India (NFHS-III). It is to be mentioned that growth before adolescence is more sensitive to environmental factors, whereas growth during adolescence is a result of the complex interaction between biological and environmental factors (WHO, 1995; Bogin, 1999; Khongsdier *et al.*, 2005; Medhi *et al.*, 2007). Moreover, adolescence is a time where the lifestyle and food habits are influenced by socio-cultural factors resulting in nutrient intake imbalance and inadequacy can result in delayed physical development and maturation and can arrest or slows linear growth. Therefore, the consumption of inadequate quality of diets and nutrients plays very vital role in the manifestation of under-nutrition (e.g., stunting and thinness) among early stages and adolescents (Venkaiah *et al.*, 2002; Deshmukh *et al.*, 2006; Rao *et al.*, 2006; Malhotra and Passi, 2007; Kawade, 2012; Jacob and Nair, 2012). It is evident that the female adolescents in rural areas are more vulnerable than the urban counterparts, due to the inadequate food intake, poor healthcare promotional facilities and socio-economic inconvenience among population propagate vicious cycle of under-nutrition (Rao, 2001; Rao *et al.*, 2006; Medhi *et al.*, 2007; Mondal and Sen, 2010; Maiti *et. al.*, 2011). In almost all Indian populations, boys have better access to food and basic amenities than girls and there is found to be a pronounced preference for the male child (Kishor, 1993). Several studies have reported discrimination in diet, basic amenities, education and health care against the girl child in India (Devendra, 1995; Borooah, 2004; Khongsdier *et al.*, 2005) and there is found to be a pronounced preference for male child in Indian societies (Kishor 1993; Mishra *et al.*, 2004). These socio-cultural difference leads to nutritional variation across the populations in early age groups and adolescent populations including North East India.

Recommendation

The weight and height increases with ages are consistent with distinct biological process in well nourished individual subjects but the discussion above reveals a poor growth pattern as manifested in greater prevalence of stunting and thinness in Indian adolescents including north eastern India. This poor growth pattern among adolescents will be apparent as multi-dimensional adverse physical and social condition leads to delay in the onset of puberty and poor work capacity in adulthood (WHO, 1995; Strickland, 2002). Poor socio-economic status, early marriage, high prevalence of anaemia and under-nutrition compound the consequent effect to reduce the reproductive, physical, and mental capacities of adolescent girls and continue to result in low birth weights and foetal loss in adolescents including North East India. Even during late adolescence, the physiques continue to mature, with most still putting on height (Bogin, 1999), adequate nutrition supply in the form of a balanced diet rich in nutrients (e.g., iron) is key to improve such critical situations (Parasuraman *et al.*, 2009; Bharati *et al.*, 2013). The existing literature reveals a significant proportion of Indian adolescents found to have iron deficiency and was suffering from anaemia (Rao, 2001; Rao *et al.*, 2006; Parasuraman *et al.*, 2009). The National Sample Survey (NFHS-III) data confirmed (Parasuraman *et al.*, 2009) that prevalence of anaemia among the adolescent (15-24 years) is very critical in the north-eastern States of Assam (68.0 per cent), Sikkim (64.0 per cent), Tripura (61.0 per cent), Arunachal Pradesh (52.0 per cent) and Meghalaya (48.0 per cent). Moreover, undernourished adolescents are unlikely to contribute to full potential for the economic growth of the country, but their subsequent manifestation related can threaten the vicious cycle of adverse health condition and nutrition status of next generation. It is generally accepted that with the improvement of health services, food availability and nutrition awareness that new generation would be the taller and heavier than their predecessor. Similarly, the radical shifts in diet pattern especially processed and fast foods habits and reduced physical activity responsible for increased incidence of overweight-obesity thereby increase the NCDs in sub-urban and urban population in India.

The existing data suggested significant proportion of Indian adolescents found to be undernourished including north-eastern regions (e.g., Khongsdier *et al.*, 2005; Medhi *et al.*, 2006, 2007; Sil *et al.*, 2011; Singh and Mondal, 2013). The literature review reveals significant paucity of literature particularly in nutrition assessment issues of adolescent nutrition, but the national data (NFHS-II and III) reported high prevalence of undernourishment observed among adolescents and young adults (aged 20-24 years) in North East India. Therefore, the adolescents should be recognised as priority target group an integral part of health promotion and optimal nutrition through balanced diet and nutrient supplementation should be promoted in conjunction with healthy eating habits and physical activity. There is no easy solution to overcoming these confounding problems, but successful strategies need to incorporate increased dependence on the local resources through integrative approach across the States including North East India. A comprehensive multi-disciplinary approach in terms of dietary evaluation, biochemical analysis, nutritional assessment, medical diagnosis, psychological and cultural evaluation for effective understanding of such issues of double burden of malnutrition among Indian adolescents including North East India. Intervention programme mention the physical growth and health related issues should be implemented to ameliorate the nutritional status and achieve optimum growth potential. These intervention programmes can be launched in the early age group children and adolescents to break the vicious cycle of under-nutrition in Indian as well as in north-eastern populations. The programmes that need to be initiated are briefly stated below :

1. Multi-disciplinary health-service offering varied healthcare and promotional service to the early age groups and adolescents should be organised at regular intervals, especially in the rural and sub-urban regions. These services should include physician, dieticians and nutritionists and be able to provide regular and free medical diagnosis, medicines and nutrition supplements (e.g., iron).
2. The current research should highlight the need for re-examining existing healthcare programmes, identifying limitations, ensuring logistics and feasibility rather than proposing new programmes among target groups especially children, adolescents and early pregnant women.
3. Efforts should be made to disseminate knowledge related to nutritional requirements during early ages and adolescents under the community based reach out health services. Creating nutritional and health related awareness will help to improve the better quality of life among early stages and adolescents in India.

References

Anand, K., S. Kant, and S. K. Kapoor. 1999. 'Nutritional status of adolescent school children in rural North India'. *Indian Pediatr.* 36:810-815.

Antony, G.M., and A. Laxmaiah. 2008. 'Human development, poverty, health and nutrition situation in India'. *Indian J Med Res.* 128:198-205.

Bamji, M.S., 2003. 'Early nutrition and health–Indian perspective'. *Curr Sci.* 85:1137–1142.

Banerjee, S., A. Dias, R. Shinkre, and V. Patel. 2011. 'Under-nutrition among adolescents: A survey in five secondary schools in rural Goa'. *Natl Med J India.*24, 1:8-11.

Basu, D., I. Banerjee, D. Sun, M.S. Bartwal, and R.K. Neeta Devi. 2013. 'Cross-sectional reference values for BMI among Khasi tribal adolescents of Meghalaya, India'. *Anthrop Anz.* 70:179–191.

Bogin, B. 1999. *Patterns of Human Growth.* 2nd Edition. Cambridge: Cambridge University Press.

Borooah, V.K. 2004. 'Gender bias among children in India in their diet and immunisation against disease'. *Soc. Sci. Med.* 58:1719–1731.

Bose, K., S. Biswas, S. Bisai, S. Ganguli, A. Khatun, A. Mukhopadhyay, and M. Bhadra. 2007. 'Stunting, underweight and wasting among Integrated Child Development Services (ICDS) scheme children aged 3-5 years of Chapra, Nadia District, West Bengal, India'. *Matern Child Nutr.* 3:216-221.

Chhatwal, J., M. Verma and S. K. Riar. 2004. 'Obesity among pre-adolescent and adolescents of a developing country (India)'. *Asia. Pac. J. Clin. Nutr.* 13:231-235.

Cole, T.J., M.C. Bellizzi, K. M. Flegal, and W. H. Dietz. 2000. 'Establishing a standard definition for child overweight and obesity worldwide: International survey'. *British Medical Journal.* 320:1240–3.

Cole, T.Z., K.M. Flegal, D. Nicholls and A. A. Jackson. 2007. 'Body mass index cut offs to define thinness in children and adolescents: International survey'. *British Medical Journal.* 335:194.

Das, D.K., and R. Biswas. 2005. 'Nutritional status of adolescent girls in a rural area of North 24 Parganas district, West Bengal'. *Indian J Public Health*.49, 1:18-21.

Das, P., S.K. Ray, G.K. Joardar and S. Dasgupta. 2007. 'Nutritional profiles of adolescents in a rural community of Hooghly district in West Bengal'. *Indian J Public Health*. 51:120-1.

de Onis M., P. Dasgupta, S. Saha, D. Sengupta, and M. Blossner. 2001. 'The National Center for Health Statistics reference and the growth of Indian adolescent boys'. *Am J Clin Nutr*. 74: 248-53.

Deshmukh P.R., S.S. Gupta, M.S. Bharambe, A.R. Dongre, C. Maliye, S. Kaur and B. S. Garg. 2006. 'Nutritional status of adolescents in rural Wardha'. *Indian J Pediatr*. 73:139-41.

Devendra K., 1995. 'Girl child in rural India'. *Soc Change*. 25:189–196.

Ghosh A., 2011. 'Rural-urban comparison in prevalence of overweight and obesity among children and adolescents of Asian Indian origin'. *Asia Pac J Public Health*. 23:928-35.

Ghosh A., 2011. Rural-urban comparison in prevalence of overweight and obesity among children and adolescents of Asian Indian origin. *Asia Pac J Public Health*. 23, 6:928-35. doi: 10.1177/1010539511428697.

Goyal J. P., N. Kumar, I. Parmar, V.B. Shah, and B. Patel. 2011. 'Determinants of overweight and obesity in affluent adolescent in Surat City, South Gujarat region, India'. *Indian J Community Med*. 36:296-300.

Goyal R.K.,V.N. Shah, B.D. Saboo, S.R. Phatak, N.N. Shah, M. C. Gohel, P. B. Raval and S. S. Patel. 2010. 'Prevalence of overweight and obesity in Indian adolescent school going children: Its relationship with socio-economic status and associated lifestyle factors'. *J Assoc Physicians India*. 58:151-158.

International Association of Study of Obesity (IASO). 2010. *Extended International (IOTF) Body Mass Index Cut-Offs for Thinness, Overweight and Obesity in Children*. http://www.iaso.org/resources/aboutobesity/child-obesity/newchildcutoffs.

International Institute for Population Sciences (IIPS) and Macro International. [Online] 2007; *National Family Health Survey (NFHS-III), India*, Vol.1. pp.192-222. Available from: http://www.nfhsindia.org [Last cited on 2007].

International Institute for Population Sciences (IIPS) *National Family Health Survey (NFHS-II)-, India* 1998-1999. India, IIPS, Mumbai, 2000.

Jacob J.A., and M. K. Nair. 2012. 'Protein and micronutrient supplementation in complementing pubertal growth'. *Indian J Pediatr*. 79 Suppl. 1:S84-91.

Jain S., B. Pant, H. Chopra and R. Tiwari. 2010. 'Obesity among adolescents of affluent public schools in Meerut'. *Indian J Public Health*. 54:158-60.

Kapil U., and H. P. Sachdev. 2012. 'Urgent need to orient public health response to rapid nutrition transition'. *Indian J Community Med*. 37, 4:207-10.

Kapil U., P. Singh, P. Pathak and S. N. Dwivedi. 2001. 'Prevalence of obesity amongst affluent adolescent school children'. *Indian Pediatr* 39:449–52.

Kawade R.2012. 'Zinc status and its association with the health of adolescents: A review of studies in India'. *Glob Health Action*. 5:7353.

Khongsdier R., R. Varte and N. Mukherjee.2005. 'Excess male chronic energy deficiency among adolescents: A cross-sectional study in the context of patrilineal and matrilineal societies in Northeast India'. *Eur J Clin Nutr*. 59:1007–1014.

Kishor, S. 1993. 'May God give sons to all: Gender and child mortality in India'. *Am Sociol Rev*. 58:247–265.

Kraemer, S .2000. 'The fragile male'. *Br. Med. J.* 321, 1609–1612.

Kuczmarski, R.J., C. L. Ogden, S. S. Guo, *et al*., 2002. 'CDC growth charts for the United States: Methods and development'. National Center for Health Statistics. *Vital Health Stat*. 11: 246.

Maiti S., D. De, K. Chatterjee, K. Jana, D. Ghosh, and S. Paul. 2011. 'Prevalence of stunting and thinness among early adolescent school girls of Paschim Medinipur district, West Bengal'. *Int J Biol Med Res*. 2: 781-783.

Malhotra A, and S. J. Passi. 2007. 'Diet quality and nutritional status of rural adolescent girl beneficiaries of ICDS in north India'. *Asia Pac J Clin Nutr*. 16, Suppl 1:8-16.

Mandot, S., D. Mandot and J. K. Sonesh.2009. 'Nutritional status of tribal (Garasia) school children of Sirohi district, Rajasthan'. *Indian Pediatr*.46, 5:437-8.

Measham A.R,, and M. Chatterjee. 1999. *Wasting Away: The Crisis of Malnutrition in India*. Washington DC: The World Bank.

Medhi G.K, N. C. Hazarika and J. Mahanta. 2007. 'Nutritional status of adolescents among tea garden workers'. *Indian J Pediatr*. 74:343-7.

Medhi G.K., A. Barua and J. Mahanta. 2006. 'Growth and nutritional status of school age children (6-14 Years) of Tea garden worker of Assam'. *J Hum Ecol*. 19:83-85.

Ministry of Human Resource Development, Department of Youth and Social Affairs – *National Youth Policy, 2000*. Government of India, New Delhi, 2000.

Mishra, V., T. K. Roy and R. D. Retherford. 2004. 'Sex differences in childhood feeding, health care, and nutritional status in India'. *Popul. Dev. Rev*. 30, 269–275.

Mondal N, and J. Sen. 2010a. 'Prevalence of undernutrition among children (5-12 years) belonging to three communities residing in a similar habitat in North Bengal, India'. *Ann Hum Biol*. 37:198-216.

Mondal N., and J. Sen. 2010b. 'Assessment of nutritional status among rural adolescents of Darjeeling district, West Bengal, India using anthropometry'. *Italian Journal of Public Health*. 7:54-61.

Must A., G. E. Dallal and W. H. Dietz. 1991a. 'Reference data for obesity: 85th and 95th percentiles of body mass index (wt/ht^2) - A correction'. *American Journal of Clinical Nutrition*, 54:773.

Must A., G. E. Dallal and W. H. Dietz.1991b. 'Reference data for obesity: 85th and 95th percentiles of body mass index (wt/ht^2) and triceps skinfold thickness'. *American Journal of Clinical Nutrition*, 53:839-846.

Nandy S., M. Irving, D. Gordon, S. V. Subramanian and G. D. Smith. 2005. 'Poverty, child undernutrition and morbidity: New evidence from India'. *Bull World Health Organ*. 83:210–16.

Parasuraman S., S. Kishor, S. K. Singh, and Y. Vaidehi. 2005-2006. *A Profile of Youth in India. National Family Health Survey (NFHS-3), India, 2005-06.* Mumbai: International Institute for Population Sciences; Calverton, Maryland, USA: ICF Macro, 2009.

Popkin B. M. 2002. 'The shift in stages of the nutrition transition in the developing world differs from past experiences!'. *Public Health Nutr.* 5, 1A:205-14.

Ramachandran, P. 2007. 'Poverty nutrition linkages'. *Indian J Med Res.* 126:249-61.

Rao K.M., A. Laxmaiah, K. Venkaiah, and G. N. Brahmam. 2006. 'Diet and nutritional status of adolescent tribal population in nine states of India'. *Asia Pac J Clin Nutr.* 15:64-71.

Rao, S. 2001. 'Nutritional status of the Indian population'. *J Bio Sci* 26: 481–489.

Sen J., and N. Mondal. 2012. 'Socio-economic and demographic factors affecting the Composite Index of Anthropometric Failure (CIAF)'. *Ann Hum Biol.* 39:129-36.

Shivaramakrishna, H. R., A. V. Deepa, and M. Sarithareddy. 2011. 'Nutritional status of adolescent girls in rural area of Kolar District -A cross-sectional study'. *Al. Ameen. J. Med. Sci.* 4, 3: 243 -246.

Sidhu, S., N. Kaur and R. Kaur. 2006. 'Overweight and obesity in affluent school children of Punjab'. *Ann Hum Biol.* 33:255-9.

Sil, S.K., S. R. Sarkar, S. Saha, and S. Roy. 2011. 'Assessment of nutritional status of rural tribal children in Tripura'. *Indian Pediatr.* 48,6:488-9.

Singh, J and N. Mondal, 2013. 'Assessment of nutritional status: A case of tribal children in Assam, Northeast India'. *Nepal J Pedtr. Soc.* 33:1-7.

Singh, N., and C.P. Mishra. 2001. 'Nutritional status of adolescent girls of a slum community of Varanasi'. *Indian J Public Health.* 45:128-34.

Strickland, S.S. 2002.'Functional consequences of adult malnutrition in developing countries: a review'. *J Physiol Anthropol.* 21:1-9.

Subramanian, S.V.; I. Kawachi; and G. D. Smith. 2007. 'Income inequality and the double burden of under and over-nutrition in India'. *J Epidemiol Community Health.* 61:802-9.

Venkaiah K., K. Damayanti, M. U. Nayakand and K. Vijayaraghavan. 2002. 'Diet and nutritional status of rural adolescents in India'. *Eur J Clin Nutr*. 56:1119-25.

World Health Organisation 2007. *WHO Child Growth Standards: Head Circumference- for-Age, Arm Circumference – for - Age, Triceps Skinfold -for-Age and Subscapular Skinfold – for - Age: Methods and Development.* Geneva, World Health Organisation, 2007.

World Health Organisation. 1983. *Measuring Change in Nutritional Status*. Geneva: World Health Organisation.

World Health Organisation. 1995. *Physical Status: The Use and Interpretation of Anthropometry*. Technical Report Series No. 854. World Health Organisation: Geneva

World Health Organisation. 1998. *Nutritional Status of Adolescents Girls and Women of Reproductive Age*. Report of Regional Consultation. Geneva: World Health Organisation,SEA, SEA/NUT/14, 1998.

12
Biparietal Diameter between Meitei and North-Eastern Thai Foetuses

– *Thokchom Ursa* and *S. Jibonkumar Singh*

Introduction

Measurements of the fetal biparietal diameter and head circumference are used in assessing fetal growth, dating pregnancies and in the detection of foetal abnormalities. (Chitty *et al.*, 1994). The study of biparietal diameter of foetus in obstetrics and anti-natal care with the help of ultrasound in utero has afforded modern obstetricians to know beforehand the relation between the size and shape of foetal head and pelvic brim of the expectant mother. It helps in forecasting whether spontaneous delivery through vagina would be possible or not thereby helping obstetricians to take right decision during labour and delivery (Mador *et al.*, 2011)

Biparietal diameter is the most important measurement of feotal head as its values are significantly superior to that of the average cranial circumference (Hadlock *et al.*, 1982). Apart from that several other applications in clinical practice which include determining the gestational age, estimation of foetal weight and evaluation of growth can be known through the study of biparietal diameter.

Biparietal diameter derived from one population cannot be used as the basis for decision making for different population as it leads to incorrect decision and mismanagement in anti-natal care. There are more than 25 different biparietal diameter charts available from all over the world (Shah *et al.*, 1991). Therefore, it is important that each population establish its own normal growth curve and nomogram of biparietal diameter. Keeping this view in mind, the present study aims at observing population-specific growth pattern of biparietal diameter of the Meitei foetuses. At the same time, it also aims at comparing the growth pattern of biparietal diameter of foetuses between the Meitei and north-eastern Thailand population, who basically belong to the same racial stock.

Materials and Methods

The present study is a cross-sectional one with prospective data collected from 535 pregnant Meitei women. The Meiteis are a major ethnic group from the Indian north eastern State of Manipur and belong to Mongoloid group of race. The obstetrics ultrasound examination is taken from the Regional Institute of Medical Sciences, Imphal from Meitei women with normal singleton pregnancy from 14 weeks of gestational age to 40 weeks. Gestational age is about 280 days calculated from the first day of last normal menstrual cycle (Dutta, 2004). Gestational age relates to age of the foetus and is counted as the time elapsed since 14 days prior to conception, assuming ovulation occurred on day 14th of the menstrual cycle. To confirm the actual gestational age of foetus, history of regular menstruation with exact date of the last menstrual period was taken. Complicated pregnancies like hypertension pre-eclampsia, diabetes mellitus, foetuses with congenital malformation, chromosomal abnormality or intra uterine growth restriction are excluded.

The biparietal diameter is the distance between parietal eminences on either side of skull and is the widest diameter of skull from side to side. Using scans at different angles, the transverse section will be recognised when the shape of foetal skull is ovoid and the middle echo from *flax cerebri* is interrupted by the *cavum septi pellucidi* and the *thalami*. When this plane is found, measurement is made from the outer table of the proximal skull to the inner table of distal skull (Palmer, 1995). The measurement of the biparietal diameter was undertaken with the help of Siemens and Samsung Ultrasound machine equipped with 3.5 mhz.

For comparison of BPD corresponding to different gestational age between the Meitei foetuses and the north eastern Thailand foetuses, the data given in Table 11.2 is from (Saksiriwuttho *et al.*, 2007).

Results

Table 12.1 and 12.2 show the Mean and Standard Deviation of the BPD of the Meitei and North Eastern Thailand Foetuses respectively. It is evident from Table 12.1 that among the Meitei foetuses, there is a progressive increase in the mean of biparietal diameter with increasing gestational age. In Table 12.2, except for the gestational age of 25 and 26 weeks, where there is a decrease of the mean of biparietal diameter, the mean of biparietal diameter among the North Eastern Thailand foetuses increases with increasing gestational age.

Table 12.1: Mean and Standard Deviation of BPD of the Meitei foetuses

G.A (in weeks)	*Sample Size*	*Mean (in mm)*	*S.D.*
14	13	26.52	2.706
15	7	29.814	1.282
16	7	34.76	1.801
17	17	37.672	1.740
18	12	41.025	1.616
19	18	44.64	1.867
20	20	47.807	3.942
21	29	51.158	2.721
22	22	55.386	3.217
23	12	57.325	3.384
24	18	59.933	1.175
25	11	62.936	1.927
26	16	65.906	1.205
27	10	68.69	1.631
28	11	73.245	3.537
29	16	74.49	2.190
30	22	77.054	2.577
31	23	77.804	2.400
32	24	81.095	2.803
33	25	83.328	2.578
34	34	85.638	2.465
35	44	87.613	2.320
36	45	89.528	1.398
37	36	91.944	1.372
38	29	94.062	1.538
39	10	95.6	1.915
40	4	97.1	0.574

Table 12.2: Mean and Standard Deviation of the BPD of the North Eastern Thai Foetuses

G.A (in weeks)	*Sample Size*	*Mean (in mm)*	*S.D.*
14	12	28.75	0.95
15	11	32.09	2.06
16	11	34.85	3.04
17	13	39.96	3.51
18	16	42.00	1.73
19	20	43.69	3.46
20	14	48.86	2.40
21	11	50.09	3.24
22	12	53.25	2.09
23	15	56.53	3.14
24	13	59.05	2.55
25	15	64.98	4.97
26	20	63.66	3.79
27	19	67.81	2.71
28	23	71.25	4.61
29	23	73.52	2.68
30	26	79.93	3.79
31	29	79.38	3.98
32	31	81.58	3.91
33	32	82.31	2.66
34	31	84.02	3.77
35	33	87.50	2.26
36	31	88.34	2.69
37	29	88.81	3.09
38	31	90.31	2.87
39	35	91.63	3.46
40	35	95.29	4.34

Table 12.3 shows the results of t and z test for testing whether

there is significant difference in the growth of biparietal diameter between two samples. It can be known from the table that in the second trimester of 14th to 24th week, significant difference in the biparietal diameter growth can be seen at the beginning of second trimester i.e., 14th and 17th week of gestation, where the north Eastern Thailand foetus shows having greater growth of biparietal diameter. But towards the end of second trimester i.e., at the 22nd week of gestation, the Meitei foetuses seem to draw alongside and overtake its north Eastern Thailand counterpart showing greater growth of biparietal diameter with significant difference. In the beginning of the third trimester, the Meitei foetuses show significantly greater growth of biparietal diameter at the 26th week of gestation, but this is overtaken by the north Eastern Thailand foetuses at the 31st week of gestation. Towards the term and ending of the third trimester i.e., 34th, 36th, 37th, 38th, 39th and 40th weeks of gestation, the Meitei fetuses show greater growth of biparietal diameter with significant difference.

Table 12.3: Calculation of *t* and *z* tests of mean of BPD of Meitei and North Eastern Thailand foetuses

G.A. (in wks)	*Mean[1] (mm)*	*S.D.[1] σ_1 (mm)*	*Mean[2] (mm)*	*S.D.[2] σ_2 (mm)*	*d.f.*	*Calculated t or z*	*Table t or z at 5 percent*	*Results*
14	26.52	2.706	28.75	0.95	15	2.680	1.753	Significant
15	29.814	1.282	32.09	2.06	15	2.723	1.753	Non significant
16	34.76	1.801	34.85	3.04	15	.074	1.753	Non significant
17	37.672	1.740	39.96	3.51	16	2.074	1.746	Significant
18	41.025	1.616	42.00	1.73	18	1.475	1.734	Non significant
19	44.64	1.867	43.69	3.46	29	1.137	1.699	Non significant
20	47.807	3.942	48.86	2.40	31	.047	1.695	Non significant
21	51.158	2.721	50.09	3.24	15	.093	1.753	Non significant
22	55.386	3.217	53.25	2.09	30	2.264	1.697	Significant

23	57.325	3.384	56.53	3.14	22	.601	1.717	Non significant
24	59.933	1.175	59.05	2.55	15	1.118	1.753	Non significant
25	62.936	1.927	64.98	4.97	19	.714	1.729	Non significant
26	65.906	1.205	63.66	3.79	23	2.432	1.714	Significant
27	68.69	1.631	67.81	2.71	26	1.049	1.706	Non significant
28	73.245	3.537	71.25	4.61	24	0.746	1.711	Non significant
29	74.49	2.190	73.52	2.68	35	1.206	1.695	Non significant
30	77.054	2.577	79.93	3.79	62	1.141	1.670	Non significant
31	77.804	2.400	79.38	3.98	47	1.732	1.679	Significant
32	81.095	2.803	81.58	3.91	52	.525	1.775	Non significant
33	83.328	2.578	82.31	2.66	52	1.432	1.775	Non significant
34	85.638	2.465	84.02	3.77		2.026	1.96	Significant
35	87.613	2.320	87.50	2.26		.214	1.96	Non significant
36	89.528	1.398	88.34	2.69		2.257	1.96	Significant
37	91.944	1.372	88.81	3.09	36	4.987	1.694	Significant
38	94.062	1.538	90.31	2.87	46	6.261	1.684	Significant
39	95.6	1.915	91.63	3.46	26	4.555	1.76	Significant
40	97.1	0.574	95.29	4.34	33	2.221	1.681	Significant

1. stands for the mean of bi parietal diameter of the Meitei foetuses.
2. stand for the mean of bi parietal diameter of the North Eastern Thailand foetuses.

* t- test is applied when one of the sample size or both are less than thirty.

** Z- test is applied when both the sample sizes are more than thirty.

*** For gestational age 34 and 35, *z*-test is applied where the degrees of freedom is not necessary.

Discussion

It is a known fact that the growth of foetus is related to genetically determined intrinsic growth potential and the environment in which it develops. By environment, it is related to the maternal dietary and nutrient intake and physical wellbeing. It also includes the maternal constrains caused by teratogens and other factors, which can affect the growth and development of foetus. A study of biparietal growth from different populations shows different findings. Campbell in 1971 established the mean biparietal diameter at 40th week was 98.1mm among the Caucasoid. Hadlock *et al.*, in 1984 gave estimated measurements by week's gestations in which the mean biparietal diameter at the 40th week was 94.8mm. Chan and Yeo in 1991, studied among the Chinese foetuses of Singapore and establish a mean of 92.89 mm at the 40th week. In India, study on the southern region by Rajan *et al.*, in 1991 and Karanth and Kumar in 1993 established mean biparietal diameter of 90.00 mm in the studies. Shah *et al.*, in 1991 in their study among the Indian women based in Bombay established a mean biparietal diameter of 91.4 mm at 40th week.

In the above studies, the mean of biparietal diameter at the 40th week were different for each population and the authors had argued that for the reference of growth and assessing of gestational age from foetus biparietal diameter should not be based from of a different population. Size and maturity of foetus varies from one population to another.

The Meiteis of Manipur, who are dominant caste group found settling in the north eastern part of India, racially belong to Mongoloid stock. Therefore, it is again questionable whether the monograms established for foetuses from mainland India, who are racially different can be applied to a Mongoloid population. On the other hand, though Meitei population of Manipur and Thai population of Thailand belong to same racial stock, seldom they share a common gene pool and does not stand any chance of being genetically very close. The maternal environment are not similar as they have different socio-economic and ethnic background. When the tests of significance are being applied to see the difference in growth of biparietal diameter in both samples, the mean values give varied results of being not significantly different and significantly different in the different gestational weeks until at the term or ending of the third trimester i.e., from 36th to 40th week, the Meitei foetuses show significantly higher mean values of biparietal diameter. The higher value may be an indicator of secular trend of growth inside utero as the mean value of 97.1 mm exceed even from the values found from Chinese and other Indian population studies. We cannot conclude that the north Eastern Thailand foetuses are having poor growth and development of the biparietal diameter.

Conclusion

In contemporary obstetrics, the measurement of the biparietal diameter offers an index in assessing gestational age, monitoring foetal growth and estimating foetal weight. The shape and size of the foetal head depends on the gene pool, which it shares and also the environment which the maternal as well as the developing foetus is sharing at the same time. Although from the same racial stock, but different ethnicity, geographical and socio-economic background, the two samples in the present chapter shows different mean values at each gestational week. Therefore, it is recommended to establish a standard value of nomogram for different population groups to study the growth and maturity of the foetus of corresponding population. Therefore, by establishing standardised norm for specific population would help in avoiding discrepancies between gestational age and ultra-sonographically measured maturity of the foetus, which one often come across while depending on other work.

References

Campbell, S. 1971. 'Growth of the fetal biparietal diameter during normal pregnancy'. *J Obstet Gynaecol Br Cwlt,* 78:513-519.

Chan,W.B, and G.S.H. Yeo. 1991. 'A comparison of fetal biparietal diameter measurements between local Chinese and Caucasian populations'. *Singapore Med J.* 32:214-217

Chitty, L.S, and D.G. Altman, A. Hendeson, and S. Campbell. 1994. 'Charts of fetal size'. *British Journal of Obstretics and Gynaecology.*101 35-43.

Dutta, D.C.2004. *Textbook of Obstetrics.* New Central Book Agency (P) Ltd. Kolkata.

Hadlock, R.P., R.L. Deter, R.B. Harrist, and S.K. Park, 1982. 'Fetal biparietal diameter: A critical re-evaluation of the relation to menstrual age by means of real time Ultrasound'. *J. Ultrasound Med;* 1: 97-104.

Hadlock, R.P., R.L. Deter, R.B. Harrist, and S.K. Park, 1984. 'Hadlock Formulas'. *Radiology* 152:497-501.

Karanth, L.K. and P. Kumar, 1993. 'Ultrasound estimation of fetal parameters in Coastal Karnataka'. *J. of Obst and Gyn. of India.*43, 1-3: 328-331.

Mador, E.S., C. C. Ekwempu, J. T. Mutihir, G. L. Adoga, and J. O. Ogunranti. 2011. 'Ultrasonographic biometry: Biparietal diameter of Nigerian fetuses'. *Niger Med J.* 52, 1: 41-44.

Palmer, P.E.S.1995. *Manual of Diagnostic Ultrasound.* World Health Organisation.

Rajan, R., B. Girija and R. Vasantha, 1991. 'Ultrasound fetal growth parameters'. . *J. of Obst and Gyn. of India.* 41, 1-3: 139-145.

Saksiriwuttho, P. T. Ratanasiri, and R. Komwilaisak, 2007. 'Fetal biometry chart for normal pregnant women in Northeastern Thailand'. *J Med Assoc Thai* 90, 10: 963-1999.

Shah, P.K., N. Fonseca, P. R. Vaidya, and S. G. Shah. 1991. 'Ultrasound cephalometry in Indian pregnant women'. *J. of Obst and Gyn. of India.* 41, 1-3: 311-316.

13
Cardio-Vascular Risk Profiles in Sikkim, India

– *Barun Mukhopadhyay* and *Sovanjan Sarkar*

The Setting : Sikkim

Formerly a tiny Himalayan kingdom, Sikkim became the 22nd State of the Indian Union in May 1975. Presently, it is considered as one of the North-Eastern States of India. As a mountainous State of the Eastern Himalaya, Sikkim is bounded by national and international boundaries: In the west by Nepal, in the north by Tibet (China), in the east by Chumbi valley of Tibet and Bhutan and in the south by Darjeeling district of the State of West Bengal. Sikkim is located between 27^0 00' 46" and 28^0 07' 48" north latitude and 88^0 00' 58" and 88^0 55' 25" east longitude. Sikkim forms part of the Eastern Himalayan range of mountains, which projects southwards having varied elevations that range from 300 to 7,000 metres above sea level. The northern portion deeply cuts into escarpments while the highest portion of the State is in the northwest that includes Kanchenjunga (8,598 metres), the third highest peak in the world. Most of the peaks are above 5,300 metres and snow covered. Sikkim is primarily a catchment area of the Teesta drainage system, the largest river in the State that flows in a north-south direction. Sikkim stretches over 112 kms. from north to south and 64 kms. from east to west.

The climate of the State has been roughly divided into the tropical, temperate and alpine zones. Sikkim is subjected to heavy rainfall owing to its location in the direct path of the monsoons. High degree of variation in climate and vegetation is observed that ranges from sub-tropical to alpine depending upon the altitude. Altitude is the main factor controlling the climate of State. Low temperature, high rainfall on windward slopes, the comparatively dry leeward side and heavy precipitation in the form of snow at mountain tops are the main features of climate in Sikkim.

The Sikkim Himalaya has its richness of flora and fauna, which really is unique. It shows tremendous biological diversity.

It is appropriately acknowledged as India's most significant biodiversity hotspots (Shenga, 1994) and one of world's critical centers of biodiversity (WCMC, 1992). The total area of the State is 7,096 km^2, which is 0.22 per cent of the total geographic area of India and thus happens to be the smallest State in India. According to 2001 census, the State has a population of 5, 40,493 (288,217 males and 252,276 females) which is 0.05 per cent of the total population of India. The population density is 76 persons per km^2 (Census, 2001). According to Dhamala *et al.*, (1993) 25 different communities presently form Sikkimese population. Nepalese, Bhutias, Lepchas and Limbus constitute the majority of the population of Sikkim, of which, Bhutias and Lepchas are notified as Scheduled tribes.

General Health Scenario

For health care, mostly curative, of the population inhabiting Sikkim, development of health infrastructure has been one of the important and priority measures by successive governments of the State since 1975 when merger with the Indian Union took place. General health services during pre-merger days were not elaborate and therefore much was needed to accomplish in this area. Over the years, attention was paid to establish health institutions of different types, developing health manpower, initiating different health programmes. Expenditure on health and family welfare has also been consistently increased. Governmental activities in expanding health care services have been geared to achieve primarily national goal of 'Health for All by 2000 AD' as envisaged in Alma-Ata declaration in 1978 (Mukhopadhyay, 1998). Since 1979-80, considerable increases in number of health institutions, provide adequate health care services to both rural and urban populations. Presently, there are 24 Primary Health Centres (PHCs), 147 Primary Health Sub-centres (PHSCs) and four Community Health Centres. The State Referral Hospital (300 bedded) and the Central Referral Hospital (500 bedded) cum Medical College are located in Gangtok and Tadong, respectively (Government of Sikkim, 2003). A health survey conducted in 1979 (Deodhar *et al.*, 1982) identified with the general population, the following ten leading causes of morbidity in the descending order of magnitude: Intestinal worms, goiter, skin diseases, measles, venereal diseases, pulmonary tuberculosis, respiratory illnesses, cough and fever, malnutrition and asthma (including bronchitis). Diseases related to inadequate environmental sanitation (for example gastrointestinal infections, worm infestations etc.) tuberculosis, iodine deficiency disorders as well as alcoholism and related disorders continue to be major current health problems. Presently, the major concerns in the health sector appear to be related to the changing nature of health requirements and the pressure on the existing health amenities. Health problems pertaining to environmental pollution, improper sanitation and portable water supply remain a reality in the rural areas of Sikkim. Again, gradual emergence of communicable and non-communicable diseases like stronger strains of tuberculosis and malaria and HIV/AIDS as well as hypertension, obesity and other cardiac illnesses and diabetes pose important health problems relatively more in the urban areas (Mukhopadhyay, 1998; Lama, 2001).

Sikkim has witnessed substantial positive changes in its political and social structure, economic and cultural life during the last 100 years. The merger of Sikkim with Indian Union, in 1975, enhanced the process of socio-political changes and developmental scenario. The net State domestic product of Sikkim at constant prices increased by three times between 1981 and 1991 and per-capita income doubled during the period. This trend is continuing. The East district of the State is the most developed in which a huge variety of developmental programmes are available. South district is in the next position so far as the developmental inputs are concerned. The North district remains least populous and relatively ill-developed. The West district is more or less similar to the North District in most of the features. Lama (1994) has observed, "Since the mid-seventies, the entire fulcrum of development in Sikkim has undergone a metamorphosis in social, economic and ecological fronts".

The Study Population: The Bhutias

The Bhutias of Sikkim are distributed in all the four districts of the State. Major concentrations of Bhutias are found in some specific areas of each district. Gangtok, Ranka, Rongli, Rhenok in the East; Yoksum, Tashiding, Dzongri in the West; Kabi, Lachen, Lachung in the North and Ben, Ralong, Namlung, Lingding in the South are important examples.

Bhutias, according to Risley (1928), are the immigrants from Tibet. It is believed that the word 'Bhutia' is derived from a place in Tibet called 'Bhot'. According to Joshi (2004), the Bhutias started entering Sikkim as traders and farmers long before 15th century. The missionary Lamas were believed to be the earliest immigrants to Sikkim. They were followed by the traders, who came for bartering goods. Finally, the Bhutia peasants came in search of rich rice fields. All these stocks are now found in Demazong (or Denzong – the valley of rice - a Tibetan term of Sikkim). Another belief regarding the immigration of the Bhutias in Sikkim is that Bhutias are descendents of immigrants from Kham (Tibet) and Bhutan in the middle of 17th century.

During the latter half of 15th century, a Bhutia patriarch named Khye Bumsa from Phari (Chumbi valley, Tibet) came to Sikkim and established brotherhood with the then Lepcha chief Tho – Kung – Tek. Meanwhile, the Bhutia lamas of different sects felt the necessity of establishing a central authority to their liking and fortunately they could find such quality of leadership in one Bhutia peasant named Phuntsoh Namgyal. He belonged to the sixth generation of Khye Bumsa. Lastly, beginning of Bhutia control over Sikkim was established in the year 1642, when a band of lamas crowned him as the first Bhutia ruler.

Buddhism was introduced during this time. Lepchas, who are believed to be indigenous to the Sikkim Himalaya (Gorer, 1938), started sharing the new ideas of the Bhutias beginning an era of cultural co-existence and showing some evidences of acculturation. Continuous immigration of Bhutias to Sikkim was observed for quite some time.

The Bhutias of Sikkim presently enjoy the status of scheduled tribe. This was possible after the annexation of Sikkim with the Indian Union as the 22nd State. In present day Sikkim, the Bhutias are definitely one of the socio-politically significant ethnic groups that have been successful in making relatively better economic and social progress. As a consequence, Bhutias are exposed to differing lifestyles characterised by differential exposures to forces of modernisation.

Bhutias of rural Sikkim are generally habituated with different lifestyle from that of urban Sikkim. The socio-political standing and economic status of many Bhutias of these areas differ to a large extent, due to differential exposure to forces of modernisation. Educational and occupational status as well as associated behavioural aspects can represent the forces pertaining to modernisation. Bhutias are mostly Buddhists. Most of the rural Bhutias are agriculturists, while a few are engaged as wage labourers. Many of those who are educated got the opportunity to work as employees of various designations in both Central and State government departments. A number of rural Bhutias are engaged in business. Private jobs like driving of other's car or cab, teaching in a private school, working in a private company or factory and the like are common. Most of the Bhutias, residing in the capital Gangtok and neighbourhood are engaged in different departments of both Central and State governments. Agricultural and other type of day labourer are rarely found in urban area. Business is not uncommon so as the private jobs which include teaching in private schools, working in private commercial establishments and so on.

Studies on biological characteristics of the Bhutias are extremely rare. Bhutias show Mongoloid physical features. A study by Bhasin *et al.*, (1987) considered examining inherited traits like colour blindness, earlobe attachments, mid-phalangeal hair and behavioural traits. Information on ABO and MN blood group systems among the Bhutias of Sikkim is available. Further, data is on genetic markers such as red-cell enzymes like Glyoxalose (glo), Adenosine Aminose (Adi), Acid phosphates (ACP), Phosphoglucommutase 1 (PGM 1), Phosphexose Isomerseo (PHI), 6 Phosphoglucommutase De-hydrogenase (PGD) are also available for the Bhutias of Sikkim (Morpurgo *et al.*, 1983). Another study on genetic markers was conducted by Bhasin *et al.* (1986).

A short ethnographic note on the Bhutias of Sikkim has been provided by Dhamala *et al.* (1993). Bhasin (1989) studied ecological and cultural aspects of Bhutias of Sikkim and emphasised culture changes over time. Further, Bhasin (1990) provided detailed account of ecological, socio-cultural health and habitation aspects of Sikkimese population including Bhutias. Bhutias generally live in an extended family, where male and female share the domestic chores. Due to the effect of modernisation, particularly in the urban vicinity, nuclear families are continually increasing. The property is divided equally among the sons. They follow tribe endogamy and clan exogamy. Monogamy is the norm. However, multiple marriages sometimes occur. Clan exogamy is the general norm.

The mother tongue of Bhutias is "*Sikkimese*", as called by them. This language belongs to Tibeto-Burman group of languages (Grierson, 1927). The script of their language is Tibetan. Elderly people staying in the remote villages prefer to use Sikkimese language exclusively. While, the younger generation can speak '*Nepali*', '*Hindi*' and even English. '*Nepali*' is the language of communication with other local communities. '*Hindi*' and English are spoken by majority of urban Bhutias and rural Bhutias.

For the present study, Gangtok and neighbourhood (radius of 5 kms. from the centre of the town) was chosen since this is the largest urban centre having considerable facilities available in an urban area. The three revenue blocks, namely, Ralong, Namlung and Lingding of Ravongla sub-division of the South district were chosen as rural study area where there are large Bhutia concentration. From the urban area, a total of 100 males and 100 females were selected from 100 systematically selected households. From the rural area, 114 males and 114 females were selected from among all the 92 households located in the selected revenue blocks (villages). From each individual data on socioeconomic and demographic characteristics, exposure to mass media, physical activity level, dietary practices, perceived stress level, tobacco use in terms of smoking and tobacco (chewing), and consumption of alcohol, anthropometrics, blood pressure, blood glucose, and blood lipids were obtained following appropriate and standard techniques and protocols.

The Cardiovascular Risk Profile: The Bhutia Case

The Metabolic Syndrome (MS) also known as Syndrome X, is the combination of metabolic disorders that occur in the same individual (Eschwege, 2003). MS represents a constellation of metabolic derangement including central obesity, glucose intolerance, hyperinsulinemia, low HDL cholesterol, high triglycerides, and hypertension (Reaven, 1988). MS increases the risk of non-insulin dependent diabetes mellitus (NIDDM) and cardiovascular disease. MS is considered as one of the major problems leading to cardiovascular diseases particularly among the people who have adopted modernised lifestyle. Epidemiological studies have recorded a higher prevalence of metabolic syndrome (McKeigue *et al.*, 1992; Misra and Vikram, 2002; Deepa *et al.*, 2002) among Indians, including those settled outside India. We conducted study on MS among the Bhutias of Sikkim, as part of broader research project on cardiovascular risk vis-à-vis lifestyles. Present study follows the recommended criteria of the National Cholesterol Education Programme (NCEP, 2001) for the diagnosis of the MS (WC: >102 cm for males and >88 cm for females; TG: ≥150 mg/dL; HDL: <40 mg/dL for males and <50mg/dL for females; SBP≥130 mm Hg and/or DBP≥ 85 mm Hg; Fasting blood glucose ≥ 110 mg/dL). Individuals, who satisfied any of three or more of the combination above five criteria, were considered as having MS.

Findings of our study suggests that MS is an important health problem among the Bhutias, as revealed by higher prevalence especially among the urban Bhutias, middle-aged elderly individuals and females, inhabiting both urban and rural areas (Tables 13.1, 13.2 and 13.3). It also appears that triglyceridemia [TG (>= 150 mg/dL): Rural male: 27.59 per cent, Rural female: 23.91 per cent; Urban male: 64.71 per cent, Urban female: 37.50 per cent], low HDL cholesterol [HDLC (M <40 mg/dL; F <50 mg/dL): Rural male: 82.76 per cent, Rural female: 100.00 per cent; Urban male: 64.71 per cent, Urban female: 99.22 per cent], and hyperglycemia/impaired fasting glycemia[FBG (>= 110 mg/dL): Rural male: 20.70 per cent, Rural female: 41.30 per cent; Urban male: 19.61 per cent, Urban female: 7.03 per cent] are conspicuous problems in the study population.

Diabetes Risk Score (DRS)

DRS has been proposed by the Indian Diabetes Research Society (IDRS, 2005) based on certain modifiable and non-modifiable risk criteria viz., age, central obesity, measured in terms of waist circumference(WC), regular physical exercise, nature of work and family history of diabetes. Relative scores are assigned on the gradients of these selected criteria [Age: < 35years = 0, 35- 49 years = 20, ≥ 50 = 30; WC: male: < 80 cm. = 0, 80-89 cm. = 10, ≥ 90 cm. = 20, female: < 90 cm. = 0, 90-99 cm. = 10, ≥ 100 cm. = 20;

Regular physical exercise and strenuous work = 0, Regular physical exercise or strenuous work = 20, No regular physical exercise and sedentary work = 30; Family history of diabetes: Neither of the parents diabetic= 0, Either of the parents diabetic = 10, Both of the parents diabetic = 20] and if the total score reaches or exceeds 60, by adding up obtained scores of individual criteria, the person is considered to have high diabetes risk score. Below 60, the score is assigned to be low diabetes risk score.

We calculated DRS among the urban and rural Bhutias of both sexes aged 20 years and above. Our findings clearly suggest that very high percentage of urban males as well as females; especially middle aged and older individuals have risk of diabetes. Considerably high percentage of middle aged and older rural females also show risk of diabetes (Tables, 13.1, 13.2, and 13.3).

Table 13.1: Prevalence of MS and High Diabetes Risk Score (HDRS), by gender

URBAN						
	20 – 35 years			≤ 36 years		
	Male (35)	Female (65)	z	Male (44)	Female (56)	z
MS	31.4	45.5	1.30	67.7	78.6	1.37
HDRS	5.7	6.8	0.20	72.3	92.9	3.16**
RURAL						
	20 – 35 years			≤ 36 years		
	Male (50)	Female (64)	z	Male (43)	Female (71)	z
MS	14.0	14.0	0	40.6	47.9	0.86
HDRS	0.0	0.0	–	6.6	41.7	5.30***

** Significant at 0.01 level; *** Significant at 0.001 level

Figures in parentheses are sample sizes.

Table 13.2: Prevalence of MS and High Diabetes Risk Score (HDRS), by age group

	URBAN					
	Male			Female		
	20-35 years (35)	≤ 36 years (65)	z	20-35 years (44)	≤ 36 years (56)	z
MS	31.4	67.7	3.72***	45.5	78.6	3.56***
HDRS	5.7	72.3	9.80***	6.8	92.9	16.80***
	RURAL					
	Male			Female		
	20-35 years (50)	≤ 36 years (64)	z	20-35 years (43)	≤ 36 years (71)	z
MS	14.0	40.6	3.38***	14.0	47.9	4.26***
HDRS	0.0	6.6	2.12*	0	41.7	7.12***

** Significant at 0.01 level; *** Significant at 0.001 level

Figures in parentheses are sample sizes.

Table 13.3: Prevalence of MS and High Diabetes Risk Score (HDRS), by habitat

	MALE					
	20-35 years			≤ 36 years		
	Urban (35)	Rural (50)	z	Urban (65)	Rural (64)	z
MS	31.4	14.0	1.88	67.7	40.6	3.21**
HDRS	5.7	0.0	1.45	72.3	6.6	10.93***
	FEMALE					
	20-35 years			≤ 36 year		
	Urban (44)	Rural (43)	z	Urban (56)	Rural (71)	z
MS	45.5	14.0	3.43***	78.6	47.9	3.80***
HDRS	6.8	0.0	1.79	92.9	41.7	7.55***

** Significant at 0.01 level; *** Significant at 0.001 level

Figures in parentheses are sample sizes.

Table 13.4: Results of multiple logistic regression analysis

Independent Variable	*MS Odds Ratio (95 Per cent CI)*	*HDRS Odds Ratio (95 Per cent CI)*
Age Group	4.57 (2.90- 7.18)	143.98 (46.52-445.58)
Gender	1.49 (0.97- 2.27)	6.01 (2.87-12.62)
Habitat	0.28 (0.18-0.43)	0.04 (0.02-0.09)

It is clearly evident from the results of multiple logistic regression analysis (Table 13.4) that the urban middle-aged and older female individuals have much higher chance of experiencing diabetes. An overwhelming majority of Urban Bhutias lead sedentary lifestyle with much less strenuous work supposedly an important factor behind developing obesity, especially when they are habituated to fat-rich and calorie-dense diet. Along with sedentary lifestyles, they are definitely exposed to stressful environment, which may affect blood pressure, blood lipid and blood glucose levels. It is indeed observed that perceived psychosocial stress significantly affects cardiovascular risk factors in the study population (Sarkar and Mukhopadhyay, 2008). It is also clear that the rural individuals, especially females suffer from MS in relatively higher percentage, when compared with males. It appears that possibly owing to certain socioeconomic development as reflection of in-situ modernisation, females have better opportunities for lessening physical activities without restriction on calorie-dense diet, leading to obesity that exacerbate cardiovascular risk.

Cardio-vascular Health Education: Some Possibilities

To our understanding, the Bhutia cardiovascular health problems, as delineated above certainly call for sustained cardiovascular and metabolic health education involving both adults, young and old as well as adolescents in an appropriate manner. Although, information on cardiovascular diseases and risk factors are not available for other communities in Sikkim, many other communities viz., Rai, Chhetri, Newar, Gurung, Limboo and so on, who are at the higher socio-political ladder, are expected to have similar situations since they are equally exposed to the forces of modernisation and consequently lead a modernised lifestyle. Therefore, arguably, the situation warrants attention from health planners to provide sustained education to mitigate and reduce cardiovascular risk.

It is generally accepted that imparting health education will put emphasis on the following: behaviours targeted for change, the community settings in which interventions are implemented and the specific interventions that are perceivable culturally.

For cardiovascular health education, the behaviours targeted should include diets high in saturated fat, cholesterol, salt, and calorie-dense foods; sedentary lifestyle characterised by less than half an hour of moderate-intensity physical activity per day; tobacco use, alcohol use, mitigation of psycho-social stress; lack of screening, counseling and for prevention and treatment of hyperlipidemia, hypertension, hyperglycemia and other risk factors. The community settings should include entire community but could also include establishments wherein population attend for study or work such as schools, work sites (offices), religious organisations, and health care facilities. The specific interventions include assessment of the community's CVD burden to increase community awareness. It is noted that the education at the individual level or with mass media campaign communicates the burden, causes and corrective steps that can be taken to reduce cardiovascular risk. It is further observed that the community organisations can play an important role in mobilising media campaigns, resource development as well as environmental changes or legislative decisions.

The dietary practices of the Bhutias and for that matter many of other Sikkimese communities revolve round almost exclusive non-vegetarianism, with red meat (beef, pork, and mutton) eating as well as consumption of chicken with skin and almost absence of eating fish. Eggs, Milk and milk products of several types are regularly consumed. They eat a whole lot of *ghee* (clarified fat), butter and indigenously made cheese (*churpee)* in addition to rice, and flour. Potato is almost like a staple, and there has been a lack of variability in vegetables. Fruits are also not very common in the average household. Many traditional recipes do have large amounts of fat content in a serving. Recent additions of snacks and other food items in the urban Gangtok are comparable with any other Indian cities. Fast food centers are coming up and urban nuclear families are taking advantage of such avenues and increase possibly out of home eating restaurant. Children and young people are almost becoming addicted to packaged junk foods. In the rural area, situation is relatively better, but those who constantly visit urban area are changing their dietary pattern. Furthermore, packaged foods are available in most of the nearby urban centers because of the fact that Sikkim is a tourist destination and packaged snacks and food items, even exported ones are favoured by tourists. Consumption of salt is substantial among Bhutias and other communities in Sikkim. Consumption of free salt, tea with salt, and salt in general foods are extremely common. The practice starts from childhood and continues thereafter. Consequently, the chance of elevated blood pressure in the community (Mukhopadhyay and Mukhopadhyay, 2001).

Under this scenario, any programme encouraging heart healthy diet in the community will be extremely necessary. For the present, no such programme exists in Sikkim at the level of any community. Mass media advertisements and/or hoardings in the hospitals or health centre are rarely seen. And some posters on special days, viz., World Heart Day, etc., are visible possibly only in the main urban hospital, located in Gangtok.

Sustained programmes on heart healthy dietary practices for children, adolescents and adults of the Bhutia and other communities can be envisaged and implemented through involvement of the Department of Health Care, Human Services and Family Welfare, Government of Sikkim in collaboration with the NGO sector with a lead by the Voluntary Health Association of Sikkim. Community Organisations, Traditional Tribal Organisations, local monasteries and schools should also play active role in this endeavour. In fact, the activities of the School Health Programme of the Government should be expanded to accommodate learning of appropriate behavior modification for avoiding non-communicable diseases, beginning from dietary changes for health augmentation. It is a fact that local news papers and magazines, in addition to national dailies and magazines make some people informative but generally their effect is too small. The only local television channel occasionally show programmes that advocate healthy diet, but a sustained programme incorporating local problems at the level of the community is not possibly evident but will be welcome.

The use of tobacco and alcohol among Bhutias and other communities are very common. Tobacco use both in terms of smoking and chewing are increasing day by day. The shops selling cigarettes and processed tobacco (*khaini*) are located all around the urban centers, tourist spots and even in the villages. Although among our study population frequency of smoking among adults have not been overwhelmingly high, chewing has higher prevalence. Young male individuals are increasingly becoming smokers and tobacco chewers. Young female individuals are relatively in less risk. 'Quit Smoking' or 'Leave Tobacco' programmes are essential but they are not in sight, at the moment. School Health Programmes should be geared to address this problem. Catching them young will be the utmost necessity.

Alcohol consumption is a regular feature among Bhutias and most of all other communities. Consumption of alcohol in moderation is most often not the case and therefore it becomes a cardiovascular risk enhancing practice. Traditional millet beer and hard liquor are prepared in the households, especially in the rural ones, and consumed in most cases from the adolescence. Each and every social and religious ceremony is a time to consume these alcoholic beverages. And on the top of it, plenty of Sikkimese and other Indian brands of beer and hard liquor are available at relatively cheaper rate. Therefore, huge calorie is gained through consumption of alcohol and associated food stuff. Alcoholism has been an additional problem for many in the State. Some programmes are available in this regard, but consolidation is necessary. The physical activity level of sedentary urban workers is becoming conspicuously low. Using motor vehicle has been a practice to commute for the office, but of could help if they move either in pool car or in city bus, or a cab even for a distance of a kilometere or two from home to office or the place of business. Females are ahead of males in this regard. In the urban as well as rural areas domestic and other field help can do much of chores in Bhutia households and agricultural fields consequently reducing activity level of females, and males, as well. It appears that institutional arrangements for physical exercise or yoga or meditation are yet not a regular practice in Sikkim.

Such arrangements could be of much help. The urban milieu has been considerably stress generating in the midst of competitive and aspiring environment. Status incongruity can occur out, which will affect health, especially cardiovascular health. It is observed that perceived psychosocial stress independently affects Bhutia adults, especially in the urban setting (Sarkar and Mukhopadhyay, 2008). Government offices and local NGOs can implement counselling and stress reduction programmes.

Cardivascular risk assessment programme at the community level on a regular basis will be necessary in order to identify the degree of burden and implementing prevention strategies for prevention of cardiovascular/metabolic diseases. Neither the urban hospital nor rural health centers have such activities in place. Integrated health management programme ideally should include non-communicable disease management of the communities, but it has not been possible as yet to implement. The State should have begun such programme in collaboration with the NGOs, keeping in mind of the importance of such programme. Schools should be encouraged to regularly screen blood pressure, cholesterol and blood glucose for secondary and higher class students. Colleges and the Sikkim University should also come forward with CVD risk screening programmes in collaboration with the government or NGO sector. Awareness generation camps for CVD risk in its entirety should be regularly organised at the community setting in a culturally appropriate manner as the essential public health function.

Concluding Remarks

Bhutias, a tribal population of the small State of Sikkim showed marked cardiovascular risk profiles through adverse lifestyle choices, especially in the urban areas. Similar profiles may not be uncommon among many other Sikkimese communities, since they have chosen similar lifestyles. Continuous *in-situ* modernisation in the rural areas has put a section of rural population also in adverse profiles. Some items of traditional culture and others borrowed from modernised environment created a scenario that exacerbates the cardiovascular/metabolic health risk. This necessitates inclusion of comprehensive cardiovascular health education in Sikkim, a public health necessity. Government, NGO sector, religious, educational and civil society organisations are needed to play their respective roles in accomplishing this goal in sustained manner. Sikkim has been successful in making inroads to many health and environmental issues in the past. It is possible, in the near future to implement this important public health agenda with success.

References

Bhasin M. K. 1990. *Habitat, Habitation and Health in the Himalayas*. Delhi: Kamla-Raj Enterprises.

Bhasin M.K, A.P. Shil , M.B.Sharma , H. Walter , H. Daniker-Hopfe, I.P. Singh, V. Bhasin , V. Bharadwaj , K. Sudhakar, and D. Wadhavan . 1987. 'Biology of the people of Sikkim, India. 2. Colour blindness, ear lobe attachment, mid phalangeal hair and behavioural traits'. *Anthropologischer Anzieger*. 45:351-360.

Bhasin M.K, H. Walter, S.M. S. Chahal, V. Bharadwaj , K. Sudhakar, H. Daniker-Hopfe, A. Dannewitz, I.P. Singh, V. Bhasin, A. P. Shil, M. B. Sharma, and D. Wadhavan. 1986. 'Biology of the people of Sikkim, India.1. Studies on the variability of genetic markers'. *Zeitschrift für Morphologie und Anthropologie*. 77:49-86.

Bhasin V. 1989. *Ecology, Culture and Change: Tribals of Sikkim Himalayas*. New Delhi: Inter India Publications.

Census of India. 2001. *Provisional Population Totals*. Census of India, Series 12, Sikkim: Directorate of Census Operations.

Deepa R, C., S. Shanthirani, G. Premalatha, N.G. Sastry, and V.Mohan. 2002. 'Prevalence of insulin resistance syndrome in a selected south Indian population–the Chennai urban population study-7 (CUPS-7)'. *Indian Journal of Medical Research*. 115: 118-127.

Deodhar N.S., S. S. Srivastava ,Srivastava, S. Phadke, and A. K. Sen. 1982. *Health Conditions of Mothers and Children in Sikkim*. Calcutta: All India Institute of Hygiene and Public Health.

Dhamala R.R., C. D. Rai, M.S. Dutta, and S. Ghatak. 1993. *People of India: Sikkim*, Vol. XXXIX. Calcutta: Anthropological Survey of India and Seagull Books.

Eschwege E. 2003. 'The dysmetabolic syndrome, insulin resistance and increased cardiovascular (CV) morbidity and mortality in type 2 diabetes: Aetiological factors in the development of CV complications'. *Diabetes and Metabolism*. 29:19-27.

Gorer G.1938. *Himalayan Village. An Account of the Lepchas of Sikkim*. London: Joseph.

Government of Sikkim. 2003. *Health Information Bulletin Sikkim 2003*. Planning, Monitoring and Evaluation Division. Department of Health and Family Welfare. Gangtok: Government of Sikkim.

Grierson G. 1927. *A Linguistic Survey of India*. Vol. III. Tibeto-Burman Family. Calcutta: Superintendent of Government Printing.

Joshi H.G. 2004. *Sikkim Past and Present*. New Delhi: Mittal Publication.

Lama M. P, 1994. *Sikkim: Society, Polity, Economy, Environment*. New Delhi: Indus Publications.

Lama M. P. 2001. *Sikkim: Human Development Report*. New Delhi: Social Science Press.

McKeigue P. M, T. Pierpoint, J. E. Ferrie, and M. G. Marmot. 1992. 'Relationship of glucose intolerance and hyperinsulinaemia to body fat pattern in south Asians and Europeans'. *Diabetologia*. 35: 785-791.

Misra A, and N. K. Vikram. 2002. 'Insulin resistance syndrome (metabolic syndrome) and Asian Indians'. *Current Science*, 83: 1483-1487.

Morpurgo G, G. Modiano, P. Arese, G. N. Ranzani, L. Felicetti, F. Tozzi, G. Mura, and A. S. Santachiara-Benerecetti. 1983. 'Population genetic studies in Sikkim'. *Journal of Human Evolution*. 12: 425-437.

Mukhopadhyay B. 1998. 'Health scenario in Sikkim: An assessment'. In: S. C. Rai, R. C. Sundriyal, and E. Sharma (Eds.): *Sikkim Perspectives for Planning and Development*. Sikkim: Sikkim Science Society.

NCEP, 2001 'Executive summary of the third report of the National Cholesterol Education Programme (NCEP) Expert Panel on Detection, Evaluation, and Treatment of high blood cholesterol in adults' (Adult Treatment Panel III). *Journal of American Medical Association*. 285: 2479-2486.

Reaven G.M. 1988. 'Banting lecture: Role of insulin resistance in human disease'. *Diabetes*. 37: 1595-1607.

Risley H.H. 1928. (Reprinted 1999). *The Gazetteer of Sikkim*. Delhi: Low Price Publications.

Shenga N.C. 1994.' Status paper on biodiversity in Sikkim'. *Panda*. 1:5-10.

World Confederation and Monitoring Center (WCMC). 1992. *Global Biodiversity: State of the World's Living Resources*. London: Chapman and Hall.

14

Upper Limb Indirect Anthropometry among Khasi Adolescents of Meghalaya, India

– *Debashis Basu, Deimaphishisha Sun, Indraneel Banerjee, Y.M. Singh, J.G. Kalita* and *V.R. Rao*

The nutritional status of children and adolescents in North East India is changing rapidly following a period of recent economic growth in the region. Nutritional survey in this community of this region was estimated by Bhowmik *et al*., (1984) but no nutritional status based on either by direct or indirect method among children of this tribal population has been conducted during the then period and particularly more precisely in a pure Khasi sample. After a gap of a few decades a very few papers describing nutritional assessment based on nutrients intake and nutritional anthropometry in this population are reported by Agrahar-Murugkar and Pal (2004), Agrahar-Murugkar (2005), Khongsdier and Mukherjee (2003). In those papers, nutritional anthropometric status of this tribal children has been conducted by other nutritional parameters but not with indirect anthropometric measurements being derived from mid-upper arm circumference and triceps skin fold thickness. As more recently, the anthropometric evaluation of upper limb has become significantly valuable in the assessment of nutritional status of children and adults. As Frisancho (1981) opines that 'the utility of the measurements taken on upper limb to assess the nutritional status is based on the evidence that the organisms, when faced with nutritional restrictions utilises its nutritional reserves stored in the form of skeletal muscle protein, visceral protein, and fat'. It is well known that the triceps skin fold thickness indicates the calorie reserves stored in the form of fat (Jelliffe, 1966; Frisancho, 1974 and 1980; and Garn *et al*., 1975,) and arm muscle size reflects the reserves of muscle protein (Jelliffe, 1966 and Frisancho, 1974 and 1980). However, in the evaluation of health and nutritional status, one of the specific measures that uses anthropometry is that of body mass index (BMI) which is an indicator of thinness or fatness and is calculated as weight (kg) is divided by square of height (m) ÷ (kg/m^2). Although, the simpler measurements like height or weight serve significant purposes but independently any single measurement does not fulfill its requirement like it is reported by Weekly Epidemiological Record (1987) and even among the patients with COPD by Soler-Cataluia *et al*. (2005). It is well known that the environmental factors like socio-economic condition, dietary pattern, effect of heterosis, religion etc., have to some extent, bearings on nutritional status (Martorell *et al.,* 1984; Gross and Monteiro, 1989; Ahmed *et al.,* 1991; Getaneh *et al.,* 1998; Khongsdier and Mukherjee, 2003; Agrahar-Murugkar and Pal, 2004; Nemati *et al.,* 2008; etc.). Hence, it would be important to assess nutritional status of children in this region in the backdrop of an improving economic circumstance. In the present chapter, an attempt has been made to explore nutritional status based on indirect anthropometric measurements among the Khasi tribal adolescents of Meghalaya.

Material and Method

Population: The Khasis are a group of people, who are racially distinct and are geographically relatively isolated in existence from the rest of the country. The Khasi people belong to one of the earliest groups of races migrated to Assam (undivided). The homeland of the Khasis is in the Khasi and Jaintia Hills of Meghalaya. It is bounded by Assam on the East and North and Northwest and by Bangladesh on the South and Southwest. The northern part of the Khasi territory is known as Ri-Bhoi, which is formed of hillocks, and flat lands amidst them. The central portion as known as Ri-Lum, which is dominated by ranges of hills and the Southern region constitutes the Ri-War region marked by stiff slopes descending towards Sylhet area of Bangladesh. The Khasis are identified with the Mon-Khmer people of the Far East mainly on the basis of the language, megalithic culture and iron smelting. Modern linguistics study show that there exist some important relation between the Khasi and Mon-Khmer groups of the languages. In the opinion of world-renowned linguist like Pater Schmidt, Khasi in origin is Mon-Khmer of the Austric family (Austro-Asiatic). Close sisters of Khasi are probably the *Paluang–Riang- Wa* dialects of Burma (Myanmar). The conformity of Khasi to Mon-Khmer is shown also in respect of gender, Syntax, monosyllabic and also morphological construction (Bareh, 1964). A majority of Khasis depend on agriculture for livelihood with Jhum cultivation of land still in current practice. The Khasis cultivate paddy, potatoes and maize as main crops. Rice is their staple diet, while consumption of animal proteins such as pork and beef is common. It is not known, although anticipated that such dietary practices may have changed over preceding decade.

We have studied a cohort of Khasi adolescents from geographically distinct area in the State of Meghalaya and assessed their nutritional status using four indirect anthropometric measurements viz., Total upper arm area (TUA), Upper arm muscle area (UMA), Upper arm fat area (UFA), and Arm fat index (AFI). The present nutritional anthropometric investigation by cross-sectional method has been carried out among Khasi adolescent children living in Nongpoh, district capital of Ri-Bhoi district, and Shillong, state capital of Meghalaya during March-April, 2003 and June, 2008. The anthropometric measurements were taken on 335 boys and 335 girls respectively between ages 11+ and 17+ years. Maximum care was taken in collecting measurements from the subjects of Khasi parents thereby sampling a pure ethnic group. In the present sample, subjects were selected irrespective of sub-groups viz., Khynriam, Pnar, Bhoi and War Khasi rather the sample included subjects from all sub-groups studying in two districts; and a few children could not participate in this exercise for being physically challenged. The children between 8.00 yrs. and 8.99 yrs., 9.00 yrs. and 9.99 yrs., 10.00 yrs. and 10.99 yrs. are designated as 8+ yrs., 9+ yrs., and 10+ yrs. etc., age categories (Eveleth and Tanner, 1976). The methods for anthropometric measurements are described elsewhere (Basu and Sun, 2004). We have studied a cohort of Khasi adolescents from a geographically distinct area in the state of Meghalaya and assessed their nutritional status using four indirect anthropometric measurements viz., Total upper arm area (TUA), Upper arm muscle area (UMA), Upper arm fat area (UFA), and Arm fat index (AFI). These four indirect measurements were derived from upper arm circumference and triceps skin fold thickness following Frisancho (1990). The derived measurements or indirect anthropometric measurements are calculated as follows;

Total Upper Arm Area (TUA) = $C^2 / (4 \times \pi)$

[Supposing C = value of upper arm circumference

T = value of triceps skin fold thickness]

Upper Arm Muscle Area (UMA) = $[C - (Ts \times \pi)]^2 / (4 \times \pi)$

To adjust the area of the bone and to obtain the bone-free arm muscle area, the values are adjusted by subtraction of 10.0 cm^2 for males and so do by 6.5 cm^2 for females.

Here the upper arm fat area is calculated by subtraction :

Upper Arm Fat Area (UFA) = Total Upper Arm Area – Upper Arm Muscle Area

The arm fat index (or percentage of fat in the upper arm) is derived by this equation:

Arm fat index (AFI) = (Upper Arm Fat Area / Total Arm Area) × 100.

LMS method (Cole and Green, 1992) which summarises the centiles by three smooth curves representing skewness (L curve), the median (M curve) and coefficient of variation (S curve), has been applied here to construct the mean curves. The choice of the smoothing parameters for the L, M, and S curves was made on the basis of detrended QQ plots. Growth Analyser 3.5 2.0 (version 3.5 build 204) (2.0, build 61) software was instrumental for LMS curve fitting. Since the data on these measurements at regional or National level is lacking, the present population has been compared with NHANES I and II sample (Frisancho, 1990). In terms of assessment of muscle and fat status of the Khasi children, the classification of nutritional status being framed by Frisancho (1990) has been followed. The particulars of the assessment of nutritional status are given in the following Tables :

Table 14 (A): Anthropometric classification for evaluation of the nutritional status

Levels	*Percentile*	*Z-score*	*Muscle status*[a]
Category I	0.0 to 5.0	$Z < -1.650$	Low muscle wasted
Category II	5.1 to 15.0	$-1.645 < Z < -1.040$	Below average
Category III	15.1 to 85.0	$-1.036 < Z < +1.030$	Average
Category IV	85.1 to 95.0	$+1.036 < Z < +1.640$	Above average
Category 1V	95.1 to 100.0	$Z > 1.645$	High Muscle: Good nutrition

(a) Muscle status defined with reference to sex-specific standards of UMA by age and/or frame area.

Table 14 (B): Anthropometric classification for evaluation of the fat status

Levels	*Percentile*	*Z-score*	*Fat status*[b]
Category I	0.0 to 5.0	Z<-1.650	Lean
Category II	5.1 to 15.0	-1.645<Z<-1.040	Below average
Category III	15.1 to 75.0	-1.036<Z<+0.670	Average
Category IV	75.1 to 85.0	+0.675<Z<+1.030	Above average
Category 1V	85.1 to 100.0	Z>1.036	Excess Fat

(b) Fat status defined with reference to sex- and age- specific standards of sum of triceps and Subscapular skinfold thickness, UMA, AFI, and/or per cent fat weight.

Results

Table 14.1 shows sample size, mean, SD values of four indirect anthropometric measurements viz. Total upper arm area (TUA), Upper arm muscle area (UMA), Upper arm fat area (UFA), and Arm fat index (AFI), of the Khasi adolescents by age and sex. The edf values of *l*, *m*, and *s* for UMAC, TSF, TUA, UMA, UFA, and AFI among the Khasi Adolescents are shown in Table 14.2. Table 14.3 exhibits LMS values of TUA, UMA, UFA and AFI among the Khasi Adolescents. The mean values of the measurements of UMAC, TSF, TUA, UMA, UFA, and AFI for both the populations are plotted in Fig 14.1 to 14.6 respectively, which also show the comparative assessment. Fig. 14.7 and 14.8 exhibit the plotting of Z-scores in Khasi adolescent boys and girls respectively with reference to NHANES I and II boys and girls respectively. Figs.14.9 and 14.10 shows the MUAC- for –age smoothed curves for Khasi adolescent boys and girls respectively. Figs.14.11 and 14.12 shows the TSF- for–age smoothed curves for Khasi adolescent boys and girls respectively.

Table 14.1 indicates that the mean values of UMAC, TUA, UMA, among the boys increase with the increase of age while the same values of TSF and AFI decrease with the increase of age. In both cases the variations are linear in nature. Among the girls the mean values of UMAC, TSF, TUA, UMA, UFA and AFI increase with the increase of age. In all the measurements among the girls, the variations being positive are linear in nature. It is worthwhile to mention that the mean values by age and sex-wise of TSF are higher among the girls in comparison to their boys' counterpart. And at the same time the mean values of AFI among the boys decrease as the age increases, while this phenomenon is vice-versa among the adolescent girls.

The difference between mean values of TUA at age 11+ years and 17+years among the boys (23.05 cm^2) is much higher as compared to those of girls aged between 11+ years and 17+years (16.50 cm^2). While in case of UMA the same trend of UMA among the boys (20.65 cm^2) is observed and the difference of same value among the girls is (8.70 cm^2) - indicating more muscle development among the boys. At the same time the mean values of AFI among the girls aged between 11+ years and 17+ years increase with the increase of age as compared to those of boys the same values decrease with the increase of age – indicating more fat deposition among the girls.

Discussion

In the present chapter an attempt has been made to explore the nutritional anthropometric status among the Khasi tribal adolescent children resorting to the four indirect anthropometric measurements of which the mean values are lagging far behind the International Reference (NHANES I and II sample) and over all, those values over the age groups barring the value of UFA at 16+ yrs. are consistent as consistent the NHANES I and II sample values are. The differences between 11+yrs. and 17+ yrs. for all four measurements in the present tribal girls while compared to those of the same values for the girls of the respective age groups of International Reference (NHANES I and II sample) do not differ much, rather, the values of UMA of the girls of International reference are very inconsistent –which indicates that the development of muscle and fat areas in the present girls is regular, or in other words, one can reach the inference that not necessarily, on the basis of lower values of the four measurements while compared to that International Reference (NHANES I and II sample), the girls of the present sample suffer from a little degree of nutritional deficiency or chronic energy deficiency (CED). So far the muscle status among the Khasi children is concerned it indicates that both the Khasi boys and girls belong to the category of <Below average> and their fat status belong to the category of <Average>, respectively. It may lead to an option that both boys and girls contingents of the present sample have lower values of all measurements as compared to those of the International reference, may be due to the later different ethnic or racial affiliation as well as socio-economic condition. The difference between muscle and fat Z- scores between the boys and girls and between Khasis and NCHS data. – as it is observed, both boys and girls have relatively normal fat in the upper arm but the muscle bulk if rather low. This suggests relative peripheral adiposity in preference to muscle bulk, an important factor in predicting insulin resistance. The fat area as compared to that of muscle area out of total arm area is lower as it is observed in other populations too (Basu, 2004a and 2004b; Frisancho, 1990). This phenomenon in the case of the present tribal children lies perhaps in food habit coupled with poor socio-economic condition meant for the children or, in other words, they could not afford to have sufficient essential nutrients being responsible for muscle development and calorie reserve in the form of fat deposition. It is worthwhile to mention that the members of this population consume proportionately higher amount of leafy vegetables in the food items, perhaps, due to their limited resources. Taking the factors or results for all the indirect measurements into consideration, it can be inferred that the children of the present population having lower mean values of upper arm circumference and triceps skin fold thickness while compared to that of International reference, do not seem to have suffered from acute nutritional deficiency remarkably as the balance between 'calorie required' and 'calorie expenditure', as presumed, comply with the height as they are shorter to their International counterparts. So far the values of AFI (proportion of fat area by total upper arm area multiplied by 100) is concerned, the higher value of this ratio reflects greater deposition of fat with respect to total upper arm area. The mean values of AFI among the boys by age wise decrease with the increase of age –indicating the replacement of fat by muscle being contributed by consumption of protein; while among the girls the mean values of the same ratio increases with the increase of age- reflecting more deposition of fat which supplies calorie-leading to the gender specific phenomenon. Both fat area and arm area comprised soft tissues that indicate the protein and calorie reserve in the body (Frisancho, 1981; Gunay *et al.*, 1990; Macias-Tomei *et al.*, 2001). Taking the values of AFI by age and sex wise in to consideration, it indicates that the children as they grow have proportionately more muscle area than that of deposition of fat draws attention to the deficiency of protein existing in their dietary pattern leading to nutritional problem. In this regard, it is suggested that the phenomenon of calorie requirement as well as expenditure according to height or per-population can be justified after a large scale anthropometrically valid investigation. But, the standard score analysis with reference to the NHANES I and II sample shows that the children in the present tribal population suffers a little extent of chronic energy deficiency (CED). Hence, the overall observation in Khasi children was that of chronic energy deficiency, the relative difference between muscle and fat status may provide an indication of a shift in the type of malnutrition. It is well recognised that obesity and malnutrition are simultaneously present in emerging economies like India (Kelishadi, 2007; Singh and Mechirova *et al.*, 2007) and it is possible that our observation reflects overlapping markers of over and under nutrition. The children under this study are very much vulnerable to suffer from acute malnutrition- the undesired consequences of nutritional restrictions.

References

Agrahar-Murugkar D, and P. P. Pal 2004. 'Intake of nutrients and food sources of nutrients among the Khasi tribal women of India'. *Nutrition*, 20,3: 268-273.

Agrahar-Murugkar D. 2005. 'Nutritional status of Khasi school girls in Meghalaya'. *Nutrition*, 21,4:425, 4:425-431.

Ahmed F, M. A. Bhuyan, N. Shaheen S. Barua, B.M. Margetts and A.A. Jackson. 1991. 'Effect of socio-demographic conditions on growth of urban school children of Bangladesh'. *Eur. J. Clin. Nutr.* 45, 6:327-330.

Bareh H. 1964. *Khasi Democracy*. Shillong: Ri-Khasi Press.

Basu D and D. Sun, 2004. *Physical Growth of Adolescents: The Khasi of Meghalaya.* Report Submitted to the Department. Anthropological Survey of India. Kolkata.

Bhatt S.C. 1997. *The Encyclopaedic District Gazetteers of India, North-Eastern Zone,* Vol.11. Gyan Publishing House, New Delhi.

Bhowmik D.C, M.M. Das and P. Ganguly. 1984. 'Food habits of Khasi people: A study of tradition and change'. *Human Science*, 33:263-269.

Cole T.J and P.J. Green 1992. 'Smoothing reference centile curves: The LMS methods and penalizeised likelihood'. *Stat Med*, 11:1305-1319.

Eveleth P.B and J. M. Tanner 1976. *Worldwide Variation in Human Growth*. Cambridge: Cambridge University Press.

Frisancho A.R. 1974. 'Triceps skin fold and upper arm muscle size norms for assessment of nutritional status'. *Am. J. Clin. Nutr*. 27: 1052-1057.

Frisancho A.R. 1980. 'Role of calorie and protein reserves on human growth during childhood and adolescence in a Mestize Peruvian population'. In L. S. Greene and F. E. Johnston (Eds): *Social and Biological Predictors of Nutritional Status, Physical Growth and Behavioural Development*. pp.49-58. New York: Academic Press.

Frisancho A.R. 1981. 'New norms of upper limb fat and muscle areas for assessment of nutritional status'. *Am. J. Clin. Nutr*. 34: 2540-45.

Frisancho A.R. 1990. *Anthropometric Standards for the Assessment of Growth and Nutritional Status*. Ann Arbor, Michigan University Press.

Garn S.M, D. Clark and K. Guire. 1975. 'Growth, body composition and development of obese and lean children'. In M. Winick (Ed): *Childhood Obesity*. New York: John Wiley and Sons. pp. 23-46.

Getaneh T, A. Assefa and Z. Tadesse 1998. 'Protein-energy malnutrition in urban children prevalence and determinants'. *Ethiop. Med. J*. 36, 3:153-166.

Gross R, and C. A. Monteiro 1989. 'Urban nutrition in developing countries some lessons to learn'. *Food Nutr. Bull. WHO*. 11, [http://www. Un.edu/unupress/food/8F112e/8F112E03. htm# Urban nutrition in developing countries some lessons to learn.].

Gunay U, N. Sapan; C. Sallh and H. Dogruyol, 1990. 'Determination of arm fat area and arm muscle area in children 6-12 years of age in Bursa'. *Turk J. Pediatrics*. 32,2: 93-100.

Jelliffe D.B. 1966. *The Assessment of the Nutritional Status of the Community*. World Health Organisation, Geneva.

Kelishadi R. 2007. 'Childhood overweight, obesity, and the metabolic syndrome in developing countries'. *Epidemiol Rev*. 2007; 29:62-76 E Pub 2007 May Review.

Khongsdier R and N. Mukherjee 2003. 'Growth and nutritional status of Khasi boys in Northeast India relating to exogamous marriages and socio-economic classes'. *Am. J. Phys. Anthropol.* 122:162-170.

Macias-Tomei C, M. Lopez-Blanco and L. Blanco-Cedres, 2001. 'Patterns of body mass and muscular components in children and adolescents of Caracas'. *Acta Med. Auxol.* 33,3 : 139-144.

Martorell R, J. Lesbi, and P.R. Moock, . 1984, 'Characteristics and determinants of child nutritional status in Nepal'. *Am. J. Clin. Nutr.* 39,1:74, 1:74-86.

Nemati A, M. Barak, A. Baghi, N. Naghizadeh, Abbasgholizadeh, F.S. Homapour, V. Hazarati, Sepehram and B. Shakiba, 2008. 'Relationships between anthropometric indices and socio-economic differences for children at 6 years old living in urban areas of Ardebil, Iran'. *J. Applied Sciences*, 8, 20 :3748-3752.

Singh R. B, D. Pella, V. Mechirova , K. Kartikey, F. Demeester, R.S. Tomar, R. Begom, A. S. Mehta, S. B. Gupta, Amit K. De, N. S. Neki, M. Haque, J. Nayse, S. Singh, A. S. Thakur, S. S. Rastogi, K Singh, and A. Krishna, 2007. 'Prevalence of obesity, physical inactivity and under nutrition, a triple burden of diseases during transition in a developing economy. The Five City Study Group'. *Acta Cardiol.* 62,2:119, 2:119-27.

Soler-Cataluia J. J, L. Sanchez-Sanchez, M. A. Martinez-Garcia, P. R. Sanchez, E. Salcedo, and M. Navarro. 2005. 'Mid-arm muscle area is better predictor of mortality than body mass index in COPD'. *Chest* 128:2108-2115.

Weekly Epidemiological Record. 1987. 'Weekly Epidemiological Record: Nutrition. 1987. Global Surveillance through anthropometric measurements, Part I', *World Health Organisation*, 62: 37-38.

Table 14.1: Mean and SD values of UMAC, TSF, TUA, UMA, UFA, and AFI among the Khasi Adolescents

Age (yrs)		*Boys*											
		UMAC(cm)		*TSF(mm)*		*TUA(cm)^2*		*UMA(cm)^2*		*UFA(cm)^2*		*AFI (%)*	
	N	M	SD	M	SD	M	SD	M	SD	M	SD	M	SD
11+	45	17.56	1.67	7.8	2.56	24.76	5.06	18.32	3.44	6.44	2.64	25.71	6.29
12+	47	18.86	2.76	7.4	2.19	28.91	9.76	22.42	8.95	6.48	2.07	23.21	6.59
13+	52	20.15	2.44	8.1	3.5	32.31	8.41	25.03	6.21	7.74	4.18	23.63	7.03
14+	43	20.74	2.18	6.8	1.46	35.59	7.33	27.87	6.57	6.72	1.61	19.69	4.16
15+	51	21.90	1.97	6.9	1.98	38.48	6.83	31.26	6.21	7.22	2.12	18.87	5.05
16+	52	23.45	2.28	7.2	2.07	44.16	9.35	36.18	8.44	9.98	2.47	18.32	5.17
17+	45	24.44	1.92	7.6	2.6	47.81	7.76	38.97	6.63	8.84	3.20	18.45	5.67
		Girls											
11+	43	17.92	1.40	9.34	2.05	25.70	4.00	17.97	2.91	7.72	1.93	29.93	5.39
12+	50	18.91	2.35	10.56	3.34	28.89	7.38	19.59	4.53	9.30	3.75	31.48	6.94
13+	45	19.90	2.01	12.62	4.24	31.82	6.39	20.54	5.25	11.28	3.89	35.54	10.56
14+	53	21.41	1.64	13.66	4.44	36.67	5.72	23.45	3.83	13.22	4.64	35.51	9.02
15+	52	22.00	1.75	14.42	3.85	38.75	6.08	24.47	4.26	14.28	4.15	36.59	7.55
16+	48	22.19	1.95	13.62	4.01	39.47	6.83	25.70	4.36	1.77	4.55	34.37	7.43
17+	44	22.97	1.70	15.04	3.89	42.20	6.21	26.61	3.92	15.59	4.49	36.52	6.98

Table 14.2: edf values of *l*, *m*, and *s* for UMAC, TSF, TUA, UMA, UFA, and AFI among the Khasi Adolescents

Measurements	*Boys*			*Girls*		
	l	*m*	*s*	*l*	*m*	*s*
MUAC	1.5	3	2.1	2	3	2.3
TSF	1.6	3	2.4	2	3.2	2
TUA	1	3.1	2.0	2.6	3	2.1
UMA	1.9	3.0	2.0	1.9	3.0	2.0
UFA	1.6	3.0	2.1	1.5	3.0	2.1
AFI	1.5	3.1	2.1	2.0	3.0	2.0

Table 14.3: LMS values of TUA, UMA, UFA and AFI among the Khasi Adolescents

Age (yrs)	*Boys*			*Girls*		
	l	*m*	*s*	*l*	*m*	*s*
	UMAC			UMAC		
11+	-2.36	17.45	0.10	-0.81	17.78	0.10
12+	-2.36	18.45	0.10	-0.23	18.94	0.10
13+	-2.36	19.46	0.10	0.30	20.03	0.09
14+	-2.36	20.52	0.09	0.80	21.03	0.09
15+	-2.36	21.69	0.09	1.25	21.82	0.08
16+	-2.36	22.99	0.09	1.68	22.48	0.08
17+	-2.36	24.29	0.08	2.08	23.06	0.08
	TSF			TSF		
11+	-0.64	0.72	0.27	0.62	0.91	0.30
12+	-0.64	0.71	0.27	0.50	1.06	0.30
13+	-0.64	0.69	0.27	0.39	1.20	0.30
14+	-0.64	0.68	0.27	0.28	1.30	0.29
15+	-0.64	0.67	0.27	0.17	1.36	0.29
16+	-0.64	0.67	0.27	0.07	1.40	0.29
17+	-0.64	0.68	0.27	-0.04	1.43	0.29

	TUA			TUA		
11+	-1.15	24.18	0.20	-0.32	25.07	0.21
12+	-1.15	27.16	0.20	-0.09	28.60	0.20
13+	-1.15	30.23	0.19	0.16	32.00	0.19
14+	-1.15	33.60	0.18	0.39	35.23	0.18
15+	-1.15	37.51	0.18	0.62	37.91	0.17
16+	-1.15	42.08	0.17	0.84	40.20	0.16
17+	-1.15	46.77	0.16	1.03	42.27	0.15
	UMA			UMA		
11+	-0.82	17.91	0.23	1.24	18.14	0.23
12+	-0.82	20.69	0.22	1.24	19.74	0.22
13+	-0.82	23.61	0.21	1.24	21.35	0.20
14+	-0.82	26.81	0.21	1.24	23.01	0.19
15+	-0.82	30.37	0.20	1.24	24.47	0.18
16+	-0.82	34.31	0.19	1.24	25.77	0.16
17+	-0.82	38.26	0.19	1.24	26.94	0.15
	UFA			UFA		
11+	-0.65	5.90	0.29	0.23	7.39	0.34
12+	-0.65	6.16	0.29	0.23	9.15	0.34
13+	-0.65	6.41	0.29	0.23	10.80	0.34
14+	-0.65	6.64	0.29	0.23	12.18	0.33
15+	-0.65	6.95	0.29	0.23	13.26	0.32
16+	-0.65	7.43	0.29	0.23	14.14	0.32
17+	-0.65	7.98	0.29	0.23	14.94	0.31
	AFI			AFI		
11+	-0.30	24.46	0.26	0.74	29.48	0.24
12+	-0.30	22.68	0.26	0.64	31.94	0.23
13+	-0.30	21.13	0.26	0.54	33.98	0.23
14+	-0.30	19.60	0.26	0.47	34.96	0.23

15+	-0.30	18.39	0.26	0.40	35.31	0.23
16+	-0.30	17.64	0.26	0.35	35.43	0.23
17+	-0.30	17.13	0.26	0.30	35.56	0.22

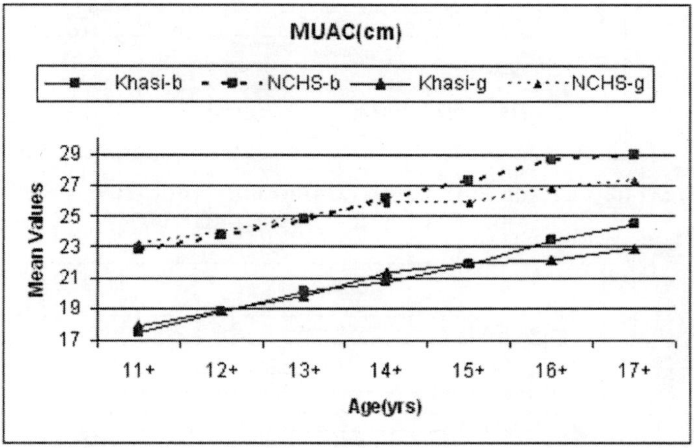

Fig. 14.1 MUAC (cm) in Khasi adolescents and NHANES I and II population (b = Boys; g = Girls)

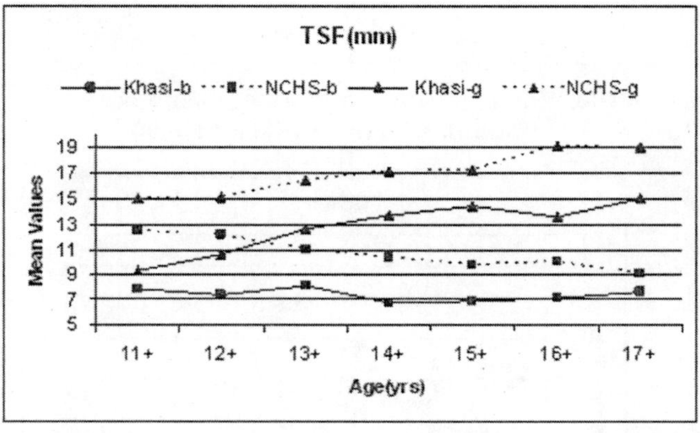

Fig. 14.2 TSF (mm) in Khasi adolescents and NHANES I and II population (b = Boys; g = Girls)

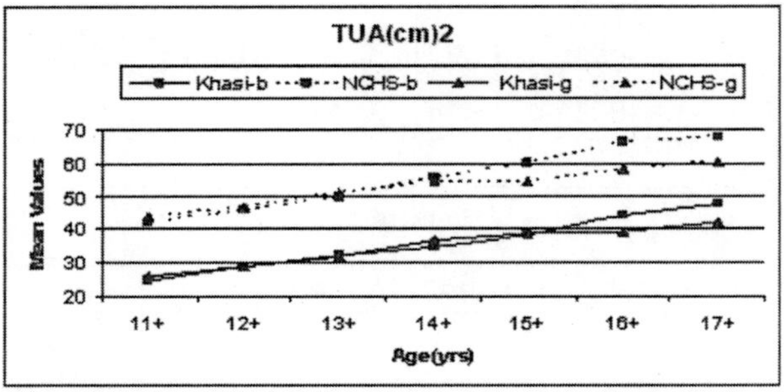

Fig. 14.3 TUA (cm)^2 in Khasi adolescents and NHANES I and II population (b = Boys; g = Girls)

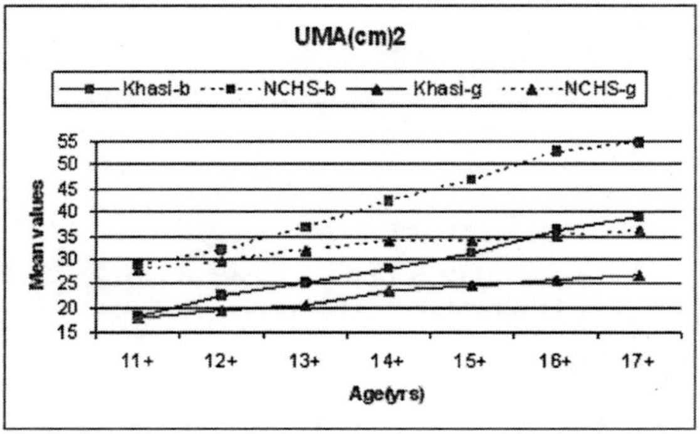

Fig. 14.4 UMA (cm)^2 in Khasi adolescents and NHANES I and II population (b = Boys; g = Girls)

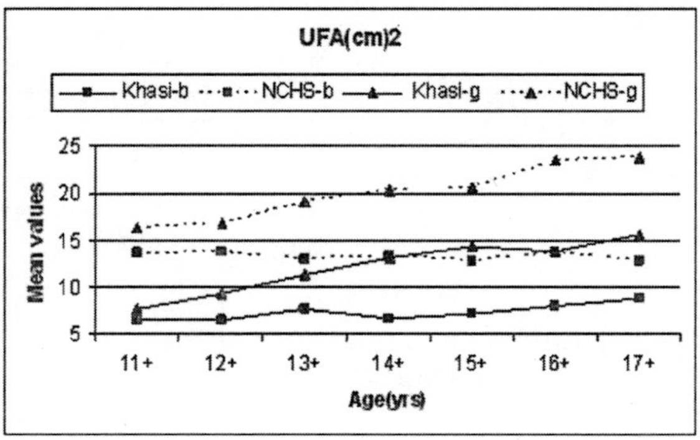

Fig. 14.5 UFA (cm)^2 in Khasi adolescents and NHANES I and II population (b = Boys; g = Girls)

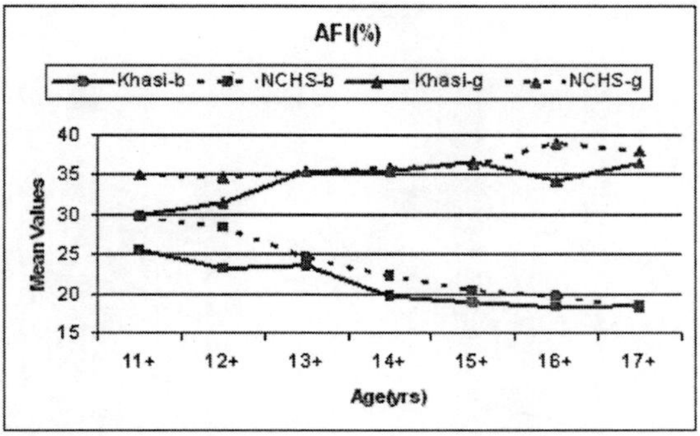

Fig. 14.6 AFI (per cent) in Khasi adolescents and NHANES I and II population (b = Boys; g = Girls)

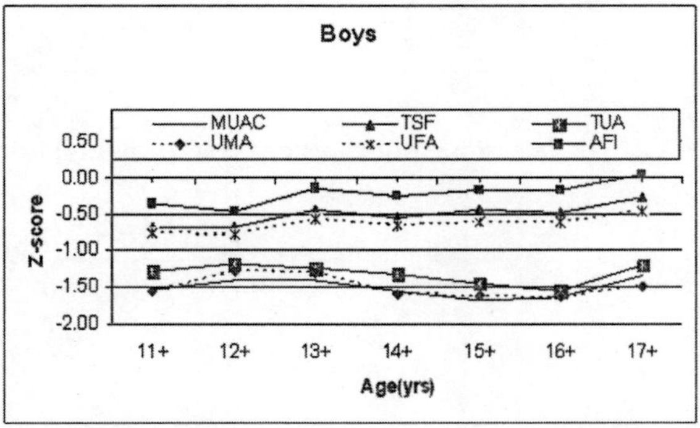

Fig. 14.7 Z-score in Khasi adolescent boys with reference to NHANES I and II Boys

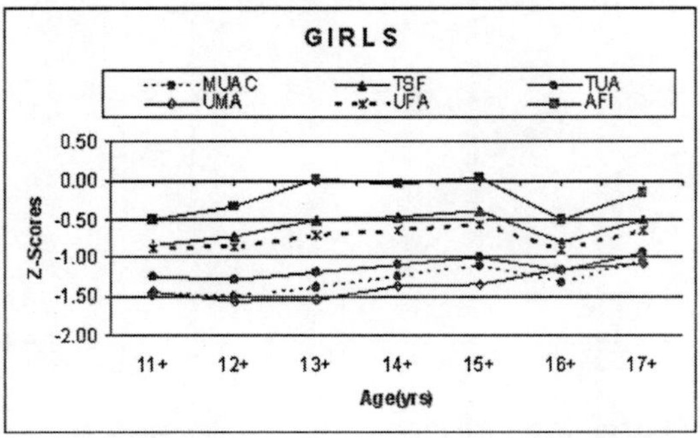

Fig. 14.8 Z-score in Khasi adolescent Girls with reference to NHANES I and II Girls

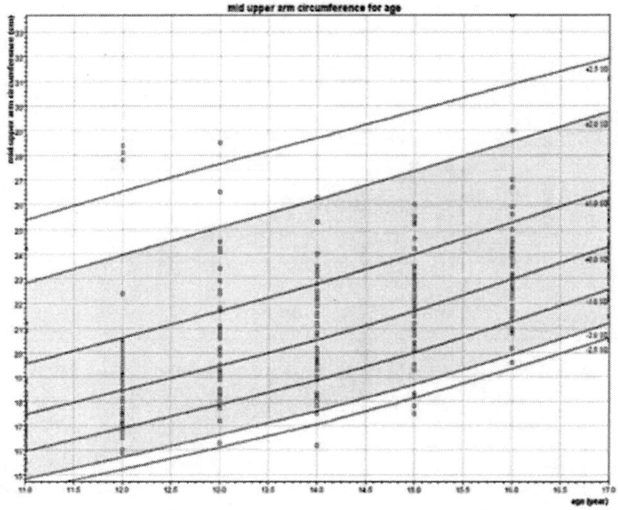

Fig.14.9 MUAC-for–age smoothed curves for Khasi adolescent Boys

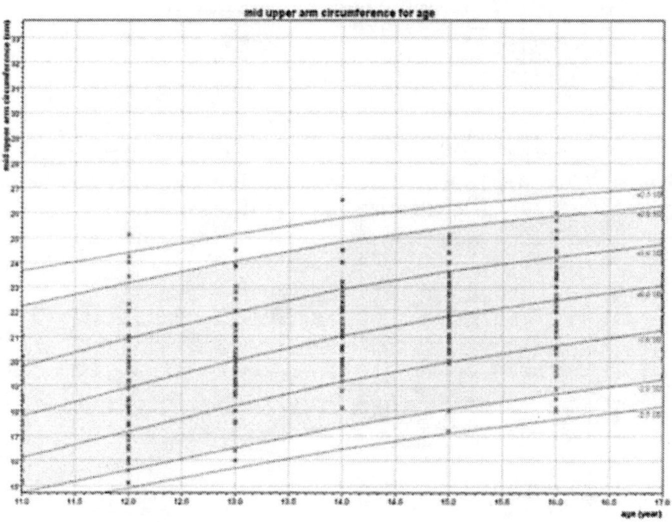

Fig.14.10 MUAC-for–age smoothed curves for Khasi adolescent Girls

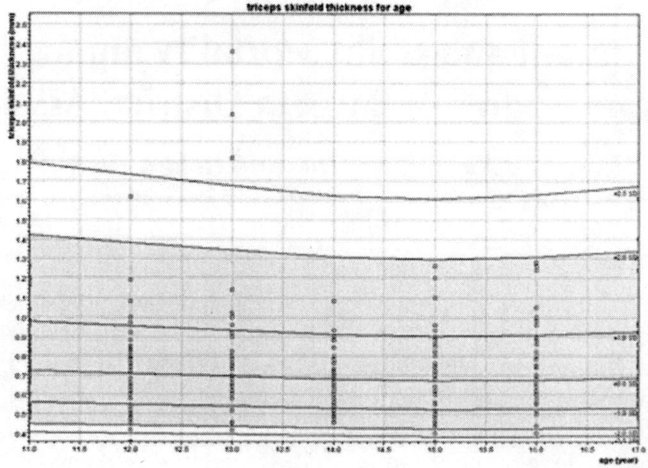

Fig.14.11 TSF- for–age smoothed curves for Khasi adolescent Boys.

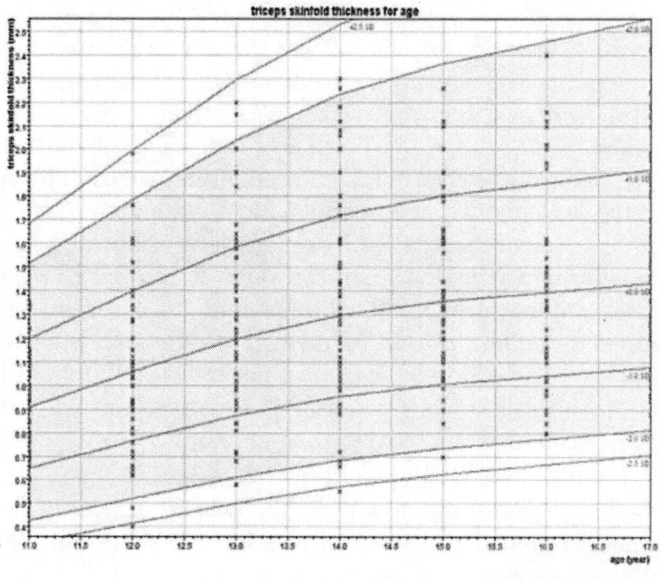

Fig.14.12 TSF- for–age smoothed curves for Khasi adolescent Girls.

15
Infant and Child Mortality among Namasudras of Barpeta District, Assam

– *Nabajit Kr. Das and Rekha Das*

Introduction

Children are an important asset of a nation. Reduction in infant and child mortality is likely the most important objective of the Millennium Developmental Goal-4 (UNICEF, 2012). It is one of the important indicators of country's general medical and public health conditions. Consequently, the country's level of socio-economic development befall on it. Its decline is, therefore, not only desirable but also indicative of an improvement in general living standards. Many biological and socio-cultural factors are responsible for high mortality rate of children, especially of infants. The economically advanced countries were able to reduce their death rate to less than ten per thousand largely by providing people with adequate and wholesome food, pure drinking water, better hospital facilities, better sewage disposal and taking proper measures to control various diseases (Agarwala, 1988). India is among the countries where child mortality rate is alarmingly high. The Sample Registration System, in 2010, estimated that, out of the total deaths reported, 14.5 per cent are infant deaths (< 1 years), 3.9 per cent deaths are of 1 - 4 years children, 18.4 per cent deaths are of children of 0 - 4 years and 2.7 per cent deaths pertained to children of 5 -14 years. As mortality is comparatively high among and likely to vary in different social and cultural groups, within and between States, there is a need for undertaking mortality studies in different parts of the country.

For infant and young children, the risk of dying is closely related to the environment where they live, because they are ill-equipped to deal with infection. Inadequate food and lack of elementary hygiene are other factors. While the baby is in her mother's womb, the health and nutrition of mother, her age, the number of children she already had, the interval in between and the care during pregnancy, have profound influence on survival. Inadequate care during delivery, incomplete or no immunisation, inadequate or no breast feeding and improper supplement feeding practices enhance the child hazard. Thus, the determinants of child survival vary according to socio-economic, cultural, demographic and health care factors. In reference to the above background in the present chapter an attempt has been made to see whether infant and child mortality in relation to some demographic and socio-economic factors exists.

Material and Method

Interview with structured schedule was the prime method of data collection. Altogether 112 eligible couples, having 0-14 years aged children were selected and the mothers were interviewed for collecting the data on child mortality. The study aims at assessing child mortality pattern along with demographic and socio-economic affecting factors. The chi-square test was used to see the impact of infant and child mortality. The logistic regression model was used to estimate the odds-ratios for different independent factors influencing child mortality.

The study was undertaken in three different villages viz. Palashartal, Baradi and Bheraldi of Barpeta district. The villages were selected purposively. Eligible couples from villages were included in the study. A total of 112 Namasudra mothers of reproductive age group were interviewed. Demographic and socio-economic variables viz., mothers age at child birth, birth order, and attendant at the time of delivery, status of immunisation, mothers' education, fathers' education and fathers' occupation are considered.

Results and Discussion

Out of total 397 live births, 353 are surviving children and 44 are dead children. The percentages of surviving and death children stood at 88.92 per cent and 11.08 per cent respectively.

Mortality of children (0-14 years) is shown in four different stages: neo-natal (upto 28 days), post neo-natal (1 month to 1 year), '1-4' years and '5-14' years age groups. The percentage of infant mortality is 6.05, of which 3.78 per cent are neo-natal mortality and 2.27 per cent are post neo-natal mortality. The percentages of mortality in '1-4' years age group and '5-14' age group are 2.01 and 3.02 respectively (Table 15.1). The infant mortality of the Namasudras of present study is quite higher in percentage than that of India which is 4.70 (UNICEF, 2012).

Table15.1: Child mortality according to age

Categories	*Male*		*Female*		*Total*		*Per cent Child Mortality against*
		%		%		%	
Infant mortality	10	52.63	14	56.00	24	54.55	6.05
(i) Neo- natal (upto 28 days)	7	36.84	8	32.00	15	34.09	3.78
(ii) Post neo- natal (1 month to 1 year)	3	15.79	6	24.00	9	20.45	2.27
1-4 year	4	21.05	4	16.00	8	18.18	2.01
5-14 year	5	26.32	7	28.00	12	27.27	3.02
Total	**19**	**100.00**	**25**	**100.00**	**44**	**100.00**	**11.08**

Studies of infant and child mortality reveal that a few demographic characteristics have certain impact on infant and child mortality. A number of researches have established the importance of demographic variables in the study of early mortality (Basavarajappa *et al.*, 1962; Basu and Puri, 1963; Karn and Penrose, 1951; Mahadevan, 1985; Mills and Seng, 1954; Puffer, 1982). The distributions of child mortality by demographic and socio-economic variables are shown in Table 15.2. From the chi square tests, it is observed that of all the variables - birth order and the status of immunizaisation are significantly associated with child mortality. However, there is no significant association of child mortality with other potential risk factors viz., mother's age at birth, attendant at the time of delivery, type of family, parents' education and occupation of the parents.

Table 15.2: Demographic and socio-economic factor influencing child mortality

Factors	*Child Survival*			$\chi 2$		*Significant*
	Live	*Alive*	*Death*			
1. Mothers age at birth						
<20	73	64 (87.67)	9(12.33)	**0.141**	**0.707**	Not Significant
20+	324	289 (89.20)	35(10.80)			
2. Birth order						
1	49	44(89.80)	5(10.20)	**7.097**	**0.029**	**Significant**
2—3	176	164(93.18)	12(6.82)			
4+	172	145(84.30)	27(15.70)			
3. Attendant at the time of delivery						
Doctor	146	133(91.10)	13(8.90)	**1.142**	**0.565**	Not Significant
Untrained dhai	38	33(86.84)	5(13.16)			
4. Status of Immunisation						
Still Continuing	57	52(91.23)	5(8.77)	**9.531**	**0.023**	**Significant**
Completely immunised	92	87(94.57)	5(5.43)			
Half-done	133	120(90.23)	13(9.77)			
Not immunised	115	94(81.74)	21(18.26)			
5. Mother's education						
Illiterate	190	165 (86.84)	25(13.16)	**1.897**	**0.102**	Not Significant
Primary	130	117(90.00)	13(10.00)			
Secondary	34	31(91.18)	3(8.82)			
Higher	43	40(93.02)	3(6.98)			
6. Father's education						
Illiterate	50	44 (88.00)	6(12.00)	**0.748**	**0.249**	Not Significant
Primary	228	201(88.16)	27(11.84)			
Secondary	91	82 (90.11)	9(9.89)			
Higher	28	26(92.86)	2(7.14)			
7. Father's occupation						
Farmer	253	230(90.91)	23(9.09)	**2.922**	**0.097**	Not Significant
Labour	73	62(84.93)	11(15.07)			
Bussiness	31	27(87.10)	4(12.90)			
Carpenter	40	34(85.00)	6(15.00)			

The age of mother at time of child birth is an important factor for infant and child survival. Infants born to mothers who are less than 20 years of age are at higher risk of dying in infancy (Caldwell, 1979). In the present study the proportion of child death (12.33 per cent) is found to be higher among those mothers age at child birth was less than 20 years as compared to those whose age at child birth was more than 20 years (10.8 per cent). However, the difference is not statistically significant. Birth order plays a very vital role on child mortality. Studies had reported the risk of dying for neonates is very high for first order births, which is reversed for the childhood mortality, where the risk of dying is high for birth orders greater than three (Basavarajappa *et al.*, 1962; Pradhan and Arokiasamy, 2006). Proportion of child mortality i.e., 10.20 per cent and 6.83 per cent occurs in birth order number 1 and 2 - 3, while in case of birth order number four and above the child mortality is found to be 15.70 per cent. Therefore, it can be said that child mortality is higher when mothers have more conceptions. Place of delivery is also an important determinant of child survival. Child mortality is found to be the highest when deliveries are conducted by untrained *dhai* (13.16 per cent). It is found to be 8.90 per cent when deliveries are attended by doctor and it is 12.12 per cent when attended by trained *dhai*. Thus, it is clear that trained *dhai* or doctor's assistance is necessary for safe child birth and safe motherhood. The immunisation of children against six serious but preventable diseases viz. tuberculosis, diphtheria, pertusis, tetanus, poliomyetelis and measles is an important aspect of child health care system in India. According to National Family Health Survey report of 2005 - 06 only 43.5 per cent children in India and 31.4 per cent in Assam are vaccinated against the six dreadful diseases. A strong significant relationship is found between child mortality and status of immunisation. The child mortality is the highest i.e., 18.26 per cent for the children who are not at all immunised. The percentage of child mortality for half immunised, completely immunised and still continuing immunisation categories are 9.77 per cent, 5.43 per cent and 8.77 per cent respectively. Maternal education is another important factor which affects child mortality. Children of illiterate mothers have higher risk of dying during infancy compared to literate mothers, as a strong link is seen between female education and child survival (Alam, 2011; Bhattacharya, 1999). Negative association is found to exist between mothers' education and child mortality among the Namusudras. Child mortality when studied in relation to mothers' education it is found to be the highest, i.e., 13.36 per cent for the illiterate mothers, 10.00 per centfor primary educated mothers, 8.82 per cent for secondary educated mothers and 6.98 per cent for the mothers having higher education. Like mothers' education, fathers' education has also played a significant role on child mortality. When child mortality is studied in relation to fathers' educational status, the illiterate fathers have experienced the highest incidence of child death and the percentage is 12.00 per cent. Child mortality when studied in relation to fathers' occupation, the highest mortality is found among the labour category, i.e., 15.07 per cent and the lowest is found among the farmer category, i.e., 9.09 per cent. Present finding is in conformity with the study of Alam, 2011 who found child mortality to be highest among the labour categories.

The results of logistic regression analysis are shown in Table 15.3. Status of immunisation is one of the important factors which have a very significant impact on child mortality. When child mortality of non immunised children is compared with the immunised children the risk is found to be 3.887 times higher in non-immunised. However the risk is found 1.673 times and 1.885 times higher for still continuing, half immunised children.

Table 15.3: Logistic regression estimates for the effects of some selected variables on child mortality

Explanatory variables	*Coefficient*	*S.E.*	*p-value*	*Odds ratio*	*95 Per cent CI*
1. Birth order					
1 (ref.)	--	--	--	1.000	--
2-3	-0.44	0.559	0.431	0.644	0.215-1.925
4+	0.494	0.516	0.339	1.639	0.596-4.509

Cont.

2. Immunisation status					
Completely immunised (ref.)	--	--	--	1.000	--
Still Continuing	0.515	0.656	0.433	1.673	0.462-6.056
Half immunised	0.634	0.545	0.245	1.885	0.648-5.483
Not immunised	1.358	0.519	0.009	3.887	1.405-10.758

The risk of child mortality is found 0.644 times lower for birth order 2-3 but it is 1.639 times higher for the birth order 4 and above as compared with first birth order (Table15.3).

Conclusion

From the present finding it can be concluded that infant and child mortality are affected by demographic and socio-economic factors. Among them, birth order and status of immunisation have found significant role in infant and child mortality.

References

Agarwala, S. N. 1988. *India's Population Problems*, New Delhi; Tata Mc.Graw Hill Publishing Company Limited.

Alam, R. 2011. 'Parent's education and its impact on child mortality: A case study at Thakurgaon district in Bangladesh', *Pakistan Journal of Social Sciences*, 8, 1: 55-61.

Basavarajappa, K.G., V.A. Despandey and K.V. Ramcharan. 1962. 'Effect of sex, maternal age, birth order and socio-economic status on the birth weight of live-born infant', *Indian Journal of Child Health*, 6:18-27.

Basu A.K. and R. K. Puri. 1963. 'Relation on some material factors to birth weight of offspring', *Indian Journal of Child Health*, 12: 233-241.

Bhattacharya, P.C. 1999. 'Socio-economic determinants of early childhood mortality: A study of three Indian states', *Demography India*, 28:47-63.

Caldwell, J.C. 1979. 'Education as a factor in mortality decline: An examination of Nigeria data'. *Population Studies*, 33, 2: 395-413.

International Institute for Population Studies (IIPS) and Macro International. 2007. *National Family Health Survey (NFHS-III), India, 2005-06.*

Karn, M.N and L. S. Penrose. 1951. 'Birth weight and gestation time in relation to maternal age, parity and survival role', *Annals of Eugenics*.39: 144-150.

Mahadevan, K. 1985, *Infant and Childhood Mortality in India*, Delhi; Mittal Publications.

Mills, Jean and Y. P. Seng 1954. 'The effect of age and impact of the mother on the birth weight of the offspring', *Annals of Human Genetics*, 19: 58-73.

Office of the Registrar General, *Sample Registration System, Statistical Report 2010*, New Delhi.

Pradhan, J and P. Arokiasamy. 2006. 'High infant and child mortality rates in Orissa: An assessment of major reasons', *Population, Space and Place*, 12:187-200.

Puffer, R. R. 1982, *Mortality of Infants and Children Under Five Years of Age in India*, New Delhi, UZAID.

UNICEF. 2012. *Level and Trends in Child Mortality, Report 2012*, New York; 3 UN Plaza.

16

Demographic Study among the Deoris of Assam

– *Dali Dutta, Runjun Patir* and *S. Sengupta*

Demographic study is an important field of research in physical anthropology. Study of demographic parameters is very important to understand genetic structure of a population. Unfortunately, in North East India, excepting a few, this area fails to attract much attention from anthropologists to understand the demographic makeup of varied population groups. It is worth mentioning that Zubro (1976) has called for urgent descriptive demographic studies of wide range of population types.

In the present chapter, an attempt has been made to look into the variation that exists with regard to few demographic variables amongst three territorial groups of Deoris of upper Assam.

Ethnically, the Deori are affiliated to the Tibeto-Mongoloid tribal groups and one of the scheduled tribes in the plain districts of Assam. There are three sub-divisions or territorial groups of the Deori-the Tengaponiya, the Dibongiya, and the Borgonya. The name of each sub-division owes its origin from a particular river of their original homeland. The Deori are mainly found in Lakhimpur, Dibrugarh, Tinsukia, Sibsagar, Jorhat and Shonitpur districts of Assam. Besides, they were also concentrated in Mahadevpur area of Lohit district, Arunachal Pradesh. According to 2001 Census, the total population of the Deori in Assam is 41,161 of which 20,809 are male and 20,352 are female. They are bilingual and only Dibongiya group preserved traditional dialect.

Material and Method

The villages selected for present study are Kolowloa Deori *Gaon* of Dibrugarh district; Upor Deori *Gaon* of Jorhaut District and Bormuria Deori *Gaon* of Dhemaji District, Assam. Data on bio-events and pregnancy outcome were collected through in-depth interview with each of the married women or head of the household, using fertility and household schedule, taking into consideration those demographic data as suggested by W.H.O (1964, 1968).

Women whose husbands are alive and have at least one child are only interviewed. Abortion cases reported in the present investigation are those of spontaneous abortion only. In cases, where the subjects were not aware of their real age, it was estimated in correlation with certain local events and thus is approximate only. Information given by mothers were cross checked and verified from their respective husbands or/and elderly women of the household. Thus, there are chances of minor recall lapses in information.

While analysing data on selection intensity, we have taken cognisance of only those mothers, who are aged 40 years and above in the Deori population. In this context, it is worth mentioning that most of the earlier workers has considered the mothers aged 40 years and above for calculation of the total selection intensity. They observed that in Indian women, fertility declines drastically when a mother reaches 40 years of age. In order to estimate the total selection intensity, we have followed the method proposed by Crow (1958). We have used the modified formula of Johnston and Kensinger (1971), which takes care of embryonic deaths. This has been done with a view to identifying how these two estimates of total selection intensity in the Deori population, differ from each other. No statistical sampling technique was applied for the selection of the village.

Results

Table 16.1A to 16.1.C shows the percentage distribution of Deori population in terms of age, sex and marital status. The Borgonya section of the Deori seems to have the highest percentage of child population (27.77 per cent), followed by the Dibongya (24.52 per cent) and the Tengaponiya (22.65 per cent). In the age groups of 15 - 49 years comprising the population at fertile ages, the Borgonya Deori (58.62 per cent) registered the highest percentage, followed by the Dibongya (56.79 per cent) and the Tengaponiya (54.23 per cent). This high incidence may be attributed to the falling mortality and survival of persons to the age of reproduction. These findings signify potential upward thrust on fertility and population growth. With regard to persons aged 50 years and above, the Tengaponiya Deori has shown a higher proportion (23.12 per cent), followed by the Dibongya (18.69 per cent) and the Borgonya

(13.59 per cent) and there by the later two sub-population of Deori implying relatively low survival to the old ages or low life expectancy. Low proportion of population in old ages is also an indicator of young age composition. Although, the sex ratio for India is highly masculine, the overall sex ratio (i.e., number of females per thousand males) is in favour of females in Dibongya and Borgonya Deori. As per 2010 census, the sex ratio for the Indian population is 933 and for the State of Assam are 932. Following Sundberg's classification, all the three populations considered for the present investigation may be categorised as 'Stationary' type. The age and sex structure in the three sub-populations depicts the base which is quite narrow in female side. It may be due to lower birth rate or higher infant and child mortality rate. However, the higher age group only in Dibongya Deori exhibit greater number of aged females.

Table 16.1A: Distribution of Tengaponiya Deori population by Age, Sex and Marital Status

Age Group	*Unmarried Male*		*Unmarried Female*		*Married Male*		*Married Female*		*DSW/ Male*		*DSW/ Female*		*Total*	
	No.	%	No.	%	No.	%	No.	%	No.	%	No.	%	No.	%
0-4	38	4.46	27	3.17									65	7.63
5-9	40	4.69	23	2.70									63	7.39
10-14	37	4.34	28	3.29									65	7.63
0-14	115	13.49	78	9.16									193	22.65
S.R	678													
X^2	0.62													
15-19	37	4.34	30	3.52			3	0.35					70	8.22
20-24	23	2.70	15	1.76	4	0.47	16	1.88					58	6.81
25-29	19	2.23	7	0.82	12	1.41	21	2.46					59	6.92
30-34	11	1.29	6	0.70	17	2	37	4.34					71	8.33
35-39	4	0.47	7	0.82	44	5.16	49	5.75			1	0.12	105	12.32
40-44			1	0.12	39	4.58	15	1.76					55	6.46

45-49	1	0.12	1	0.12	19	2.23	22	2.58			1	0.12	44	5.17
15-49	95	11.15	67	7.86	135	15.85	163	19.13			2	0.24	462	54.23
S.R	1009													
X^2	14.58													
50-54			2	0.23	26	3.05	12	1.41	1	0.12	1	0.12	42	4.93
55-59					13	1.53	15	1.76			2	0.23	30	3.52
60+					52	6.10	39	4.58	8	0.94	26	3.05	125	14.67
50+			2	0.23	91	10.68	66	7.75	9	1.06	29	3.40	197	23.12
S.R	970													
X^2	4.12													
Total person	210	24.64	147	17.25	226	26.53	229	26.87	9	1.06	31	3.64	852	100.00
S.R	915													

Table 16.1B: Distribution of Dibongiya Deori Population by Age, Sex and Marital Status

Age group	*Unmarried Male*		*Unmarried Female*		*Married Male*		*Married Female*		*DSW/ Male*		*DSW/ Female*		*Total*	
	No.	%	No.	%	No.	%	No.	%	No.	%	No.	%	No.	%
0-4	23	4.06	15	2.65									38	6.71
5-9	30	5.29	24	4.23									54	9.52
10-14	24	4.23	23	4.06									47	8.29
0-14	77	13.58	62	10.94									139	24.52
S.R	805													
X^2	0.77													
15-19	13	2.29	21	3.70			1	0.18					35	6.17
20-24	18	3.17	17	2.99	3	0.53	13	2.29					51	8.99
25-29	18	3.17	19	3.35	9	1.59	23	4.06					69	12.17
30-34	16	2.82	2	0.35	15	2.65	19	3.35					52	9.17
35-39	9	1.59	6	1.06	24	4.23	20	3.52	1	0.18			60	10.58

40-44	1	0.18	2	0.35	17	2.99	9	1.59					29	5.11
45-49					16	2.82	8	1.41			2	0.35	26	4.58
15-49	75	13.22	67	11.81	84	14.81	93	16.40	1	0.18	2	0.35	322	56.79
S.R	1013													
X^2	13.21													
50-54					5	0.88	11	1.94			4	0.71	20	3.53
55-59			3	0.53	6	1.06	7	1.24			5	0.88	21	3.71
60+	1	0.18	3	0.53	27	4.76	11	1.94	2	0.35	21	3.71	65	11.46
50+	1	0.18	6	1.06	38	6.70	29	5.12	2	0.35	30	5.29	106	18.69
S.R	1585													
X^2	4.02													
Total person	153	26.98	135	23.81	122	21.51	122	21.52	3	0.53	32	5.64	567	100.00
S.R	1040													

Table 16.1C: Distribution of Borgoniya Deori population by Age, Sex and Marital Status

Age group	*Unmarried Male*		*Unmarried Female*		*Married Male*		*Married Female*		*DSW/ Male*		*DSW/ Female*		*Total*	
	No.	%	No.	%	No.	%	No.	%	No.	%	No.	%	No.	%
0-4	28	4.09	21	3.07									49	7.16
5-9	31	4.53	26	3.80									57	8.33
10-14	43	6.29	41	5.99									84	12.28
0-14	102	14.91	88	12.86									190	27.77
S.R	863													
X^2	0.46													
15-19	28	4.09	38	5.56	1	0.15	2	0.29					69	10.09
20-24	29	4.24	23	3.36	4	0.58	9	1.32					65	9.50
25-29	19	2.78	13	1.90	7	1.02	20	2.92					59	8.62

30-34	5	0.73	6	0.88	17	2.48	21	3.07			2	0.29	51	7.45
35-39	1	0.15	1	0.15	27	3.95	41	5.99			1	0.15	71	10.39
40-44	1	0.15			29	4.24	16	2.34			1	0.15	47	6.87
45-49			2	0.29	21	3.07	15	2.19			1	0.15	39	5.70
15-49	83	12.14	83	12.14	106	15.49	124	18.13			5	0.73	401	58.62
S.R	1122													
X^2	9.27													
50-54					13	1.90	7	1.02			1	0.15	21	3.07
55-59					10	1.46	9	1.32			1	0.15	20	2.93
60+					19	2.78	9	1.32	6	0.88	18	2.63	52	7.60
50+					42	6.14	25	3.65	6	0.88	20	2.92	93	13.59
S.R	938													
X^2	1.17													
Total person	185	27.05	171	25.00	148	21.69	149	21.78	6	0.88	25	3.65	684	100.00
S.R	1018													

The young age dependency ratio is relatively higher in the Borgonya Deori (42.99) than the Dibongya Deori (38.29) and the Tengaponiya Deori (36.14), which may be explained in terms of relatively young age composition and high fertility in them than the other two sub-samples. The old age dependency load for the Tengaponiya Deori has been observed to be higher (23.41) than the Dibongya Deori (17.31) and the Borgonya Deori (11.76). These estimates suggest low survival to old ages among the Borgonya and Dibongya Deori compared to the Tengaponiya Deori. The index of aging is found to be as 64.78 in the Tengaponiya, 46.77 in the Dibongya and 27.36 in the Borgonya Deori.

Table 16.2: Population distribution by sex among Deori population

Name of the Community	*Male*	*Female*	*Sex Ratio*	*Child Dependency Ratio*	*Old Dependency Ratio*	*Index of Aging*
TENGAPONIYA DEORI	445 52.23%	407 47.77%	915	36.14	23.41	64.78
DIBONGYA DEORI	278 49.03%	289 50.97%	1040	38.29	17.91	46.77
BORGONYA DEORI	339 49.56%	345 50.44%	1018	42.99	11.76	27.36

The frequency of nuclear family predominates than the joint family in Dibongya and Borgonya Deori (Table 16.3). Frequency of joint family is relatively high in the Tengaponiya Deori (61.64 per cent), on the other hand the Dibongya Deori (52.88 per cent) and Borgonya Deori (64.80 per cent) records very high incidence of nuclear family than the former sub-sample. Statistically significant differences of Tengapaniya Deori exists with each of Dibongya Deori ($X^2 = 5.19$) and Borgonya Deori ($X^2 = 18.84$)

Table 16.3: Pattern of family types among Deori population

Name of the Community	*Joint Family*	*Nuclear Family*
TENGAPONIYADEORI	90 61.64%	56 38.36%
DIBONGYADEORI	49 47.12%	55 52.88%
BORGONYADEORI	44 35.20%	81 64.80%

Table 16.4 shows the pattern of family size among the Deori population of Assam. It is found that the pattern of family size in majority is moderate consisting of 4 - 6 members while the least incidence occurs with regard to large category (consisting 10 > members) which is recorded only in few families. Test of significance are not marked suggesting similarities among them.

Table 16.4: Pattern of family sizes among Deori population

Name of the Community	*Small (1–3)*	*Medium (4–6)*	Large (7–9)	*Very Large (10>)*	*Total*
TENGAPONIYA DEORI	11 (7.53%)	90 (61.64%)	36 (24.66%)	9 (6.16%)	146
DIBONGYA DEORI	15 (14.42%)	65 (62.50%)	18 (17.31%)	6 (5.77%)	104
BORGONYA DEORI	19 (15.20%)	77 (61.60%)	25 (20.00%)	4 (3.20%)	125

In all the population groups, most of the villagers attained education up to High School Standard (VIII - X). The rate of illiteracy in the Borgonya Deori (16.41 per cent) is found to be more than the Tengaponiya (11.21 per cent) and Dibongya Deori (12.68 per cent). Only 16.56 per cent of the Borgonya Deori, 11.46 per cent of the Tengaponiya Deori and 5.04 per cent of the Dibongya Deori completed the level of graduation. Incidence of Post Graduates is very rare among all the territorial group of the Deori under consideration.

Table 16.5: Educational status among Deori population

Name of the Community ,sex	*Education Level*						
		Primary	*Secondary*		*Higher*		
	Illiterate	*Standard I-IV*	*Standard V-VII*	*Stan-dard VIII-IX*	*Stan-dard XI-*	*Gradu-ate*	*Post gradunt*
TENGAPONIYA DEORI	KOLOWLOWA DEORI GAON						
Male	14	62	36	155	80	58	2
%	3.44	15.23	8.85	38.08	19.66	14.25	0.49
Female	74	48	25	140	59	32	0
%	19.58	12.70	6.61	37.04	15.61	8.47	0
Total	88	110	61	295	139	90	2
%	11.21	14.01	7.77	37.58	17.71	11.46	0.25

DIBONGYA	UPORDEORIGAON						
Male	20	48	26	48	106	11	1
%	7.69	18.46	10.00	18.46	40.77	4.24	0.38
Female	48	50	17	65	80	16	0
%	17.39	18.12	6.16	23.56	28.98	5.79	0
Total	**68**	**98**	**43**	**113**	**186**	**27**	**1**
%	**12.68**	**18.28**	**8.03**	**21.08**	**34.71**	**5.04**	**0.18**
BORGONYA DEORI	BORMURIADEORIGAON						
Male	29	48	32	95	48	61	1
%	9.24	15.29	10.19	30.25	15.29	19.43	0.32
Female	76	45	26	98	35	45	1
%	23.31	13.80	7.98	30.06	10.74	13.80	0.31
Total	**105**	**93**	**58**	**193**	**83**	**106**	**2**
%	**16.41**	**14.53**	**9.06**	**30.16**	**12.97**	**16.56**	**0.31**

The age at menarche is low in Dibongya Deori (12.10 ± 0.11 years). The Tengaponiya Deori girls (12.19 ± 0.10 years) follow it. Borgonya Deori girls (12.95 ± 0.20 years) menstruate relatively much later than the girls of the other two sub-populations (Table 16.19). The mean menopausal age of the Dibongya Deori (45.73 ± 0.50 years) is higher than the Tengaponiya Deori (44.59 ± 0.29 years) and the Borgonya Deori (43.50 ± 0.54 years) sub-population.

Table 16.6 shows the mean age at marriage. Among the Tengaponiya Deori the mean age at marriage is found to be 28.60 ± 0.33 years for males and 23.46 ± 0.17 years for females, where as among the Dibongya Deori it is 28.59 ± 0.56 years for males and 21.33 ± 0.47 years for females. The mean age at marriage in the Borgonya Deori is 26.49 ± 0.43 years for males and 21.44 ± 0.38 years in females. The variations that exist among different sub-samples are statistically significant.

Table 16.6: Mean age at marriage among Deori population

Name of the Community	*Sex*	*Number*	*Mean ±S.E*
TENGAPONIYA DEORI	Male	226	28.60 ± 0.33
	Female	229	23.46 ± 0.17
DIBONGYA DEORI	Male	122	28.59 ± 0.56
	Female	122	21.33 ± 0.47
BORGONYA DEORI	Male	148	26.49 ± 0.43
	Female	149	21.44 ± 0.38

Table 16.7 shows the mean age at first childbirth. **The mean age at first child birth in the Tengaponiya Deori females is found** to be 24.65 ± 0.48 years, while among the Dibongya Deori it is 23.38 ± 0.63 years. The mean age at first child birth among the Borgonya Deori is 22.12 ± 0.49 years. The Tengaponiya Deori appear to stand statistically significantly apart from the Borgonya Deori ($t = 3.69$) by showing higher mean age at first child birth.

Table 16.7: Mean age at first child birth among Deori population

Name of the Community	*Number of women*	*Mean ± S.E.*
TENGAPONIYA DEORI	91	24.65 ± 0.48
DIBONGYA DEORI	55	23.38 ± 0.63
BORGONYA DEORI	73	22.12 ± 0.49

Table 16.8 shows the child women (fertility) ratio, i.e., number of children aged five years and below per 1,000 women aged 15-49 years irrespective of marital status. It can be observed from the table that the fertility ratio in Tengaponiya Deori population is relatively lower than the other two sub-samples. Such lower rate of fertility ratio in them may be due to a recent fertility decline, as has also been suggested by the constriction at the base of the population distribution.

Table 16.8: Child women (fertility) ratio among Deori population

Name of the Community	*Number of women aged 15 – 49 years*	*Number of Childr en below 5*	*Fertility Ratio*
TENGAPONIYA DEORI	39	43	1021.56
DIBONGYA DEORI	16	19	1871.50
BORGONYA DEORI	29	34	1721.40

Table 16.9 shows the completed family size among the Deori women of present study. It is seen that the mean number of live birth and surviving children per mother is conspicuously low in Deori, more particularly among Tengaponiya section of Deori population. However, except the difference between Tengaponiya and Borgonya Deori (t = 2.07) with regard to Live Birth, the variations observed among different sub-samples are not statistically significant.

Table 16.9: Completed family size among Deori population

Name of the Community	*Number of Mothers aged 45+*	*Number of Live Born Childr en*	*Number of Surviving Childr en*	*Mean Number of Live Births per Mother*	*Mean Number of Surviving Childr en per*
TENGAPONIYA DEORI	21	77	71	3.67 ± 0.17	3.38 ± 0.16
DIBONGYA DEORI	24	98	91	4.08 ± 0.42	3.79 ± 0.40
BORGONYA DEORI	16	79	66	4.94 ± 0.59	4.13 ± 0.39

The average number of live births per mother by age at marriage is given in Table 16.10. It is seen from the table that the average number of live birth decreases with the increase in age marriage.

Table 16.10: Number of live births by age at marriage among Deori population

Name of the Community	*Age at Marriage (in years)*	*Number of Women*	*Number of Live Births*	*Average number of live births*
TENGAPONIYA DEORI	<19	18	44	2.44
	20 – 24	38	93	2.45
	25 - 29	26	56	2.15
	30 - 34	7	10	1.43
	35 and above	2	2	1.00

DIBONGYA DEORI	<19	16	40	2.50
	20-24	23	86	3.74
	25-29	13	38	2.92
	30-34	3	6	2.00
BORGONYA DEORI	<19	28	87	311
	20-24	29	89	3.07
	25-29	14	29	2.07
	30-34	2	5	2.50

Table 16.11 presented the mean number of live births and surviving children according to educational level. It is found that mean number of live births per mother's decreases with the rise in education level of the mother.

Table 16.11: Fertility by educational level among Deori population

Name of the Community	*Educational Level*	*Number of Mother*	*Number of Live Births*	*Number of Surviving*	*Mean Number of Live Births*	*Mean Number of Surviving*
TENGAPONIYA DEORI	Illiterate	1	42	39	3.82 ± 0.48	3.55 ± 0.47
	Primary Level	2	8	8	4.00 ± 1.00	4.00 ± 1.00
	Secondary Level and Above	78	155	150	1.99 ± 0.11	1.92 ± 0.10
DIBONGYA DEORI	Illiterate	15	67	63	4.47 ± 0.65	4.20 ± 0.57
	Primary Level	6	18	16	3.00 ± 0.26	2.67 ± 0.07
	Secondary Level and Above	34	85	77	2.50 ± 0.20	2.26 ± 0.19
BORGONYA DEORI	Illiterate	22	91	76	4.14 ± 0.25	3.45 ± 0.12
	Primary Level	1	2	2	2.00 ± 0.00	2.00 ± 0.00
	Secondary Level and Above	50	117	109	2.34 ± 0.11	2.18 ± 0.09

In all the three territorial groups of Deori, the fertility rate is relatively low in the age group of < 19 years, the peak fertility is manifested in the age group of 20 - 24 years, and thereafter it declines substantially. The A.S.F.R in the age group of < 19 years and 20 - 24 years, the fertility rate is more or less similar among the Dibongya and Borgonya Deori, which can be assumed due to relatively long duration of high fertility in them as compared to the Tengaponiya Deori.

Table 16.12: Age specific fertility rate among Deori population

Age groups (in years)	*TENGAPONIYA DEORI*			*DIBONGYA DEORI*			*BORGONYA DEORI*		
	No. of mothers	No. of live births	A.S.F.R	No. of mothers	No. of live births	A.S.F.R	No. of mothers	No. of live births	A.S.F.R
<19	15	15	1.00	12	16	1.33	24	31	1.29
20-24	46	58	1.26	33	45	1.36	48	63	1.31
25-29	68	69	1.01	43	51	1.19	66	72	1.09
30-34	72	48	0.67	44	45	1.02	58	35	0.60
35-39	56	15	0.27	39	11	0.28	44	7	0.16
40-44	30	0	0	31	2	0.06	25	2	0.08
45+	21	0	0	24	0	0	16	0	0
Total fertility rate.	**4.21**			**5.24**			**4.53**		

The frequency of marriages within and outside the community is given in Table 16.13. It is found that the frequency of marriages between the Dibongya Deori with neighbouring population is relatively higher than the other two population groups. On the other hand the frequency of marriage within same population is found to be little more in Tengaponiya Deori (95.77 per cent) and Borgonya Deori (91.95 per cent).

Table 16.13: Marriage by population among Deori population

Type of Marriages	*TENGAPONIY A DEORI*	*DIBONGYA DEORI*	*BORGONY A DEORI*
a) Marriage within the population	249 (95.77%)	134 (87.01%)	160 (91.95%)
b) Marriage outside the Population	11 (4.23%)	20 (12.99%)	14 (8.05%)

Figures with in parantheses indicates percentage.

The frequency of marriages within and outside the villages (Table 16.14) shows that the incidence of village endogamy in the present Borgonya Deori sample is comparatively higher.

Table 16.14: Marriage by village level among Deori population

Type of Marriages	*TENGAPONIYA DEORI*	*DIBONGYA DEORI*	*BORGONYA DEORI*
(a) Marriage within the same village	51 (19.62)	34 (22.08)	43 (24.71)
(b) Marriage outside the village	209 (80.38)	120 (77.92)	131 (75.29)

Figures with in parantheses indicates percentage.

Table 16.15 presents the admixture rate among the Deori population of Assam. The admixture rate in the present Borgonya population sample is found to be little higher than the other two sub-samples.

Table 16.15: Village Level Admixture Rate in Deori population

Items	*TENGAPONIYA DEORI*	*DIBONGYA DEORI*	*BORGONY A DEORI*
(a) Total Population	852	567	684
(b) Number of Parents whose one of the parents is from another population or sub-population	11	20	30
(c) Total number of gamets	852 X 2 = 1,704	567 X 2 = 1,134	684 X 2 = 1368
(d) Total number of gamets coming from another population	11	20	30
(e) Admixture rate = Total number of gamets coming from another population / Total number of gamets	(0.65)	(1.76)	(2.19)

Figures within parenthesis indicates percentage.

Table 16.16 shows the frequency of prenatal wastages and postnatal mortality rate in the Deori population of the present study. Incidence of miscarriage is highest among the Dibongya Deori (10.82 per cent) which is closely followed by the Tengaponiya Deori (8.07 per cent) and the Borgonya Deori (4.33 per cent). The rate of stillbirth is recorded as 6.06 per cent in the Borgonya Deori, 2.06 per cent in the Dibongya Deori and 1.79 per cent in the Tengaponiya Deori. Thus, the total embryonic wastages in Dibongya Deori (12.89 per cent) are slightly higher than that of the Borgonya Deori (10.39 per cent) and Tengaponiya Deori (9.87 per cent). The infant mortality rate is relatively higher among the Borgonya Deori (3.81 per cent). However, such incidence is quite low in Tengaponiya Deori (1.95 per cent). The child mortality is also found to be higher among the Borgonya Deori (3.81 per cent). The juvenile mortality rate on the other hand shows similar incidence both in Borgonya (2.38 per cent) and Dibongya Deori (2.35 per cent). The total pre-reproductive mortality as a whole is found to be high in Borgonya Deori (10.00 per cent), followed by the Dibogya Deori (8.24 per cent).Total pre-reproductive mortality is quite low in Tengaponiya Deori (3.42 per cent).

Table 16.16: Prenatal wastages and post natal pre-reproductive mortality in Deori population

Parameters	*TENGAPONIYA DEORI*	*DIBONGYA DEORI*	*BORGONYA DEORI*
Total Number of Mother	91	55	73
Total Number of Conception	223	194	231
Total Number of Live birth	205	170	210
Total Number of abortion/ Miscarriage	18	21	10
Rate per cent	8.07	10.82	4.33
Average	0.0807	0.1082	0.0433
Total Number of Still birth	04	04	14

Rate (per cent)	1.79	2.06	6.06
Average	0.0179	0.0206	0.0606
Total Number of Infant Mortality	04	06	8
Rate (per cent)	1.95	3.53	3.81
Average	0.0195	0.0353	0.0381
Total Number of Child Mortality	01	04	8
Rate (per cent)	0.49	2.35	3.81
Average	0.0049	0.0235	0.0381
Total Number of Juvenile Mortality	02	04	5
Rate (per cent)	0.98	2.35	2.38
Total Number of Embryonic wastages	22	25	24
Rate (per cent)	9.87	12.89	10.39
Average	0.0987	0.1289	0.1039
Total Number of Post Natal Death	07	14	21
Rate (per cent)	3.41	8.24	10.00
Average	0.0341	0.0824	0.1000

In the present study, we have taken into consideration only those mothers who have reach the age of 40 years and above. It has been reported by many scholars that fertility declines drastically when a mother reaches 40 years of age. Table 16.17 shows the parameters used in calculating selection intensity. It is seen that there are altogether 86 mothers (Tengaponiya = 30, Dibongya = 31, Borgonya = 25) who are aged 40 years and above. The mean number of live births to those mothers is found to be little higher in Borgonya Deori (4.32) with the corresponding variance of 5.06. The proportion of child mortality before the reproductive age in them is 0.1574 and that of embryonic deaths (still births and abortions) is 0.0855.

Table 16.17 : Demographic variables used in calculating selection potential in Deori population.

Age groups (in years)	*TENGAPONIYA DEORI*			*DIBONGYA DEORI*			*BORGONYA DEORI*		
	No. of mothers	No. of live births	A.S.F.R	No. of mothers	No. of live births	A.S.F.R	No. of mothers	No. of live births	A.S.F.R
<19	15	15	1.00	12	16	1.33	24	31	1.29
20-24	46	58	1.26	33	45	1.36	48	63	1.31
25-29	68	69	1.01	43	51	1.19	66	72	1.09
30-34	72	48	0.67	44	45	1.02	58	35	0.60
35-39	56	15	0.27	39	11	0.28	44	7	0.16
40-44	30	0	0	31	2	0.06	25	2	0.08
45+	21	0	0	24	0	0	16	0	0
Total fertility rate.	**4.21**			**5.24**			**4.53**		

Table 16.18 shows the index of total selection intensity calculated according to Crow's (1958) formula as well as according to the modified versions proposed by Johnston and Kensinger (1971). It is found that the total selection intensity (I) calculated according to Crow's formula, which is lower than that calculated according to the method suggested by Johnston and Kensinger. In Deori population, the relative contribution of fertility component to the index of total selection is higher than the corresponding mortality component.

Table 16.18: Indices of opportunity for selection in Deori population

Name of the Community	Crow, 1958			Johnston and Kensinger, 1971			
	I_m	I_f	I	I_{me}	I_{mc}	I_f	I
TENGAPONIYA DEORI	0.0638	0.1407	0.2135	0.0900	0.0638	0.1407	0.3226
DIBONGYA DEORI	0.0790	0.2075	0.3029	0.1220	0.0790	0.2075	0.4618
BORGONYA DEORI	0.1808	0.2711	0.5085	0.0926	0.1868	0.271	0.6435

Discussion

The mean age at menarche among the populations under study has been compared with the available data on population groups from North East India having Mongoloid ethnic affinity. The mean age at menarche of the population groups under study are not much different from the mean values in studies reported earlier. The mean value of menarche found in population groups like the Ahom (12.25 years – 12.96 years), Sonowal Kachari (12.22 years – 12.77 years), Mikir (12.75 years), Chutiya (12.54 years), Mishing (12.26 years – 12.97 years), Singpho (12.59 years) and Garo (12.55 years) are close to the mean age recorded in the present population groups. However, one Ahom sample (Srivastava and Goswami, 1968) record markedly lower mean value than those of the present sample. On the other hand, the menarcheal age is found to be higher in the Moran (13.51 years), Deori (13.03 years), Meitei (13.28 years and 14.34 years), Turung (13.03 years), Apatani (13.40 years and 13.61 years), Adi (14.45 years and 13.47 years), Christian Khasi (14.60 years), Non-Christian Khasi (14.10 years), Tangkhul Naga (13.93 years), Zemi Naga (14.13 years), Ao Naga (14.88 years), Angami Naga (15.00 years), Kabui Naga (15.15 years), Mao Naga (14.59 years), and Tarao Naga (13.46 years) of North East India.

Table 16.19: Mean age at menarche in some Mongoloid population groups of North East India

State / Population Groups	No.	Menarcheal Age Mean ± S.E.	Source
ASSAM		–	
Tengaponya Deori	91	12.19 + 0.10	Present Study
Dibongya Deori	55	12.10 + 0.11	Do

Borgonya Deori	73	12.95 ± 0.20	Do
Deori	77	13.03	Das *et al,* 1980
Ahom	164	12.24 ± 0.09	Barua and Sengupta, 2009
Ahom	50	11.65	Srivastava and Goswami, 1968
Ahom	264	12.96 ± 0.60	Gogoi, 1972
Ahom	66	12.29	Das et al., 1980
Ahom	194	12.60 ± 0.12	Sengupta, 1982
Ahom	77	12.83 ± 0.12	Das, 1983-1986
Ahom	77	12.25 ± 0.13	Balgir, 1994
Mishing	165	12.97 ± 0.08	Barua and Sengupta, 2009
Mishing	82	12.68	Das *et al,* 1980
Mishing	355	12.26 ± 0.08	Buzarbarua and Das (Unpub)
Sonowal Kachari	185	12.54 ± 0.08	Barua and Sengupta, 2009
Sonowal Kachari	200	12.77 ± 0.12	Deka, 1976
Sonowal Kachari	32	12.22 ± 0.18	Balgir, 1994
Moran	67	13.51	Das et al 1980
Chutiya	62	12.54	Do
Lalung	51	12.36 ± 0.06	Do
Turung	32	13.06 ± 0.20	Das, 1985
Khamiyang	40	12.80 ± 0.13	Do
Mikir	52	12.75 ± 0.18	Khatoniar, 1972
Garo	95	12.55 ± 0.09	Ahmed Das and Saikia, 1999
ARUNACHAL PRADESH			
Adi	109	14.45 ± 0.98	Duarah, Duara, 1969
Adi	17	13.47 ± 0.36	Balgir, 1994
Singpho	95	12.59 ± 0.15	Kar and Mahanta, 1975
Apatani	219	13.40 ± 0.08	Jaswal and Jaswal, 1981
Apatani	13	13.61 ± 0.66	Balgir, 1994

MANIPUR			
Meitei	161	12.77±0.04	Devi and Singh, 1982
Meitei	410	13.28±0.04	Devi, 1985
Meitei	487	14.34	Chakravartti, 1986
Kabui	484	15.15	Chakravartti, 1986
Tangkhul	307	13.93	Chakravartti, 1986
Tarao Naga		13.46	Singh, 1989
Mao Naga	536	14.59± 1.03	Maheo and Kalla, 2000
MEGHALAYA			
Christian Khasi	119	14.60	Nag, 1965
Non-Christian Khasi	131	14.10	Nag, 1965
Christian Rural Khasi	155	13.09±0.06	Barua and Das, 1983
Christian Urban Khasi	161	13.80±0.06	Barua and Das, 1983
Non-Christian Rural Khasi	160	13.7±0.07	Barua and Das, 1983
Non-Christian Urban Khasi	165	13.6±0.06	Barua and Das, 1983
NAGALAND			
Zemi Naga	214	14.13	Bhowmik *et al.* 1971
Angami Naga	50	15.00	Suri, 1985
Ao Naga	150	14.88±0.11	Sengupta and Purnungla, 2005
Naga	15	13.80±0.26	Balgir, 1994

The mean age at marriage in the present samples are quite deviant from each other. The mean age at marriage among females in Mongoloid population of North East India ranges from the Lalung (14.59 years) to the Sonowal Kachari (23.66 years; Sengupta and Kalita, 2001). In this regard, the present Deori population under study show close affinity with the mean marital age of the Sonowal Kachari of Assam which occupies position at the higher range of the extreme.

Marriage takes place relatively at earlier ages among the Ahom (17.98 years), Non-Christian Khasi (18.00 years), Chutiya (18.06 years) , Mishing (18.43 years), Moran (18.51 years) and Deori (18.47 years), Christian Khasi (19.00 years), Khamti (19.00 years),

Meiteis, (19.09 years), Non-Christian War Khasi (19.44 years), Boro Kachari (19.63 years), and Pnar (19.64 years) of North East India. The mean age at marriage is found to be relatively higher in the Ao Naga (21.83 years), Zemi Naga (21.80 years), and Dimasa (21.90 years).

The completed family size is 3.67 in the Tengaponiya Deori, 4.08 in Dibongya Deori and 4.94 in the Borgonya Deori. Thus, the Deori sub-populations of the present study show much lower values than those reported from other North East Indian population having Mongoloid ethnic affiliation. The completed family size among Mongoloid populations of Assam like the Ahom (5.43), Chutiya (5.29) and Moran (7.24) shows comparative higher values. Completed family size reported for the Purum-I (5.00) and Purum-II (4.23) of Manipur; Hajong (4.69) and Pnar (5.05) of Meghalaya is however somewhat close to them. It is generally suggested that fertility ratio of a population tends to decline if the total fertility rate is higher than the completed family size. Barring Borgonya Deori, in other two Deori sub-populations, the total fertility rate is little higher than the completed family size.

The fertility ratio in Tengaponiya (1103), Dibongya (1188) and Borgonya (1172) is extremely low and rests towards the lower range, whereas the other Mongoloid populations of North East India are on the other extreme. viz, Khamti (36.00, 36.70 and 37.19), Pnar (43.89), Semsa (50.23), Singpho (53.50), Christian War Khasi (61.48), Muklom Tangsha (61.68), War Khasi (61.83), non-Christian War Khasi (62.10), Dalu (86.36) and Pnar (86.96).

The mean value of conception in the Dibongya (3.53) and Borgonya (3.16) Deori of the present study shows similarities with the Pnar (3.56) and Lalung (3.61) of Assam; and one Khamti sample (3.67) of Arunachal Pradesh. The mean conception among Tengaponiya Deori (2.45) is extremely low. On the other hand, the Hajong (5.10), Khamti (5.11), Mishing (5.64), Moran (5.75), Deori (5.62), Nocte (5.68 and 5.92), Khamiyang (5.95), Turung (6.90), and Pnar (6.25) population exhibit relatively higher mean conception per mother.

The mean number of live births per married Deori women of the present study (Tengaponiya – 2.25, Dibongya – 3.09, Borgonya – 2.88) exhibit close degree of affinity with the Ahom (3.32), Sonowal Kachari (3.21) of Assam; Digaru Mishmi (3.19) of Arunachal

Pradesh. The other population of North East India like the Wancho (4.01), Khamti (3.57), and Nocte (5.23) of Arunachal Pradesh; Semsa (4.28) , Chutiya (4.40), Ahom (4.45), Mishing (3.99), Moran (5.52), and Deori (5.54) of Assam; Meiteis (4.63) of Manipur; Non-Christian War Khasi (4.73), Christian War Khasi (4.81), War Khasi, Hajong (4.99) and Pnar (6.04) of Meghalaya; Ao Naga (4.51) of Nagaland shows markedly higher mean value of live birth than the present population groups under study.

The incidence of miscarriage is comparatively higher among the Dibongya (10.82) and Tengaponiya (8.07) population than the other North East Indian population. The Borgonya (4.33) population on the other hand exhibits closer degree of approximation with the Semsa (3.34), Pnar (4.63) of Assam; and War Khasi (4.56 and 4.64) of Meghalaya. Frequency of miscarriage is low in Hajong (0.30) of Meghalaya; Deori (0.460, Mishing (0.48; Das and Das, 1982), Moran (0.84) and Ahom (0.97; Das and Das, 1982) population of Assam; and Muklom Tangsha (0.82) of Arunachal Pradesh. The rate of miscarriage among the, Pnar (1.37), Nocte (1.50), Turung (2.31), Wancho (2.37), Semsa (3.34), Christian War Khasi (4.56) and Non-Christian War Khasi (4.64) are also much lower than the present sub-samples.

Mongoloid populations of North East India generally exhibit relatively higher still birth rate than the caste (Indid) population (Sengupta and Purnungla, 2005). The still birth rate in Borgonya (6.06) is much higher than that in the Wancho (0.30), Lalung (0.58), Ao Naga (0.69), Chutiya (0.75) and Deori (0.91) population. The rate is however is not as low as found in the present Tengaponiya (1.79) and Dibongya (2.06) sub-samples and also in other North East Indian population like Nocte (1.05), Sonowal Kachari (2.09), Muklom Tangsha (1.23), Pnar (1.54), Khamiyang (2.11), Semsa (2.56), Hajong (2.80), and Moran (2.95).

The infant mortality rate in North East India varies between 2.39 per cent in the Ahom population to Digaru Mishmi (29.46 per cent) of Arunachal Pradesh. Such rate in Mizos (23.00 per cent) of Shillong, Meghalaya is also quite high. The infant mortality rate in all the Deori sub-samples (Tengaponiya – 1.95 per cent, Dibongya – 3.53 per cent, Borgonya – 3.81 per cent) population occupies position at the lower range and shows closer similarities with the Pnar (4.20 per cent), Sonowal Kachari (4.04 per cent), and Ahom

(2.39 per cent) populations of Assam. The infant mortality rate is comparatively higher among the Ao Naga (5.18 per cent), Moran (6.70 per cent), Christian War Khasi (6.89 per cent), War Khasi (7.00 per cent), Mishing (7.26 per cent), Khamti (7.37 per cent), Semsa (7.55 per cent), Muklom Tangsha (7.79 per cent), Non-Christian War Khasi (8.55 per cent), Pnar (11.92 per cent), Nocte (13.92 per cent), Hajong (15.64 per cent), and Mizo (16.80 per cent) population.

The child mortality rate is quite low among the Ahom (1.10 per cent) while the rate is relatively higher among the Semsa (13.09 per cent). The child mortality is also found to be quite high among the Moran (12.06 per cent). Like the present Tengaponiya Deori (0.49 per cent) sample, low child mortality rate is also noticed among the Khasi (1.59 per cent), Ahom (1.10 per cent), Ao Naga (1.78 per cent), Garo (2.17 per cent) and Chutiya (2.26 per cent) population. The Khamti (4.67 per cent), Mishing (3.99 per cent), Deori (3.20 per cent), and Sonowal Kachari (3.98 per cent) are little more than the lower ranges displayed by the Mongoloid population groups of North East India and shows close similarity with the Dibongya (2.35 per cent) and Borgonya Deori (3.81 per cent).

The juvenile mortality rate in the present Tengaponiya (0.98 per cent) sub-sample is low and falls in the lower limit of the ranges. The rate is appreciably high in Pnar (8.00 per cent), Mizo (8.90 per cent), Semsa (10.97 per cent), Digaru Mishmi (12.16 per cent), Nocte (12.34 per cent), Hajong (15.03 per cent), Khamti (15.21 per cent), and Semsa (10.97 per cent). The rate is found to be low in Chutiya (0.56 per cent), Khasi (0.89 per cent), Ao Naga (1.04 per cent), Ahom (0.92 per cent), Garo (1.58 per cent), Moran (1.67 per cent), Muklom Tangsha (1.84 per cent), Pnar (2.10 per cent; Khongsdier *et al.*, 2001), Lalung (2.35 per cent), and Mishing (0.30 per cent and 2.56 per cent). The War Khasi (4.85 per cent and 5.12 per cent), Non Christian War Khasi (3.64 per cent), and Christian War Khasi (3.68 per cent) however show relatively higher juvenile mortality rates in them.

Table 16.20: Pregnancy outcome in some Mongoloid population groups of North East India.

Population	*No.*	*Mean ageat marriage*	*Mean Conception*	*Mean live birth*	*Abortion*	*Still birth*	*Mortality*			*Source*
							Infant	**Child**	**Juvenile**	
ASSAM										
Tengaponiya	91	23.46	2.45	2.25	8.07	1.79	1.95	0.49	0.98	Presentstudy
DibongyaDeori	55	21.33	3.53	3.09	10.82	2.06	3.53	2.35	2.35	Do
BorgonyaDeori	73	21.44	3.16	2.88	4.33	6.06	3.81	3.81	2.38	Do
Ahom	164	20.09	3.83	3.32	12.26	1.11	2.39	1.10	0.92	Barua and Sengupta, 2009
Mishing	165	20.98	4.32	3.99	6.08	2.10	3.80	2.28	0.30	Do
SonowalKachari	185	20.17	3.63	3.21	9.84	2.09	4.04	2.02	0.67	Do
Ahom	66	17.98	4.68	4.45	0.97	3.88	5.42	1.69	2.26	Das and Das, 1982
Mishing	75	18.43	5.64	5.34	0.48	4.72	11.35	4.02	-	Do
Mishing	141	19.43	5.57	4.98	6.62	4.07	7.26	3.99	2.56	Sengupta and Dutta,
Sonowal Kachari	200	23.66	4.01	3.76	1.35	1.17	4.38	3.98	1.33	Sengupta and Kalita, 2001
Semsa	198	-	4.72	4.28	3.34	2.56	7.55	13.09	10.97	Limbu and Khongsdier, 2000
Dimasa		21.90	-	-	-	-	-	-	-	Royand Ali,1996
BoroKachari		19.63	-	-	-	-	-	-	-	Guha and Mukherjee,
Moran	65	18.51	5.75	5.52	0.84	2.95	6.70	12.0	1.67	Das and Das,1982
Lalung	47	14.59	3.61	3.55	-	0.58	-	2.35	2.35	Das *etal*., 1980
Deori	78	18.47	5.62	5.54	0.46	0.91	3.20	3.20	-	Das and Das, 1982
Chutiya	60	18.06	4.43	4.40	-	0.75	2.64	2.26	0.56	Do
Khamyang	40		5.95		6.36	2.11				Das, 1985
Turung	32		6.90		2.31	5.31				Do
Zemi		21.80								Royand Ali, 1996
Pnar	200	19.77	3.56	3.35	4.63	1.54	4.20		2.10	Khongsdier *et al*, 2001
ARUNACHALPRADESH										
Nocte	176		5.68	5.02						Buzarbarua, 1994
Nocte	169		5.92	5.23	1.50	1.05	13.92		12.34	Do
Wancho	82	-	4.12	4.01	2.37	0.30				Kar and Sharma, 1983
MuklomTangsha	123	-	4.02	3.97	0.82	1.23	7.79	-	1.84	Sarkar, 2002
Khamti	120	19.0	3.67	3.57			11.21	4.67	21.02	Choudhury *et al*, 1994
Khamti	85	-	5.11				7.37	-	15.21	Barua etal,1994
Singpho	411			3.74						Padmanabham, 1998
DigaruMishmi	152			3.19			22.89	-	12.16	Kotal and Barua, 2004
DigaruMishmi	64			3.50			29.46	-	19.20	Do

MANIPUR										
Maiteis	269	19.09		4.63						Choudhury and devi, 1977
Hmar		20.78								Varte,2006
MEGHALAYA										
Pnar	93	19.64	6.29	6.04	1.37	2.39	11.92	-	8.00	Khongsdier,1992
Hajong	196		5.10	4.99	0.30	2.80	15.64		15.03	Barua,1982
Hajong	198		5.04	4.94						Barua,1983
Khasi (C)		19.00								Nag,1965
Khasi (NC)		18.00-	-	-	-	-	-			Do
War Khasi	411			4.73			7.00		3.66	Khongsdiets and ghosh, 1194
War Khasi	144			6.30			10.47	-	4.96	Do
War Khasi							8.70		5.12	Khongsdier,1995
War Khasi							11.82		4.85	Khongsdier,1995
War Khasi (C)		20.04		4.81	4.56	3.11	6.89	-	3.68	Ghosh & Khongsdier, 1997
War Khasi (NC)		19.44-		4.66	4.64	3.46	8.55		3.64	Do
Khasi							4.20	1.59	0.89	Adak,1997
Garo							5.19	2.17	1.58	Do
Mizo							23.00		8.90	Do
Mizo							16.80			Barua,1982
NAGALAND										
Ao Naga	150	21.83	4.83	4.51	6.08	0.69	5.18	1.78	1.04	Sengupta and purnugla, 2005

Note: C = Christian; NC =Non-Christian.

The menopausal age of the present three Deori sub-sample are much lower compared to the Ahom population (46.32 years - 48.44 years), Khamiyang (46.25 years), Sonowal Kachari (47.12 and 47.22 years), and Tarao Naga (46.44 years), Mishing (48.40 years), Mao Naga (48.69 years), and Kabui Naga (48.86 years). However, they show close approximation with the Singpho (43.63 years), Turung (44.30 years), Meities (44.95 years), Tangkhul Naga (45.69 years), Garo (45.85 years), in having relatively lower value. In North East India, the highest mean age at menopause is however recorded among the Ao Naga (51.33 years) of Nagaland.

Table 16.21 : Mean age at menopause in some Mongoloid population of North East India.

Population	*No*	*Mean ±S.E.*	*Source*
Tengaponya Deori	13	44.59±0.29	Present study
Dibongya Deori	22	45.73±0.50	Do
Borgonya Deori	10	43.50±0.54	Do
Ahom	55	46.80±0.63	Barua andSengupta,2009
Ahom	36	48.44± 0.52	Gogoi, 1972
Ahom	87	46.32±0.27	Sengupta and Rajkhowa, 1996
Turung	10	44.30±0.68	Das, 1985
Khamyang	8	46.25±1.58	Das, 1985
Sonowal Kachari	66	47.22±0.29	Sengupta and Kalita, 2001
Sonowal Kachari	68	47.12±0.50	Barua and Sengupta,2009
Mishing	40	48.40± 0.60	Barua and Sengupta,2009
Mishing			
Unknown			
Garo	26	45.85±0.41	Ahmed Das and Saikia, 1999
Singpho	30	43.63±0.48	Kar and Mahanta, 1985
Meitei	64	44.95	Choudhury and Devi, 1998
Tarao Naga		46.44	Singh, 1989
Mao Naga		48.69	Maheo and Kalla, 2000
Kabui Naga		48.86	Chakravartti, 1986
Tangkhul Naga		45.69	Chakravartti, 1986
Ao Naga		51.33±0.44	Sengupta and Purnungla, 2005

The data on North East Indian population (Table 16.22) shows that among the Ahom, Boro Kachari, Tengaponiya, Borgonya, and Dibongiya Deori studied earlier, and Oraon of Assam; Khamti and Muklom Tangsa of Arunachal Pradesh; Pnar and War Khasi of Meghalaya; Hmar of Manipur; fertility component is comparatively higher than its mortality component, while it is just reverse in other population groups so far studied. It is worth mentioning that in Assam, the Ahom as well as the Sonowal Kachari population also demonstrates variations on the index due to rural - urban residence (Sengupta and Kalita, 1996; Sengupta and Chakravarty, 1998). Spuhler (1963) has suggested that socio-economic factors, particularly economic conditions, affect the index of total selection intensity. Reddy and Chopra (1990) observed that in India there is a tendency I_m for mean values of and I_f to decline with increase in degree of socio-economic development, including ready access to public health facility. Available data from North East India reveals moderately high total selection intensity in the people from Arunachal Pradesh (ranges from 0.7100 to 1.0700) mainly due to high mean live births and high mortality; relatively weak pressure of it in populations of Assam (0.1639 to 0.8700) and Manipur (0.312 to 0.377); while the people of Meghalaya (0.107 to 0.6380) and Nagaland (0.4497) the index ranges in between.

Table 16.22: Selection intensities among population groups of North East India.

Population	*According to Crow (1958)*			*According to Johnston and Kensinger (1971)*				*Source*
	I_m	I_f	I	I_{me}	I_{mc}	I_f	I	
ASSAM								
Tengaponiya Deori	0.0638	0.1407	0.2135	0.0900	0.0638	0.1407	0.3226	Present study
Dibongya Deori	0.0790	0.2075	0.3029	0.1220	0.0790	0.2075	0.4618	Present study
Borgonya Deori	0.1808	0.2711	0.5085	0.0926	0.1868	0.2711	0.6435	Present study
Tengaponiya Deori	0.108	0.181	0.309	0.073	0.108	0.181	0.403	Gogoi, 2006
Borgonya Deori	0.045	0.166	0.219	0.200	0.045	0.166	0.461	Gogoi, 2006
Dibongiya Deori	0.046	0.123	0.174	0.098	0.046	0.123	0.290	Gogoi, 2006
Ahom	0.027	0.104	0.134	0.026	0.027	0.104	0.163	Datta & sengupta, 2011
Ahom	0.043	0.167	0.217	0.051	0.043	0.167	0.280	Datta & sengupta, 2011
Ahom	0.038	0.258	0.306	0.025	0.038	0.258	0.340	Datta & sengupta, 2011
Ahom	0.083	0.118	0.218	0.074	0.083	0.118	0.308	Sengupta, 2004
Khamti	0.179	0.113	0.312	0.005	0.179	0.113	0.319	Sarkar *et al*, 1994

Sonowal	0.192	0.141	0.360					Deka, 1978
Sonowal	0.185	0.179	0.364	0.103	0.185	0.179	0.541	Deka, 1980
Sonowal	0.167	0.163	0.358	0.053	0.167	0.163	0.432	Sengupta, 2004
Boro Kachari	0.110	0.130	0.250					Guha and ukherjee, 1990
Semsa	0.320	0.250	0.650					Choudhury *et al*,2001
Semsa	0.471	0.098	0.616	0.038	0.471	0.098	0.677	Limbu and Khongsdier, 2000
Pnar Khasi	0.104	0.234	0.363	0.047	0.104	0.234	0.428	Khongsdier *et al.2001*
Oraon	0.098	0.131	0.243	0.102	0.098	0.131	0.369	Sengupta and Gogoi,1997
ARUNACHAL PRADESH								
Singpho	0.437	0.406	1.020					Padmanabham and Jaswal, 1982
Apatani (Guchi)	0.435	0.195	0.710					Padmanabham, 1982
Apatani (Guth)	0.440	0.312	0.889					Padmanabham, 1982
Gallong	0.750	0.180	1.070					Chakravarty and Ahmed, 1989
Khampti	0.388	0.398	0.934					Choudhury (Unpub)
Digaru Mishmi	0.813	0.264	1.294	0.273	0.813	0.264	1.922	Kotal and Barua, 2004
Muklom	0.107	0.188	0.315	0.021	0.107	0.188	0.342	Sarkar, 1997
MEGHALAYA								
Hajong	0.443	0.131	0.631	0.032	0.443	0.131	0.684	Barua, 1983
Jaintia	0.450	0.130	0.640					Deka, 1978
Jaintia	0.456	0.125	0.638	0.107	0.456	0.125	0.814	Deka, 1989
Pnar	0.236	0.133	0.401	0.201	0.236	0.133	0.680	Khongsdier, 1990
Pnar	0.106	0.281	0.416	0.127	0.106	0.281	0.596	Banerjee *et al*, 1994
Pnar	0.104	0.234	0.363	0.047	0.104	0.234	0.428	Khongsdier

								et al, 2001
War (Christian)	0.147	0.184	0.359	0.093	0.147	0.184	0.486	Khongsdier, 1994
War (Non Christian)	0.180	0.225	0.446	0.084	0.180	0.225	0.567	Khongsdier, 1994
Dalu	0.499	0.231	0.847	0.031	0.499	0.231	0.897	Kapoor, 1997
Sankar Koch	0.262	0.070	0.351	0.038	0.262	0.070	0.402	Kotal and Sengupta, 2003
MANIPUR								
Hmar	0.072	0.250	0.340	0.028	0.072	0.250	0.379	Varte, 1998
Chote/Purum (I)	0.198	0.095	0.312					Dasgupta *et al*, 1985
Chote/Purum (II)	0.227	0.122	0.377					Dasgupta *et al*, 1985
NAGALAND								
Kheza	0.244	0.164	0.449	0.177	0.244	0.164	0.707	Devi *et al*, 1998

The present investigation reveals that regardless of certain differences in respect of few demographic variables, the three sub-populations of Deori under study are largely similar. All the sub-samples of Deori under study as a whole are endogamous. The incidence of village endogamy in them is not very much. There is no bar against inter-marriage among the three sub-samples, but in practice, inter-marriage between sub-samples is not that frequent. The influence of physical environmental factors on the demographic traits considered in the present study may not be so significant because these three territorial sub-groups of Deori tribe mostly living in a similar ecological condition.

Acknowledgements

Financial assistance of the Indian Council of Social Science Research, New Delhi in the form of a Major Research Project (ICSSR Reference No. F.No.RP 02/082/2009/RP, dated 15 December, 2009) and Dibrugarh University authority for providing logistic support is thankfully acknowledged. Authors are also indebted to participants of Kolowloa Deori *Gaon* of Dibrugarh District; Upor Deori *Gaon* of Jorhat District and Bormuria Deori

Gaon of Dhemaji District, Assam for their sincere co-operation during data collection.

References

Crow, J. F. 1958. 'Some possibilities for measuring selection intensities in man'. *Human Biology*. 30: 1 – 13.

Johnston, F. F., and K. M. Kensiger. 1971. 'Fertility and mortality differentials and their implications for micro-evolutionary change among the Cashinahua'. *Human Biology*. 43: 356 - 364.

Reddy, B.M., and V. P. Chopra. 1990. 'Opportunity for natural selection among the Indian population'. *American Journal of Physical Anthropology*. 83: 281-296.

Sengupta, S., and K.Chakraborty. 1998. 'Selection intensity in the Ahoms of Assam'. *Journal of Human Ecology*. 9, 1: 83-85.

Sengupta,S., and M. Kalita.1996.'Selection intensity among the Sonowal of Assam'. In Sarthak Sengupta (Ed): *Peoples of North East India*, pp. 73-80, New Delhi: Gyan Publishing House.

Spuhler, J. N., 1963. 'The scope of natural selection in man'. In W.I.Schull (Ed): *Genetic Selection in Man*, pp. 1 – 111, Ann Arbor: University of Michigan Press.

Srivastava, R.P., and M. Goswami. 1968. 'The menarcheal age of Assamese girls', *Anthropologist*, 15, 1-2: 57-60.

World Health Organisation. 1964. *Research in Population Genetics of Primitive Groups*, WHO Technical Report Series No 229, Geneva: World Health Organisation.

World Health Organisation.1968. *Research in Human Population Genetics*. WHO Technical Report Series No 387, Geneva: World Health Organisation.

Zubro, E.B.W., 1976. 'Demographic anthropology: An introductory analysis'. In E.B.W. Zubro (Ed): *Demographic Anthropology: Quantitative Approaches*, pp. 1 – 26, Albuquerque: New Mexico Press.

Index